Trans-Atlantic Divide

UNIVERSITY PRESS OF
Lanham • Boulder • New York

Copyright © 2010 by
University Press of America,® Inc.
4501 Forbes Boulevard
Suite 200
Lanham, Maryland 20706
UPA Acquisitions Department (301) 459-3366

Estover Road
Plymouth PL6 7PY
United Kingdom

All rights reserved
Printed in the United States of America
British Library Cataloging in Publication Information Available

Library of Congress Control Number: 2010924900
ISBN: 978-0-7618-5138-7 (paperback : alk. paper)

∞™ The paper used in this publication meets the minimum
requirements of American National Standard for Information
Sciences—Permanence of Paper for Printed Library Materials,
ANSI Z39.48-1992

To my wife and daughter
who cheerfully endured the process

Contents

Illustrations		vii
Introduction		ix
1	The World's Sole Superpower	1
2	*Historie*—General de Gaulle, Neo-Gaullists, and America	23
3	McWorld vs. France?	44
4	Pipelines, Pershings, and Protests—Germany and the U.S.	67
5	War on Terror—Hands across the Seas?	85
6	The Iraq War and the United Nations	110
7	European Union Über Alles—The Old Versus the New Europe	136
8	Why Can't We Be Friends?	165
9	What Is to Be Done? The Road Ahead	197
Select Bibliography		219
Index		223

Illustrations

Figure I.1.   Economic Commission for Europe   xii

Figure 7.1.   Comparison of City Population Growth/Europe versus Developing World   156

Figure 8.1.   Imports from the USA/Exports to the USA in billions of dollars   169

Figure 9.1.   Convergence of Agreement between the USA and the EU Six   215

Introduction

While having breakfast in a charming Viennese Café, I glanced at the morning papers as I habitually do. Leafing thorough the respected *Die Presse* newspaper I viewed the picture of then Secretary of State Madeleine Albright arriving in Sarajevo, deplaning from a U.S. Air Force jet, wearing her trademark black brimmed Cowboy hat. She was arriving at an aid pledging conference to help the beleaguered Bosnians. As one European friend remarked with obvious exasperation, "Arriving like a *Walkerie,* all she needed was the wings on her hat!"

Albright's tenure at the State Department transpired during a very crucial geopolitical *interregnum*. Brusque, but self-assured, she epitomized the Clinton Era on the foreign policy front. Indeed many of her targets were most deserving of her wrath, but even amongst friends and allies, she created a kind of political backlash. The fact that she represented the United States of America, the world's sole military superpower, was generally unquestioned, the fact that she and her aides often acted this role with a smug brashness was uncalled for and indeed the source of smoldering resentments even among many American allies.

Not that Albright's political instincts were wrong or ill- advised. In many cases she had both the strategic and moral capacity to understand the crimes of the day-especially among the thugs running most of the cantons of ex-Yugoslavia. Her emotions and analysis were often correct, and this is in no small part due to her Czech heritage, which probably by nature brings one a special understanding of the gray areas in crises around the globe. But to assume, as many do, that the Clinton era presented a political springtime for transatlantic relations, is to see the period with rose colored glasses.

When George W. Bush took the Oath of Office of the President in January 2001, one of the more poignant messages in his Inauguration Address were the words about the *humility of great power and how to project that greatness in a humble way*. One can debate the religious intonations, but the fact remains that Great Powers don't have to remind people of their status.

I was often asked with a smirk, "Now that the Soviet Union has fallen who are our enemies?" While many would concede that Communist China could well fit into this category in the longer term future, few would admit that there was anyone who can possibly harm or threaten us. Name them! Why do we need yet more advanced generation fighter jets or new military technology, against whom? Name them! Serious people would hold this view with very few permutations.

The entire concept of post-Cold War military preparedness was viewed as *almost* negotiable. Talk of peace dividends were presented as a political given. The majority of Congressional Democrats and the Clinton Administration opposed both wider military preparedness while at the same time a grossly expanding the mission of the U.S. military in a myriad of brush fire wars and peacekeeping operations. Many Republican defense hawks meanwhile such as House Speaker Newt Gingrich quipped, "I'm a Hawk, but a cheap Hawk!" Even Defense Secretary Donald Rumsfeld, who should have known better, during the Summer 2001 was speaking about military retooling away from the old concept of U.S. military readiness as being structured to simultaneously fight two wars, Europe and East Asia. Alas, the collapse of the Soviet Union did not end threats to America. Neither did Balkan wars really pose any direct challenge. Yet in the 1990's the political perceptions were radically changed on both sides of the aisle in Washington. We had almost theologically accepted the strategic hypothesis that in the wake of the collapse of the Soviet Empire, that the *world was ours to mold, and to mind*.

Halting Ethnic genocide in places as far flung as the Balkans, Rwanda, or East Timor was viewed as the primary threat to global security, something that the U.S. military could easily handle as a kind of *Globo-Cop*. The old stereotype of Uncle Sam playing a world policeman, was ironically embraced and promoted by the Clinton Administration and given a political benediction by the Security Council. Beyond trying to stop a myriad of ethnic/regional crisis, and following up with humanitarian packages, the Administration had promoted an unfocused long-term solution. Indeed one could easily dispute that beyond the unimaginable tragedy and ethnic conflicts from Africa to Southeast Asia, but was American involvement in the national interest? Naturally then there was the comfortable isolationist view, which equally promoted a perception that America was unassailable and totally safe inside our frontiers. Few of these strategic savants could have imagined that a medieval madman on a horse but with a cell phone could possibly threaten America from of all places the Islamic Emirate of Afghanistan! Terrorists like Osama

Bin-Laden were not considered remotely threatening. After all we were the world's sole superpower!

The unimaginable horrors of September 11th was to fundamentally jolt this assumption. Moreover the continuing political consequences of September 11th and the Iraq war equally shook the traditional alliance systems to the very core of NATO. Indeed the European Union itself, the prosperous political and economic edifice of the Old World, would soon pose some very new political problems for Transatlantic relations. What I shall term *Euroland*, the often self-satisfied, morally superior and narcissistic political prodigy of the post-war era, has often challenged the traditional Transatlantic ties as much as have any actions by the White House. *Euroland*, reflecting its EU membership, sees itself as the epitome of the caring social state, views policymaking as consensus, and seeks to confront real world challenges with "soft power."

In the aftermath of the Iraq war, the trans-Atlantic dispute particularly between Washington, Paris, and Berlin had assumed a dangerous political life of its own based on *rash misperceptions and political pique*. Political classes on both sides of the Atlantic had grossly exaggerated their differences while viewing each other's common interests as seemingly unimportant. The prime issue remained Iraq, though political differences over the Balkan wars and Kyoto Treaty formed a critical part of the undercurrent. When Barack Obama entered the White House in 2009, he inherited the mistrust and the misunderstandings, as much as he brought the perception of change.

Washington needs thoughtful political damage control to solve the symptoms; a focused re-appraisal of the post WWII friendship and socio/political ties between Europe and the USA must be embarked upon to solver the deeper problem. Neither side could benefit in the long run by ratcheting up the rhetoric at the expense of the positive post-war realities. Anti-Americanism moreover could easily translate from street level and editorial rhetoric into government policy and can in the long run, be profoundly more deleterious to Europe's interests than to America's. Equally such moves will reinvigorate isolationist sentiments in the USA.

We can treat the symptoms or the problems, but we must start with the misperceptions. Smoothing of the Atlantic waters remains paramount for U.S. geopolitical and commercial relations with Europe, and for America's wider struggle with Islamic fundamentalism. Despite marked improvement in trans-Atlantic ties, the new American Administration must address this vital issue. A recommitment by the Administration to core Atlanticist values must be a first and long overdue step.

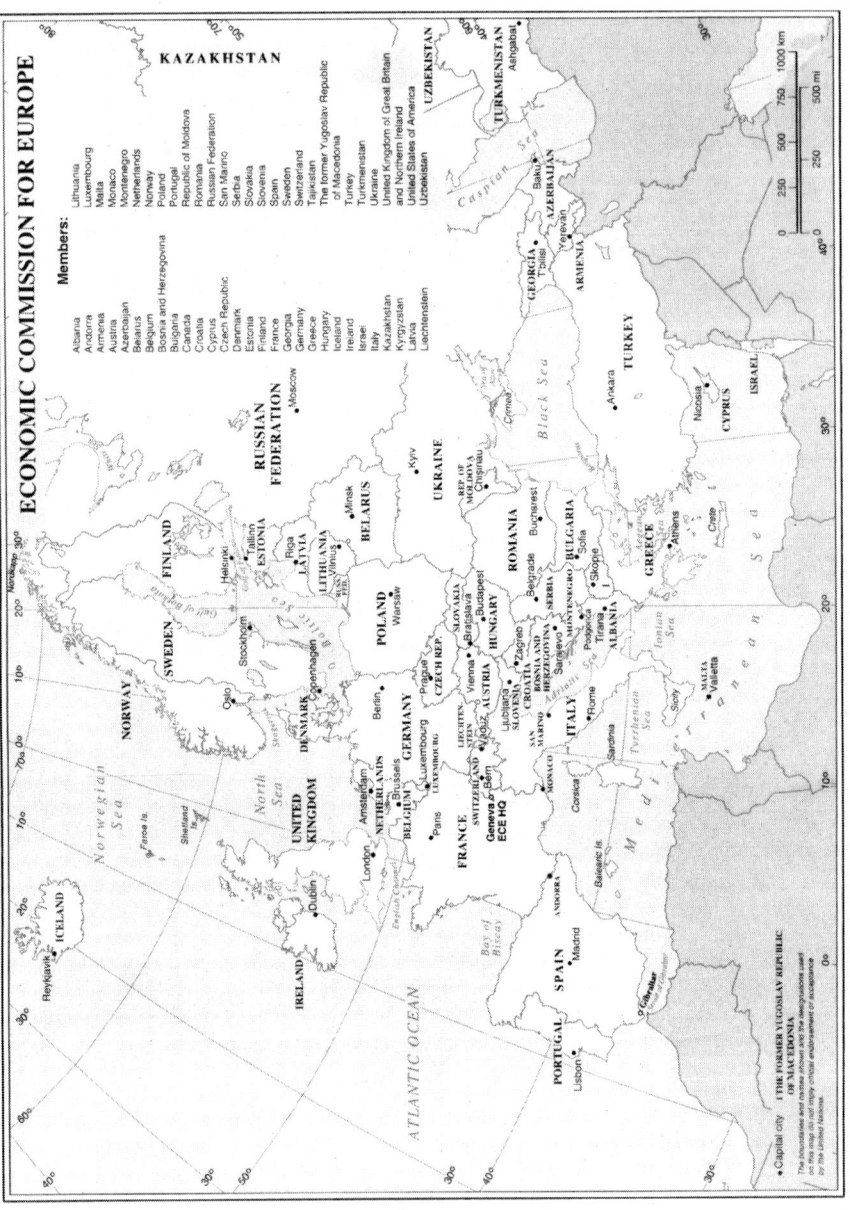

Figure I.1. Economic Commission for Europe. Map No. 3976 Rev. 11. United Nations, May 2008.

Chapter One

The World's Sole Superpower

In that gripping espionage thriller of post–war Vienna, *The Third Man*, moviegoers are treated to Orson Welles' taut and tense political drama which characterized post-WWII Europe. Cities such as Vienna provided the grist of spy movies, reflecting an unfolding geopolitical drama played out in places like Berlin, Budapest and Prague. The Cold War had clearly defined the protagonists and antagonists; backdrops would later include Korea, Cuba, Vietnam, Nicaragua, and Angola. Though regional conflicts often by proxies were catalysts for the bigger game—the East/West European divide—these violent disputes for control of the Third World played an equally strong supporting role.

But overshadowing the entire drama was the impending threat of nuclear mutual assured destruction (MAD) the doctrine which in its essence meant mutual Armageddon should the Soviets use their atomic arsenal against America. The "balance of terror" in a sense nearly assured the entire game from going nuclear, while at the same time promoting a number of conventional probing actions by the Soviets in places as varied as Korea and Cuba. During most of this geopolitical standoff—the USA and its West European allies stood shoulder to shoulder. The North Atlantic Treaty Organization (NATO), founded in 1949, became an effective military defensive pact The Atlantic Alliance not only maintained West European security and sovereignty, but preserved the longest period of peace and freedom the Old World has known. The NATO treaty—importantly enjoying strong *bi-partisan* support in Washington, moreover guaranteed the conditions for which levels of socio/economic prosperity for a Continent long plagued by "warfare, terror, murder, and bloodshed."

After extraordinary political and financial sacrifice, and through the judicious combination of diplomacy backed by a credible defense posture,

Washington and its European allies stood at the cusp of victory. The politically fortuitous combination of Ronald Reagan in America, Margaret Thatcher in Britain, and Helmut Kohl in Germany along with the spiritual powers of a Polish Pope Karol Wojtyla in the Vatican, played political midwife to the Revolutions of 1989. Soon the Soviets would collapse, but sooner again the political *raison d'etre* for European defense—that of a formidable and aggressive enemy—would disappear too. Those old ties which bound us—a common threat from Soviet communism—would soon unravel with quite unpredictable results. Along with promised peace dividends, military downsizing, and the near overnight conversion of foes into friends, both America and *Euroland* appeared confronted with the wonderful fate of the Swiss—democracy, peace, prosperity, and perhaps cuckoo clocks. Talk of trade and investment pacts replaced the long arcane discussions about strategic arms reduction treaties. Countries which had long shunned foreign investment and free trade, often in the name of socialism or self-reliance, soon became almost giddy disciples of the free market.

It appeared that the god of Mars was being eclipsed and outshone by Mercury. As for the military superpowers, the Soviet Union was out of business, People's China was nowhere near being a superpower except in their own estimation, and the USA was last man standing.

In August 1990 Saddam Hussein Iraq invaded neighboring Kuwait. Former President George Bush told Congress "Out of these troubled times... *a new world order* can emerge...freer from the threat of terror, stronger in the pursuit of justice, and more secure in the quest for peace." Yet even after his victory in the first Gulf war against Iraq in 1991, Bush warned that the world was *not* moving into "an era of perpetual peace."[1]

Still, how did we achieve this enviable position? In an important 1991 address, *Freedom and the Future*, former British Prime Minister Margaret Thatcher reminded a Washington D.C. audience of the political stakes; "Victory was not won solely in the last six months. It was the culmination of a decade's achievement, the military buildup of the 1980's, the recovery of the America's and the West's self-confidence and the revival of our economies, that made these miracles possible." She stated, "It is difficult today to conjure up the despairing and defeatist atmosphere of the post-Vietnam 1970's but in those days the West was on the decline and on the defensive." She added, "Our defenses were neglected. The Soviet Union steadily reinforced its military superiority. Our allies felt abandoned. They felt they could no longer rely on a hedonistic West." This political weakness only mirrored deeper weakness in Western societies. Margaret Thatcher stressed that by the 1980's a new direction had begun; "We wrestled with the challenge of reviving our economies. We rebuilt our shattered defenses. We faced up to the threat of a Soviet Empire at the peak of its military might, made still more dangerous by knowledge of its own economic weakness and social fragility." Margaret Thatcher added, "We made it clear that arms control would proceed on the basis of genuine equality of weaponry between East and West—or not at all. The Soviet Union built up its SS-20's. We deployed Cruise and Pershing missiles. The result, the first ever guarantee to reduce nuclear weapons. When the Soviet Union said that Germany would only be united if it left NATO, President Bush and I stayed firm. The result, a reunified Germany fully within NATO."[2]

Given her historically decisive tenure as Prime Minister between 1979 and 1990, and her unswerving commitment to reviving the Anglo/American alliance, by early 1991, Margaret Thatcher was indeed deserving of her laurels and a victory lap in Washington.

During and after the Gulf War in 1990–91, the Bush Administration's focused on establishing a *New World Order*—again a term which out of context could not only raise eyebrows, but wariness. "President Bush's successful formation of a coalition for the war against Iraq offers a paradigm for U.S. actions in the emerging complex of international relations in the new world order. Since the Gulf conflict, Washington has begun to seek diplomatic alliances to promote cooperation and security while evaluating old agreements predicated on Cold War antagonisms," writes the Hoover Institution's Thomas Henriksen adding "Whether the Iraq war was is a landmark in the sense of a turning point in America's post cold war relations is not yet clear. America's military success in the gulf war and its sole superpower status all but guaranteed that the United States will be called to be a major player in regional disputes."[3]

SOLE SUPERPOWER STATUS?

America's triumph in the Cold War was interpreted—and *misinterpreted*—in a myriad of ways. The decisive victory over Iraq in 1991 reconfirmed the obvious. By the 1990's the *monotonous mantra* began; "We are the sole superpower," "As the world's sole superpower," or "Being the world's sole superpower." The speaker or writer, through this statement, would almost religiously intone that such superpower status conveyed an almost *Olympian responsibility* for promoting good or a diabolical conspiracy to effect evil. Few American politicians or commentators on either side of the aisle realized that such absolutist statements and hubristic sentiments were and are regarded as arrogance and as a looming threat. Through history has objectively shown America's unique restraint and judiciousness in the use of its political and military power, especially after WWII--the *subjective perceptions* overseas were not so sanguine, nor informed.

On the eve of September 11th 2001, Dr. Henry Kissinger, former Secretary of State, wrote in his book *Does America Need A Foreign Policy?*, "American preeminence is a fact of life for the near and almost certainly in the mid-term future. The way the United States handles it will determine what kind of long-term future emerges."[4]

Many statesmen and traditional admirers among our allies had a disquieted feeling that the "world's sole superpower" would evolve into a unilateral political player and power-broker acting without the counsel *nor the restraint* of its longtime allies. America's overwhelming military and economic power has disquieted many Europeans.

"As the remaining superpower, the United States faces a unique political environment," wrote Dr. Henriksen of the prestigious Hoover Institution. "It is both the world's reigning hegemon and sometime villain. America's economic, military, and technological prowess endows it with what Secretary of State Madeleine K. Albright has termed *indispensability*. Whatever the political upheaval or humanitarian crisis, other states expect the United States to solve the world's problems and dispense good deeds." He advises, "Unlike most traditional nations, we do not share a common ancestry. Thus America seeks to advance ideals. Our national goals encompass more than geopolitical ends, which is why Americans are unsettled by the slaughter of innocents in faraway lands. American foreign policy debates and interventionist decisions usually include democratic values as well as our vital overseas interests."[5]

President Bill Clinton put the case of American power in candid simplicity; "We must continue to bear the responsibility for the world's leadership." In another missive he added, "Because we remain the world's indispensable nation," Clinton intoned in 1996, "we must act and we must lead. IF the United States does not lead the job will not be done." Secretary of State Madeleine Albright declared, This is a new world, "America's place is at the center of this system."[6]

Such hubris was reflected no less enthusiastically by Former Speaker of the House Newt Gingrich who stated, "As the world's only superpower, largest economy, and most aggressive culture, the United States inevitably infringes on the attention and interests of other peoples and nations. A country this large and powerful must work every day to communicate what it is doing. The world does not have to love us but it must be able to predict us."[7]

Prof. Robert Jervis of Columbia University wrote, "Worried about the aggressive and unilateral exercise of U.S. power around the world today? Fine, just don't blame President George W. Bush, September 11th, or some shadowy neo-conservative cabal. Nations enjoying unrivaled global power

have always defined their national interests in increasingly expansive terms."
In an article the *Compulsive Empire* he adds that contrary to the practice of previous administrations to cultivate allies and nurture coalitions, "the fundamental objective of the current Bush doctrine—which seeks to universalize U.S. values and defend preventively against new, nontraditional threats—is the establishment of U.S hegemony, primacy, or empire." He advises, "Great power also instills new fears in the dominant state, a hegemon tends to acquire an enormous stake in the world order." He adds "Spreading democracy and liberalism throughout the world has always been a U.S. goal, but having so much power makes this aim a more realistic one."[8]

The Clinton Administration's Chorus of *The World's Sole Superpower*, Madeleine Albright's memorable *We are the Indispensable Nation,* and her shrill calls for *Regime Change* in places varied and far, formed the political lexicon which George W. Bush would inherit and employ after September 11th.

Josef Joffe advised, "The sense that America can do anything it wants to do" was the view of the Clinton Administration, "but after 9/11 there is also a sense of *righteousness"* that Bush brought to the equation. While President Wilson spoke of "making the world safe for democracy" President Bush "wants to make the world safe through democracy."[9]

The term hegemon, a single pole or axis of power, has long been used by the Chinese to convey a malevolent power or political sphere of influence. That this term is applied to America beyond the confines of the Peking Politburo is distressing. When commentator Pat Buchanan wrote the book, *A Republic Not an Empire*, many thought his title and thesis was too jaded. From the hopeful and heralded *New World Order* of George Herbert Walker Bush in the 1990's, to the *Sole Superpower* of Bill Clinton and the early George W. Bush era, to the powerful post September 11th *Empire which Strikes Back*, American policy has undergone a revolutionary sea change. So has the rhetoric.

"The debate on Empire is back. "This is not surprising as the United States dominates the world as no state ever has. It emerged from the Cold War the only superpower, and no geopolitical and ideological contenders are in sight," opines Georgetown Professor G. John Ikenberry. Writing in the prestigious policy magazine *Foreign Affairs,* "Illusions of Empire—Defining the New American Order," he lists some current books, "The Sorrows of Empire: Militarism, Secrecy and the End of the Republic," "Colossus: The Price of America's Empire," "Incoherent Empire," and "After the Empire: The Breakdown of the American Order."[10]

There's a plethora of books describing contemporary American geopolitical power beyond the *sole superpower* rank—to that of an Empire! These are not the kooky leftwing tomes one finds in the warrens of Berkeley, Madison, or the Upper West Side, but more thoughtful and thus troubling accounts. Assessing America's role in the world or indeed finding the proper term describing U.S. power is in itself really nothing new. The *profound* difference today remains that the USA does not represent one of *many*, or of *two poles* of geo-strategic power, but alas, the *single pole* which properly leads to this unipolar reality. How to hold and judiciously use such seemingly unchallenged power naturally confronts Washington policymakers. Does America turn inwards—the clear post Cold War but pre-September 11th *temptation*, does America look outwards with militarily muscular unilateralism, viewing the chaotic global situation as presenting an azimuth of targets? Actually the Europeans feared both outcomes from their oft repeated complaint in the early 1990's that "an inward looking America was disengaging from Europe and the world," to the former *Gulliver Unbound* yammering of the German Foreign Minister Joshka Fischer, "What kind of world order do we want?" Thus without the counterbalance of the former Soviet Union to threaten European security and frighten European elites, it appears the instinctive reaction of many of America's European allies was to politically oppose Washington.

Literally on the eve of September 11th, an article "The Future of the American Pacifier," Professor John J. Mearsheimer wrote, "There is considerable evidence however, that the United States and its Cold War allies are beginning to drift apart. This trend is most apparent in Europe where NATO's 1999 war against Serbia and its messy aftermath have damaged transatlantic relations and prompted the European Union to begin building a force of its own that can operate independently of NATO, meaning the United States." He adds, " America's Cold War allies have started to act less like dependents and more like sovereign states because—being perhaps more perceptive than Washington's own foreign policy elites—they fear that the offshore balance that has protected them for so long might prove to be unreliable in a future crisis."[11]

Ironically that *unreliability factor* emerged from the European Union's continental states which when confronting the Iraq crisis during both the Clinton and George W. Bush Administrations, failed to support American military actions against Saddam. Naturally the Europeans will present a more nuanced view of their political peregrinations in the Security Council or behind the scenes in Baghdad. Yet, in the final analysis the lack of a coherent European Union response to Saddam's non-compliance with U.N. Security Council resolutions, and wavering support for subsequent American enforcement actions, led George W. Bush to call his brinksmanship bluff to Baghdad and to launch *Operation Iraqi Freedom in 2003.*

BUSH BASHING

There's also the another element beyond Washington's sole superpower mantle which particularly rankles continental Europe. Namely the U.S. President himself who was far less personally popular with the *Euroland* elites than any recent predecessor in the White House. "The loathing of Bush is extraordinary, the hatred of Blair for siding with Bush is almost as great. He is an incredibly unpopular figure in the Labor Party, and I think it is true that what is what is presented as moral opposition the war is actually political opposition to Bush," as Stephen D'Ancona of London's *Sunday Telegraph* told the popular PBS program *Frontline*.

Such emotions characterize the contemporary strategic setting and reflect a current of latent bitterness which has poisoned so very much of the trans-Atlantic debate. Even during the zenith of West Europe's "peace movement " in the late 1970's and early 1980's, the animosity level rarely reached outside the traditional communist and hard left circles. Though the press often gleefully reflected and exaggerated such opinions, the counterbalance remained a clear and present danger from the Soviet Union. Such anti-Bush emotions, and those against Blair, reflected a much wider spectrum which opposes the "superpower status" perhaps less than the actual Commander in Chief.

Europeans will usually concede that the post-September 11th world totally justified the USA to a radically transform its defense posture. The unilateral and preemptive nature of the response articulated by the Bush Administration, in other words, the aggressively pro-active nature of the defense of American interests is what the Europeans actually feared. The Administration, on the other hand, fears precisely not being able to thwart and preempt trans-border threats which can in turn bring terrorism to America's shores. Though in the immediate aftermath of September 11th it appeared as if the USA and Europe were united in active solidarity, the political fault lines reappeared as clouds of an impending confrontation with Saddam's Iraq thickened. Almost in parallel to Europe's calls for a continuing political settlement to the Iraqi problem, American policymakers saw Europe as going wobbly in the face of a clear and present danger from the Iraqi dictator. One could surmise that European attitudes favoring continued diplomacy—some would say accommodation with Saddam—sowed the seeds for yet wider American disenchantment with the "Old Europe."

"The respect American once accorded to Europeans culture, wisdom and manners has not just disappeared, it has turned into an aggressive contempt," wrote John Lloyd in the *Financial Times* article *Rowing Alone*. "The U.S., at least at the elite level, and perhaps more widely, has become seized by the idea that we Europeans are weak, whining and hopeless; ungrateful, mean and ignorant; guilty, cynical and exhausted." As Lloyd opines, "But, it is not just that the U.S. is militarily, economically, culturally and technologically hegemonic; it is also that, because of that dominance, its leaders, diplomats and soldiers regard the world from the point of view of the hub on a wheel, looking down its spokes. At the end of one of these spokes is Europe—factious at times, but united peaceful and prosperous...*Hegemons are hegemonic*."[12]

American feelings of antipathy or perhaps ambivalence towards continental Europe have grown for numerous reasons *long predating* the Iraq war. After a brief but renewed love affair between the USA and West Europe in the wake of the 1989 revolutions which toppled communism, the general impression emerged that given that the Cold War was won and over, the continued need for overseas engagement would decline correspondingly. Isolationist sentiments spread across political lines, as the lure of spending or saving the proverbial *peace dividend* appeared as a serious choice. With the possible exception of Japan bashing concerning Tokyo's whopping trade surplus at America's expense, few people outside the traditional foreign policy/ internationalist circles, appeared interested or inclined towards overseas engagements. Even Iraq's invasion and occupation or Kuwait, rather quickly overturned by an American led but United Nations sanctioned military coalition, was seen as an aberration rather than a portent of regional crises to come.

Thus when the Governor of a small southern state who was running for President, stressing his scant experience nor interest in foreign policy issues, voters could really care less. What little *was said* about foreign policy, namely about a feckless Bush Sr. policy towards Bosnia or a craven coddling of the "Butchers of Beijing" rang well with the majority of the electorate. Still in 1992, after all, "It was the economy, stupid!" But Bill Clinton as President of the United States was quickly ushered into a maze of foreign policy dilemmas which would bedevil his Administration in places as diverse as the Balkans, China, the Middle East, Haiti, North Korea, Somalia and of course Iraq. Clinton immensely enjoyed his role as Commander in Chief and Superpower *Supremo* and soon began a *whirlwind style over substance* foreign policy which put the American President on a constant worldwide road show. Given his exhausting global jaunts, setting the record for an American Chief of State, one would have never have imagined that the Governor from Little Rock would play the part so very well.

The singular lesson endures that the Clinton Administration exercised both a glaring hubris and arrogance blessed with the proverbial beginners luck of working within a world system experiencing the afterglow of the Cold War victory. Bill Clinton inherited a *seemingly stable* but soon to change international environment. He would play the part of the globetrotting President with a panache and gusto worthy of an Hollywood Oscar for Best Actor. Alas, foreign policy is not written in Hollywood-like scripts, or played by enthusiastic *amateurs*, but tempered by sober expertise and driven by often-unpredictable events. Clearly the crises Clinton inherited were not of his making but his Administration hardly made them any better. The perennial Iraq problem hovered like a desert vulture over our Middle East policy and more especially in the United Nations where the Security Council's former political solidarity against Saddam was tested by both sanctions- breaking and overall weariness from Iraqi non-compliance. Divisions in the Council precluded any serious actions against Baghdad expect by the USA and Britain. Other nations simply had either made their peace with Saddam, allowed their business bottom lines to write the policy, or could care less about what many countries considered an Anglo/ American obsession with Iraq.

CLINTON'S HUMANITARIAN CRUSADES

Naturally another vexing problems were the Balkan wars resulting from the breakup of Socialist Yugoslavia. Here was an explosive crisis—a Balkan war—on the very doorstep of the prosperous European Union! Was it America's role to solve the problem? Was the Wilsonian impulse enough to drag Washington into a region where angels feared to tread? "Clinton came into office having criticized the foreign policy of George H. W. Bush for being insufficiently true to American democratic ideals," writes Prof. Colin Dueck in his article *Hegemony on the Cheap*. He adds, "The new president promised to be more consistent that his immediate predecessor in promoting democracy and human rights in countries such as China, the former Yugoslavia, and Haiti. A leading test of the Clinton Administrations rhetorical commitment to the liberal internationalist credo was the question of humanitarian intervention." Still as Dueck warned, "Nevertheless even as President Clinton laid out his extremely ambitious foreign policy goals, he proved unwilling to support them with the necessary means. In particular, he proved reluctant to support these initiatives with the requisite amount of military force."

"In one case after another of humanitarian intervention, a pattern emerged: the Clinton administration would stake out an assertive and idealistic public position, then refuse to act on its rhetoric in a meaningful way. Yet in every such case, whether in Somalia, Haiti, Bosnia or Kosovo, the president was ultimately forced to act, if only to protect the credibility of the United States. The result was a series a remarkably half-hearted, initially low-risk interventions, which only reinforced the impression that the United States was unwilling to suffer costs or casualties on behalf of its stated interests overseas," Dueck writes in *Hegemony on the Cheap*.[13]

Part of the problem stemmed from the Administration's cutting of military budgets and resources while at the same time greatly expanding the global missions of the military. Clearly Clinton was trying to cover all bases, and indeed new bases, with a smaller and overstretched American team. The impulses of an enthusiast were starkly in contrast with world realities. The Europeans often viewed Clinton as a likable if somewhat not totally serious figure. In many cases, such as in Bosnia and Iraq, the Europeans *were* clearly on a different political wavelength.

The conflict in former-Yugoslavia dominated the UN Security Council agenda in 1992. The Security Council had mandated the UNPROFOR peacekeeping operation and later economic sanctions against Serbia. Despite UNPROFOR's mandate to protect Bosnian civilians, before long the UN was also in the business of opening supply routes to the besieged city of Sarajevo. The scourge of ethnic cleansing brought about the creation of "Safe areas" enclaves for the Muslim population. By the end of 1992, the UNPROFOR units in Croatia numbered 12,800 and 9,000 in Bosnia. Troops from 33 countries participated in the mission. Equally the humanitarian tragedy was reaching ghastly proportions. The UN High Commissioner for Refugees (UNHCR) confirmed the number of refugees and displaced persons *within* the frontiers of former Yugoslavia numbered over two million. Of these 800,000 were within Bosnia, 618,000 in Croatia and 433,000 in Serbia. Beyond this, refugees having *fled from* Yugoslavia numbered an additional 615,000 of which half had applied for political asylum. The largest number of refugees, 260,000, were in Germany and 66,000 had sought refuge in Austria.[14]

During the vicious Bosnian conflict while British and French troops served in a UN military mandate, Washington stood by the sidelines offering moralistic advice but not boots on the ground. The UNPROFOR operation deployed a large multinational force in the beleaguered Balkan land to deter, but not stop the Serb aggression. Washington was confronted by its first major foreign policy crisis in Spring 1993, and inside Europe no less. Despite its boundless energy to effect change, the Clinton Administration was now entering an Balkan imbroglio in which there would be no easy choices. Secretary of State Warren Christopher went to Europe with the announced intention to convince our NATO allies to lift the UN arms embargo against Bosnia and to commit the use of American airpower against Serb units. Despite this intent to use American power, the Euros feared that their peacekeeping units on the ground would become hostage to Serb attack and intimidation should the U.S. use its airpower. As was often the case, bickering among allies, in this case how to end the Bosnian war, soon saw Washington and Paris trading accusations. The Clinton Administration refused to bow to European pressures to force the Bosnian government to accept a peace plan and a territorial partition with the Serbs. Ironically the United States later sponsored the Dayton plan which achieved precisely that; Bosnia's ethnic partition which exists to this day.

SARAJEVO REDUX

Indeed 1993 had been a frightful year for the Balkans. The third year of bitter conflicts continued near unabated despite the deployment of the UNPROFOR, the largest peacekeeping force in UN history. In the sober tone of the Austrian Foreign Policy Yearbook, "The year 1993 bought immeasurable additional misery for the populations of Croatia and especially of Bosnia and Herzegovina , the two states most severely affected by Serbian aggression. The great majority of more than three million refugees and displaced persons from the war zone are citizens of Bosnia and Herzegovina, where the death toll is now more than 200,000." The Bosnian capital Sarajevo was under siege and thus was supplied by a UN airlift. A 1991 UN arms embargo which was imposed on all states of the former Yugoslavia had an especially negative effect on Bosnia's ability at self-defense against Serb aggression.[15]

The Sarajevo airlift in itself was a remarkable chapter in the sanguinary saga. The UN humanitarian airlift to the besieged Bosnian capital marked its 1,000 day in April 1995, thus entering the record books as the longest such relief operation in history, and serving as a both as a testament to humanitarian concerns and to diplomatic dithering. The airlift which began three years earlier has provided food and medicine for 500,000 people in the beleaguered city often in the face of withering Serb ground fire. During the airlift more than 12,000 sorties had been flown by U.S. and European aircraft making the logistical effort longer than the extraordinary Allied Berlin Airlift of 1948–1949.

Of course the Berlin blockade was broken precisely because the Soviet Union was stood down by decisive and determined American policy to keep West Berlin, a virtual island in the Soviet occupation zone of Germany free of Stalin's coercion. The USSR opposition, the stakes, and the odds to be sure were far greater than in Sarajevo. The Berlin airlift succeeded because of Allied logistical capability to sustain the operation of much larger scope than in Sarajevo and as importantly, military power combined with political willingness to effect a solution. In Bosnia the capability was there, backed by NATO's mailed fist, by micro-managed by "neutral" and some would argue incompetent, U.N. Special Representative Yasushi Akashi.

Other observers were not quite so diplomatic. David Rieff in his riveting account *Slaughterhouse; Bosnia and the Failure of the West*, paints a scathing picture of the situation; "Many United Nations officials, convinced there had never been the slightest possibility of Western military intervention, believed that Bosnia's foreign supporters—the journalists in particular—had done great harm in fostering these illusions....What would have done more to relieve the suffering of the Bosnian people, as a senior UNPROFOR civilian official once remarked to me, was a stern public declaration by the Americans that they weren't coming." He adds, "Instead the Clinton Administration continued until well into the Spring of 1994, to hold out the hope of intervention." Rieff added scathingly, "If as it seems increasingly likely in retrospect, Washington was insincere about this from the start, rather than having simply been confused or incompetent, then President Clinton and his advisors have almost as much Bosnian blood on their hands as General Mladic. It was the prospect that military aid would eventually flow in that, time and again, stiffened the Bosnian government's resolution to fight on."[16]

The third Balkan war in the 20th century confronted a mediocre political class with a defining moment in history; a defeat for diplomacy in the face of ruthless Serb aggression. In the course of a week, Washington policy reassumed its characteristic weathervane posture spinning in all directions but pointing nowhere but oblivion. Clinton's policy only tangible effect has been to create a deep rift between the U.S. and its NATO allies, quiet scorn from the Islamic world, and a condescending smirk from the Serbs. As the Serb stranglehold tightened, the U.S. even put an embargo on its rhetoric in support for the Bosnians to defend themselves!

In late 1994, Germany's *Suddeutsche Zeitung* stated caustically, "Is it possible to be blind, dumb, sanctimonious, big talking, and heartless all at once? Politicians manage it again and again!" The paper added that from the start the U.N. and NATO made two mistakes; the UN wanted to provide humanitarian aid, and the Atlantic Alliance, particularly Britain and France, wanted to support the U.N. program. The Munich paper added, "They wanted to use neither military means to keep the belligerents apart, nor use force in making aid available, faced with a determined aggressor, that is not enough. The consequences of these good intentions are political and military chaos." The U.N. agreed to suspension of even NATO pinprick air strikes on ethnic Serb targets illustrated the lack of political stamina, which squanders massive military power, which in turn encouraged Serbian armed aggression. A cartoon in the French daily *Le Monde* showed a squadron of fully armed NATO warplanes over Serbia with the line, "Let's hope our noise does not disturb the Serbs!"

In what could diplomatically be called a discreet but dangerous formula, the Clinton Administration had opened a quiet but effective back channel between Washington and Tehran which winked at Iranian weapons shipments to Bosnia's beleaguered government. The arrangement lent American support to Bosnia in its fight with the Serbs; it equally revealed a covert action which skirted the UN weapons embargo on former Yugoslavia but put the U.S. at odds with Britain and France. The operation evoked a James Bond thriller; an Iran Air 747 jumbo jet making a midnight landing at Zagreb airport unloading ostensibly "humanitarian supplies" for the besieged Bosnian Muslims. Sixty tons of guns and high explosives were in the *cache* just in time for a Spring offensive. The weapons shipment highlighted a bizarre deal between the Islamic Republic of Iran and the United States. At the same time Iran's Foreign Minister Ali Akbar Velayati was in Sarajevo opening a new $120 million Embassy for the Islamic Republic, a nerve center for Tehran's widening religious political efforts in the Balkans.

By May of 1994, persistent reports of Iran's growing influence in the Balkan war naturally would logically raise questions over whether Washington was looking the other way to what amounted to Tehran's pro-active Bosnia policy. Through its dithering diplomacy the U.S. played into the hand of extremists, especially by allowing the Islamic Republic into the equation as an arms supplier. Tehran was allowed to wedge its agenda into the Balkans to the uncomfortable chagrin of all parties. This story was largely overlooked in the U.S. press until the *Los Angeles Times,* in a piece of investigative journalism, "broke" this story in April 1996.[17]

Following the 1994 American mid-term elections, there was intense political pressure by the new Republican-led Congress to lift the arms embargo on Bosnia. Despite the moves, French and British counter-pressures from within UNPROFOR stated that "lifting the embargo would not redress the balance" and moreover that the Europeans would then withdraw from the peacekeeping force. British General Sir Michael Rose, the former force commander in Bosnia told a UN press conference that warned that if the weapons embargo was lifted, "The U.N. forces would withdraw." As I opined at the time "The world has fiddled while Bosnia has burned and the Serbs, emboldened by their sordid accomplishments, may turn next towards 'solving the problem' in ethnic Albanian Kosovo." Tragically this would happen before too long.

In Spring 1995 the situation in Bosnia came to a climax, as NATO carried out selective air strikes on the Serbs. The Serbs then retaliated by taking 300 UN troops hostage. "The Europeans accused the Clinton Administration of having jeopardized the lives of European soldiers through American demands for symbolic air strikes....the American reaction to events at the end of May/beginning of June 1995 revealed the aimlessness of the Clinton Administration's previous policy on Bosnia," wrote Georg Schild adding, "The president declared on 31 May 1995 that American ground forces could be deployed to Bosnia 'temporarily'...startled by the domestic policy discussion these remarks triggered, Clinton backtracked on a great deal of what he said a few days earlier."[18]

The Dayton diplomatic conference would eventually bring peace, or perhaps a cessation of hostilities, to Bosnia. UNPROFOR was out, IFOR was in, and America would soon have boots on Balkan soil. "The deployment of the NATO-led implementation force for Bosnia (IFOR) is a turning point not only for the former Yugoslavia but also for the Atlantic Alliance. For the first time in the Alliance's 47 year history, we are deploying ground forces in what used to be called an 'out of area operation.' " Stressed Javier Solana NATO's Secretary General. Solana added "NATO helped bring the war to an end through its support over several years to the United Nations and through its limited, but effective use of airpower. Now the Alliance is helping to implement the hard-won peace, and thus enable the reconstruction of a viable and peaceful civil society in Bosnia-Herzegovina."[19]

And for the first time, American troops served in IFOR along with a large multi-national contingent. If there was a silver lining to the Balkan thunder clouds it was that contrary to 1914, or precisely because of the lessons of 1914, that the European powers were not rushing to play political proxies. Nobody in Europe or America wished to be pulled into Bosnia. The Bosnia conflict also brought the Clinton Administration to loggerheads with UN Secretary General Boutros Boutros Ghali. Disagreement between the Egyptian SG and the U.S. Ambassador Madeleine Albright were legend to the point that Ghali accused Albright and Clinton as thwarting his election to a second term as Secretary General. In his book, "Unvanquished/ A U.S. UN Saga" the former Secretary General caustically chastises Madeleine Albright for blocking his re-election; "She carried out her campaign with determination, letting pass no opportunity to demolish my authority and tarnish my image, all the while showing a serene face, wearing a friendly smile, and repeating expressions of friendship and admiration." He equally criticized the the Clinton Administration's legacy at the U.N. and its performance in key areas such as Bosnia during the conflict.[20]

By blocking Ghali's re-election, and ultimately causing his political demise, the Clinton Administration had also challenged and confronted many unwritten rules at the United Nations. Moreover Clinton had opened a serious rift with Paris, one which would come back to haunt American administrations.

Edward Mortimer, chief speechwriter for Secretary General Kofi Annan recalls, "Memories are short. When I worked at the UN I was surprised how often I had to remind people that our relations with the Clinton Administration had been anything but smooth. President Bill Clinton blamed the UN for his own failures in Somalia and Bosnia, and thereafter systematically blocked the establishment of new UN peacekeeping operations until 1999 when he suddenly needed them in Kosovo and East Timor...in fact cooperation was often smoother with the Bush Administration which, as the historian Stephen Schlesinger has written, "has pursued a conservative but pragmatic mission at the United Nations."[21]

BACK TO THE BALKANS

Kosovo would become the new Balkan conflict. "Our region is a powder keg—we feel we are next on the ethnic genocide list of Serbia," warned Dr. Bujar Bukoshi, prime minister of the ethnic Albanian region of Kosovo. The former autonomous province of Yugoslavia where a 90% Albanian majority voted for independence from Belgrade in 1991, appeared on the verge of combustion. "We fear we will become Serbia's next victim," Bukoshi told a UN press conference in early 1993. "The carnage in Kosovo will make the current slaughter in Bosnia look pale." Before long Serbia's growing shadows over Kosovo's majority Albanian population would entangle the international community in yet another Balkan crisis. Albanian militants pressed for regained autonomy—once guaranteed by Belgrade. Here though Milosevic was playing a zero sum game in his ethnic Albanian canton. The game plan simply stated, was to force the Albanian population from their homes and out of Yugoslav Kosovo. Mass expulsion. Milosevic's ethnic cleansing in Bosnia was a well-honed strategy by the time Belgrade forces turned their guns on Kosovo. America and Europe were prepared for the Serbian moves, but again preventive political action fell far short of stopping the carnage. Sadly the Western counter-strategy was anguished indecision, diplomatic threats, and UN Security Council paralysis. The newly elected Secretary General, Kofi Annan of Ghana, was soon embroiled in the crisis.

The Clinton White House responded with its usual diplomatic tactic towards Belgrade; *Threat, Bluster, and Fumble*. The threats were clear enough especially in view of past Yugoslav actions in Croatia and Bosnia. Washington knew full well that the Serbs not only saw their backs to the wall but viewed Kosovo as the historic well-spring of the Serbian *nation*. This region, despite its overwhelming Muslim majority and its disintegration into conflict, would be a non-negotiable firewall to *sacred Serbia* itself. Milosevic would not blink here. Conversely, the international community was not ready to accept another humiliating slap from the Serbs. The actions of Belgrade's blustering tyrant and his brutal treatment of the ethnic Kosovar Albanians, would in the minds of most, justify humanitarian intervention. As in Bosnia, many of the players were the same; the Serbs and their megalomaniac socialist leader Milosevic who felt "threatened" by the people they victimize; the Muslims who fought bravely for self-determination but are deemed the troublemakers for daring to resist, and the West, may we politely use the phrase, whose endless conferences, "contact groups" and "emergency summits" always have the breathless aura of alarm but the practical effect of a model United Nations.

"The Clinton Administration made one miscalculation after another in dealing with the Kosovo crisis," writes Christopher Layne, "U.S. officials and their NATO colleagues never understood the historical and emotional importance of Kosovo to the Serbian people. Those leaders seemed to believe that Belgrade's harsh repression of the ethnic Albanian secessionist movement in Kosovo merely reflected the will of President Slobodan Milovesic of Yugoslavia." He adds that the Secretary of State Madeleine Albright "mistakenly concluded that under the threat of air strikes, the Yugoslav government would sign a dictated peace accord (the Rambouillet agreement) to be implemented by a NATO peacekeeping force in Kosovo." Layne adds, "Administration leaders believed that even if Milosevic initially refused to sign the Rambouillet Agreement, Belgrade would relent after a brief "demonstration" bombing campaign. Those calculations proved to be disastrously wrong." But as Layne stresses, "Rambouillet was a textbook example of how not to practice diplomacy. The U.S. policy, charted by Secretary Albright, was fatally flawed in a number of respects: 1) it was biased, 2) it reflected an appalling ignorance of Serbian history, nationalism and resolve, 3) it showed a culpable disregard for the foreseeable consequences of carrying out the alliance's military threat."[22]

On the night of 24 March 1999, the U.S. Air Force commenced air strikes on Yugoslavia. There was an odd surrealism in the fact that for the first time since WWII, there were sustained bombing operations on European targets, and soon the European capital of Belgrade. So less than a year before the Millennium, there was yet another Balkan war. The Allied bombing campaign against Serbia was not authorized by the UN Security Council. Moreover a series of serious *faux pas* in the actual offensive caused collateral political damage; the mistaken and tragic targeting of the Chinese Embassy, bombing Belgrade on Orthodox Easter Sunday, and numerous mistakenly hit civilian targets. Tactical Air strikes from about 15,000 ft—despite precision guided weapons—would inevitably see less than polite "collateral damage."

UN Secretary General Kofi Annan, still in political debt to Washington bristled but gave the operation qualified support. "It is indeed tragic that diplomacy has failed but there are times when the use of force may be legitimate in the pursuit of peace…but as Secretary General I have many times pointed out, not just in relation to Kosovo, that under the Charter, the Security

Council has primary responsibility for maintaining international peace and security...therefore, the Council should be involved in any decision to respect to the use of force."[23]

As Robert Kagan argues, "The Clinton Administration sent troops to Haiti in 1994 without the Security Council authorization, which came after the fact. In 1998 the Clinton Administration bombed Iraq in Operation Desert Fox without a resolution, and indeed, over strong objections registered inside the Security Council by France and Russia...The most interesting case was Kosovo...for it was the Europeans who, along with the United States went to war without obtaining the legitimizing sanction of the Security Council. Nevertheless most Europeans at the time, and even since have insisted that the Kosovo war was legitimate."[24]

"By no means are Americans the only culprits acting without UN approval: Europeans also bypass the Security Council when it suits their purposes. In Kosovo for example, it was the Europeans (who along with the United States) went to war without obtaining the Security Council's legitimizing sanction, " advises Kagan adding, "The Clinton Administration was also perfectly content to go to war in 1999 without UN authorization. Indeed many of its senior officials hoped that Kosovo would set a useful precedent for future interventions. 'Multilateral if possible, unilateral if necessary' was the catechism of the Clinton Administration, the British political scientist Christopher Coker noted."[25]

After more than six weeks of less than crippling air raids on Serbia, Milosevic was still standing. The Kremlin's Balkan troubleshooter Viktor Chernomyrdin and Finnish President Martti Ahtisaari descended upon the UN for follow-up talks with Kofi Annan. A week earlier, Annan had visited Germany and Russia to try to craft a peace deal which would bring the United Nations center stage in any Kosovo settlement. Germany's Social Democrat Chancellor Schroeder sent numerous Ministers to Moscow in hopes for forging a deal. Even the conservative *Die Welt* newspaper spoke of Moscow as "The Mecca of all Diplomacy" and added editorially that to solve the Kosovo crisis "All Roads Lead to Moscow." Likewise the center-right *Le Figaro* of Paris wrote "It's the future of Europe which is in play. The Americans have embarked in a direction which is not best for Europe. That is why Moscow must be enlisted for the exit to the war." *Le Figaro* added, "France and Europe must put all their weight behind Yeltsin and Primakov in the battle for peace."

Charting a draft resolution through the UN Security Council was complicated immeasurably after the mistaken bombing of the Belgrade Embassy of the People's Republic of China as much as it was in the Russian perception that the U.S. and the West Europeans were "ganging up" on a fellow Slav nation. While Beijing had close commercial and political links with Belgrade, the Russians had blood ties with what were often viewed as *little brothers* in Serbia. Though the Chinese communists and former Yugoslavia both basked in the heady days of the quirky non-aligned movement, the political bottom line for both Beijing and Belgrade remained *high church realpolitik*. Neither the People's Republic of China nor the Yugoslav Socialists were willing to accept any questioning of their artificial frontiers.

PRC Premier Zhu Rongji in a candid interview with a Canadian newspaper stressed that he fears the precedent set by intervention in Tibet's affairs. He told the correspondent, "The Kosovo question is an ethnic problem which of course is an internal matter, questions like this exist in many countries, you in Canada have the Question of Quebec, the United Kingdom has the Northern Ireland question, and for China there is the question of Tibet." Fearing the "very bad precedent" for the use of force, he was clearly making the moral equivalence case for China by putting Tibet on the plateau with both Quebec and Northern Ireland. The logic was clear. China's Marxist mandarins feared that the erosion of Yugoslav sovereignty in Kosovo would jolt brittle fault lines in places like Tibet, East Turkestan (Xinkiang), and even Taiwan. Thus even a year before the Kosovo crisis, tepid United Nations Security Council efforts to stop the brewing crisis were blocked by Beijing even before Moscow came to the aid of its Serbian little brothers. A Yugoslav official told me smugly that Western efforts to thwart Serbia would be blocked by the "Great Wall of China" that referring to the PRC's Security Council veto.

But before peace there would be yet more carnage. In an article "NATO's Hypocritical Humanitarianism," Doug Bandow, Senior Fellow at the libertarian CATO Institute opined, "NATO intervention in Kosovo immeasurably worsened the humanitarian situation. The alliance turned a minor tragedy into a widespread disaster, as Belgrade responded to Western aggression by killing several thousand Kosovars and turning hundreds of thousands of Kosovars into refugees." He added, "Of course after triggering massive refugee flows, Secretary of State Madeleine Albright and British Foreign Secretary Robin Cook shamelessly claimed that 'We are fighting to get the refugees home, safe under our protection.' Bandow opined, "it was the ultimate bootstrap argument: NATO intervenes, sparking a violent Serbian crackdown, which in turn causes humanitarian chaos, which then justified NATO intervention."[26]

UN Secretary General Kofi Annan was no less sanguine especially in the view that the U.S. led air offensive against Serbia lacked UN blessing; "Unless the Security Council is restored to its pre-eminent position as the sole legitimacy on the use of force" countries "are on a dangerous path to anarchy." In a speech in the Hague, reflecting his frustration over the UN's marginalization, he also cited "However, more recently, there has been a regrettable tendency for the Security Council not to be involved in efforts to maintain international peace and security. The case of Kosovo has cast into sharp relief the fact that Member States and regional organizations sometimes take enforcement action without Security Council authorization. He added specifically, "the preference for so-called "coalitions of the willing", the increasingly divergent views within the Council, and the emergence of the single super- Power and new regional Powers have all contributed to the present situation.[27]

Yet given the depth and scope of the crisis in Kosovo, force was as necessary as it was too late. The chaos was near Biblical. During May 1999 as Allied aircraft pounded Serbia, streams of beleaguered Albanian refugees poured from the forsaken Yugoslav province. UNHCR issued daily tallies; the numbers would frighten all but the most cynical and hard-hearted. The *Kosovo Emergency Updates* published daily by the UNHCR in Geneva put the numbers into frightening perspective. For example 10 June 1999, at the end of the conflict, "The number of refugees and displaced people in the region stands at 780,700 including 21,700 in Bosnia-Herzegovina, 69,700 in Montenegro, 245,100 in the FYR Macedonia, and 444,200 in Albania." Moreover humanitarian evacuations by UNHCR of the Kosovar refugees included 5,000 to Austria, 5,000 to Canada, 14,000 to Germany, and 6,000 to the USA.[28]

Such human suffering reflected not the refugee shifts at the end of WWII, nor the ethnic communal carnage in the creation of India and Pakistan in 1947, or the collapse of Saigon in 1975, but the *Brave New Europe* of 1999 less than six months before the *Millennium!* The war ended in mid-June. The international peacekeeping forces of more than 15,000 American, British, French, German, and Italians would deploy into the disputed region. So too would the Russians, whose surprise paratroop deployment seizing Pristina airport and "causing barely concealed frustration in Washington at the Russian action." Ethnic Kosovars began to return to their homes from nearby Macedonia and Albania. "But Serbs, fearful of revenge, are fleeing Kosovo on the same roads as returning ethnic Albanians," reported the *Financial Times*.[29]

Matters had come full circle. But on the political front, fissures between Washington and the United Nations had emerged. While in Russia just after the Kosovo crisis, I sensed a perceptible hostility towards the use of American power in Kosovo, not so much that it had affected *little brother* Serbs, but that again the USA was throwing its weight around and there was not much Moscow could do about it. Clearly the Russian press reflected the collective embarrassment that despite the Kremlin's political power, Russia was relegated to a near-cameo role at the end of the Balkan war. Still the surprise deployment of Russian paratroops to Pristina served both domestic and foreign policies for Moscow. "Russia Surprises NATO in Kosovo" was the headline in the *St. Petersburg Times* with the advice, "It has salved Russian feelings of inferiority caused by being ignored as NATO launched a war it opposed. It immediately boosted the morale of the Russian military who has suffered seemingly endless blows during the last decade. It gave Russia a card to play in its ongoing bargaining with the West in the post-war Balkan arrangement."[30]

A rift with France emerged too. French Foreign Minister Hubert Vedrine described the United States as a "hyper-power. An article in *Le Monde Diplomatique*, stated bluntly, "For the first time in 200 years, one country—a "hyper-power", to use an expression coined by the French foreign minister, Hubert Védrine, overwhelmingly dominates the world in the five key areas of political, economic, military, technological and cultural power. That country, the U.S., sees no reason to share or accept limits on its hegemony when it can exercise it without restriction, unchallenged by anyone, not even the UN."[31]

"In the 1990's as Clinton and Madeleine Albright were proudly dubbing the United States the 'indispensable nation,' the foreign ministers of China, France and Russia were declaring the U.S.-led unipolar world dangerous and unjust. Samuel Huntington warned about the 'arrogance' and 'unilateralism' of U.S. policies when Bush was still governor of Texas," writes Robert Kagan.[32]

Robert Kagan, the foreign policy specialist recalls "Today many Europeans view the Clinton years as a time of transatlantic harmony, but it was during those years that the Europeans began complaining about American power and arrogance in the post-Cold War world . It was during the Clinton years that then French Foreign Minister Hubert Vedrine coined the term hyperpuissance to describe an American behemoth too worryingly powerful to be designated as merely a superpower." Kagan adds, that during the 1990's that "Europeans began to view the United States as a 'hectoring hegemon' Such complaints were directed especially at Secretary of State Madeleine Albright, whom one American critic described, a bit hyperbolically, as "the first Secretary of State in American history whose specialty was …lecturing other governments, using threatening language and tastelessly bragging about the power and virtue of her country."[33]

Historian David Halberstam pointed out that the Europeans disliked even the non-threatening Bill Clinton who viewed him "as the embodiment of something they disliked greatly about America—the smug, remote superpower whose attitude on most things was, "don't call us we'll call you, and by the way, we'll make the important decisions."[34]

Thus to this backdrop, a little Balkan lesson would be forthcoming. Bill Clinton bombed the Serbs, his triumphal crusade in Europe, mostly from 15,000 feet stopped Serbian aggression, turned Kosovo into a canton of the United Nations, still failed to settle the political status question for the forsaken region, and proved U.S. military force could operate with or without the blessing of the UN Security Council.

"Twas a Famous Victory!"

NOTES

1. Thomas H. Henriksen, "The New World Order: War, Peace, Military Preparedness." Stanford, CA: Hoover Institute, 1992, p. 1.

2. Margaret Thatcher "Freedom and the Future," Address, Heritage Foundation, Washington, D.C., 8 March 1991.

3. Henriksen, The New World Order, p. 23.

4. Henry Kissinger, Does America Need a Foreign Policy; Toward a Diplomacy for the 21st Century. (New York; Simon & Schuster, 2001), p. 288.

5. Thomas H. Henriksen, "Using Power and Diplomacy To Deal with Rogue States," Stanford, CA: Hoover Institute, 1999, pp. 6–7.

6. Josef Joffe, *Uberpower; The Imperial Temptation of America*. (New York: W. Norton, 2007), pp. 37–38.

7. Newt Gingrich, "Rogue State Department," *Foreign Policy* July/August 2003, p. 46.

8. Robert Jervis, "The Compulsive Empire," *Foreign Policy* July/August 2003, pp. 83–84.

9. Josef Joffe, Lecture Council on Foreign Relations, New York 16 June 2006.

10. G. John Ikenberry, "Illusions of Empire—Defining the New American Order," *Foreign Affairs* Vol. 83 No. 2 March/April 2004, p. 144.

11. John J. Mearschimer, "The Future of the American Pacifier," *Foreign Affairs* Vol. 80 No. 5, September/October 2001, pp. 48–49.

12. John Lloyd, "Rowing Alone," *The Financial Times/FT Weekend*, 3–4 August 2002, pp. I–III.

13. Colin Dueck, "Hegemony on the Cheap; Liberal Internationalism from Wilson to Bush," *World Policy Journal* Vol. 20, No. 4 Winter 2003/04, p. 6.

14. Austrian Foreign Policy Yearbook; Report of the Austrian Federal Ministry for Foreign Affairs for the year 1992, (Vienna: Ministry for Foreign Affairs, 1992), pp. 44–46, 51.

15. Austrian Foreign Policy Yearbook; Report of the Austrian Federal Ministry for Foreign Affairs for the year 1993 (Vienna: Ministry for Foreign Affairs, 1993), pp. 52–54.

16. David Rieff, "Slaughterhouse; Bosnia and the Failure of the West", (New York: Simon & Schuster, 1995), p. 144.

17. "Did U.S. Concern for Bosnia Justify Arms Pipeline?," *Los Angeles Times* 7 April 1996 and James Risen, "House Panel to Probe Iran Arms to Bosnia," 25 April 1996, p. 12.

18. Georg Schild, "The United States and the Civil War in Bosnia," *Aussenpolitik* (47) 1/96, pp. 28–29.

19. "Speech by Secretary General Javier Solana," *NATO Review*, March 1996, p. 3.
20. Boutros-Boutros Ghali, "Unvanquished; A U.S.- U.N. Saga," (New York: Random House, 1999), pp. 333–334.
21. Edward Mortimer, "America Must Act to Swiftly to Re-Engage the World," *Financial Times* 5 November 2008, p.9.
22. Ted Galen Carpenter, Ed., "NATO's Empty Victory; A Postmortem on the Balkan War," (Washington: CATO Institute, 2000), pp. 11, 14–15.
23. "Annan Offers Qualified Endorsement of NATO Bombing," UNWire.org, 25 March 1999.
24. Robert Kagan, "Of Paradise and Power; America and the New World Order," (New York: Vintage Books, 2004), pp. 123–124.
25. Robert Kagan, "America's Crisis of Legitimacy," *Foreign Affairs*, March/April 2004, Vol. 83 No 2, p. 74.
26. Ted Galen Carpenter, Ed., "NATO's Empty Victory," p. 39.
27. Kofi Annan Address/The Hague, United Nations Press SG/SM/6997, 18 May 1999.
28. Update: Kosovo Emergency/Geneva 10 June 1999.
29. Stefan Wagstyl, "Refugees Start to Trickle Back Despite Warnings of Mines," *Financial Times*, 14 June 1999, p. 2.
30. "Russia Surprises NATO in Kosovo," *St. Petersburg Times*/Russia, 15 June 1999, p. 1.
31. Ignacio Ramonet, "New World Order," *Le Monde Diplomatique,* June1999, p. 4.
32. Robert Kagan, "America's Crisis of Legitimacy," *Foreign Affairs* Vol. 83 No 2 March/April 2004, p. 70 also see "If we have to use force," Madeleine Albright declared pompously in 1998, "it is because we are American. We are the indispensable nation. We stand tall. We see further into the future." *European Wall St. Journal*, 24–25 September 2004, p. A11.
33. Robert Kagan, "Of Paradise and Power," p. 43.
34. Alan Dowd, "Red, White and Bruised; A Brief History of European Anti-Americanism," *The American Enterprise,* Vol. 17, No. 7 October/December 2005, pp. 33–34.

Chapter Two

Histoire—General de Gaulle, Neo-Gaullists, and America

Only a philistine or a fool, cannot be impressed and awed by Paris—*The City of Light*. Alas, much of that enchantment has been translated into political postures and philosophical attitudes among France's ruling elite where visions of *Grandeur* are so easily evoked by the majestic and splendid Avenues, buildings, and monuments.

Stroll along the River Seine by night and witness an extraordinary floodlit architectural splendor lorded over by the beacon of the Eiffel Tower, crossed by beautiful bridges, and bejeweled by monuments to artistic and military achievement. Drive from the Quai d'Orsay (Foreign Ministry), passing *Les Invalides* and the grand Ministries, which cannot but impress and equally evoke visions of power and purpose. This setting of sensuousness, splendor, and standing which has motivated potentates and politicians for centuries has set the political template for French political policies. Stand in the Place de Concorde and from the azimuth of Cleopatra's obelisk view the splendid majesty of the columned National Assembly, the Navy Ministry, the Rue Royale to the Madeleine, and the beckoning beacon of the Eiffel Tower. General Charles de Gaulle and Jacques Chirac, and a host of political accolades such as Dominique de Villepin have been willingly seduced by the charms of its splendor and been quite easily convinced that *La France* is, without question, a superpower—*a nation of consequence*.

"France belongs to an elite group of nations that still believes, rightly or wrongly, not only that the world matters to them, but they matter to the world. For these nations, international identity is an essential part of national identity," opines Prof. Dominique Moisi. He adds, "They can and must make a difference on the international scene…for France, Europe is an attempt to pursue a policy of greatness through other means, a desperate search to prolong a past of influence and glory."[1]

LE GENERAL AND THE WORLD

While many Americans are decidedly unimpressed by the moral posturing of the contemporary French political class, a little history lesson recalls what often has been forgotten, namely discord in Franco/American relations during the de Gaulle era. *Le Grand Charles,* as his towering figure was known, became the embodiment of France's resplendent history; this was a clear political calculation by de Gaulle as much as it was an actual reflection of this man who had grown up in the conservative Catholic setting of Pre-1914 France. In such circles the very phrase, *La France,* was intoned with near prayerful reverence and held a singularly spiritual place. From a historical context de Gaulle felt haunted by the specter of political instability. Between 1875 and 1914, the first year of WWI, France had 49 governments whose longevity averaged nine months; between 1918 the year of victory in WWI and 1940 the date of its ignominious defeat, France had 43 governments averaging six months in office. From 1944 the year of the Liberation until 1958 with the creation of his Fifth Republic France had 19 governments. The lessons of instability were frightfully clear.

In his book "The War Memoirs," we find "a monumental self-portrait of a solitary man, who made himself the champion and knight-servant of "Our Lady France," writes Herbert Luthy. De Gaulle recounts, "All my life I have thought of France in a certain way....like the princess of fairy stories...dedicated to an exalted and exceptional destiny...France is not really herself except in the first rank...to my mind, France cannot be France without *la grandeur*."[2]

"France is only France when she is in the first rank," she can never accept less; never recognize a hegemony other than her own; never join a group as less than an equal with the greatest; never integrate—or rather "dissolve herself" in a supranational organization where her veto power would no longer come into play," advises Prof. Luthy. In a seminal article *De Gaulle: Pose and Policy* written in 1965, he sets the template for French policy, which continues to this day. "The Atlantic Alliance may be a good thing, but an "integrated" Atlantic organization under command other than de Gaulle is unacceptable. A European confederation under French leadership may be desirable, but a United States of Europe in which France might have to give in to the will of the majority is unconceivable. Partnership with the United States is something to be wished for, but an *Atlantic* partnership, in which the United States' partner would not be France, but an integrated Europe can only be rejected. A United Nations in which France has an assured veto power and a seat in the supreme directory can be useful, but an international organization in which the majority can overrule her is an abomination."[3]

Fast forward to the 21st century and we see France as a formidable member of NATO, a key power broker and force in the European Union, a formal ally of the United States but decidedly obstructionist over Anglo-Saxon Atlantic security dimensions, and vigorously vocal as a veto-holding member of the UN Security Council.

Then as now, France wanted to exercise its power through the United Nations—but a world body in which, after all, Paris held the last say. "Under de Gaulle the Quai d'Orsay has consistently sought a return to the *status quo ante*—in other words, to the primacy of the Security Council, where France has had the right of veto from the onset," wrote Andre Fontaine in 1967; "Thus she does not risk becoming involved in operations against her will."[4]

A generation later Dominique Moisi wrote, "Exploiting its position as a permanent member of the UN Security Council, France can present itself as an alternative Western voice to the nations of the Third World."

De Gaulle's Fifth Republic adopted an overtly anti-American foreign policy. "De Gaulle's energetic effort to make France master of itself and to overturn the bi-polar system of East West hegemony that divided Europe and increasingly, the world, a system that, in his view, subordinated French interests to that of an American dominated Atlantic community, brought him into conflict with Washington and the American people," writes Richard Kuisel, adding the former Fourth Republic, "much to de Gaulle's dismay had also subscribed to an integrated and Atlantic-wide defense community and to the inception of a supranational Europe. To de Gaulle both these communities NATO and the European Economic Community, deprived France of its independence and encouraged an American hegemony."[5]

The smoldering antipathy towards Anglo/Saxon power politics had as much to do with the gripping realities of de Gaulle's contemporary France, as much as any traditional Gallic antipathy towards Albion. The Anglo/American disagreements with de Gaulle date to the General's proud but politically uncompromising leadership of Free France during the Nazi occupation. Neither Winston Churchill nor Franklin D. Roosevelt, hid their personal and political animosity for the towering leader of Free France. The February 1945 Yalta Conference in the Soviet Crimea proved to be a political watershed. "Yalta was the intolerable lump which stuck in de Gaulle's throat. France, that is General de Gaulle, had been kept out of the Conference that was to determine the shape of the post-war world. The memory of this exclusion never ceased to rankle," wrote Brian Crozier in his monumental biography of the General. In fact, "Yalta was different: France's interests were involved, and the man who, all his life, had a 'certain idea of France' was not there." Indeed, "General de Gaulle's foreign policy—his systematic anti-Americanism to the point of eccentricity and beyond; its anti-British bias to the extent that

Britain followed America's lead; his taste for a deal with Russia—can largely be traced back to the giant grievance of Yalta and the accumulated pinpricks which punctured his dealings with Roosevelt and with Churchill."[6]

Later de Gaulle witnessed only tepid political/military support for France's travails in Indochina as well as more significantly the struggle in Algeria. France's fight against Arab nationalism in Algeria, or conversely as Paris viewed it, armed subversion in a constituent province of the French Republic, found little support from the Americans. Washington offered little backing for the ill-fated Franco/British Suez operation in 1956, which the Eisenhower Administration viewed a as a last gasp of colonialism. To add insult to injury Washington would give little encouragement for his idea of a French/ British/US joint command in NATO, which would control policy planning from both the Atlantic Alliance as well as its nuclear arsenal.

"Despite his age and the continuing Algerian crisis however, de Gaulle lost no time in staking France's claim to a share in world leadership, "writes Crozier, "His principal foreign policy aim was to break the American hegemony in the Western Alliance."[7]

Neither Washington nor London felt very comfortable working within de Gaulle's political playbook. The Eisenhower Administration remained adamant in not encumbering the American nuclear doctrine with French influences. Though President John F. Kennedy showed an obvious social and stylistic tilt to the whims of Paris, he hardly made the substantial political and strategic concessions de Gaulle had tried to wrest from Washington.

As Andre Fontaine wrote, "The General had already warned Washington and London in his Memorandum of 1958 that if his proposition of a three way power directorate was not acted upon he would suspend the development of French participation in that organization." In this spirit he refused any stockpiles of American nuclear weapons, and any participation in the various collective nuclear armaments plans...in 1959, beginning with the Navy, he started the process of withdrawing French forces from the integrated command, completed in 1966. In concrete terms, the policy "calls for the removal of the NATO military commands, SHAPE and AFCENT, and the expulsion of foreign troops from French territory. Some 70,000 American and other foreign troops and over 700,000 tons of stored supplies are being shifted to other bases," wrote Carl Amme.[8]

Parallel to his plans for inclusion into the Anglo/American nuclear planning Club, France independently developed its own nuclear deterrent the *Force de Frappe* and tested an atomic bomb in the Algerian desert in 1960 to the distinct displeasure of Washington and London. Development of the Atomic Bomb was clearly a geo-political reaction of the strategic setback France suffered after the Suez debacle in 1956. The ill-fated Anglo/French

Suez invasion put Paris on the defensive even in Algeria. Nonetheless in 1957 the French government had created a nuclear testing site in the Algerian Sahara; between 1960 and 1966 France carried out seventeen atomic tests. In 1961 alone there were thirteen underground tests. Even the 1962 Evian accords leading to Algerian independence contained a special clause allowing France access to facilities for another five years.[9]

LE GENERAL REMEMBERED

Franco/German Rapprochement, after the Second World War has a hallmark of the Gaullist policy. "The main conviction of General de Gaulle was the reality of nations, he was deeply convinced that a nation remains itself from century to century," stressed Alain Peyrefitte, a former Gaullist Minister (four portfolios) who directed the prestigious *Le Figaro* newspaper. Interestingly, even during the Nazi occupation of France, de Gaulle as leader of *Free France*, nonetheless saw the need for eventual reconciliation between France and Germany.

In a speech in London's Albert Hall in 1942 de Gaulle conceded that for a peaceful and prosperous future, Europe must see Franco/German rapprochement. Peyrefitte, a confident of de Gaulle outlined a historical *tour de horizon*; "The Germans are an ancient people and de Gaulle often called them not *Allemagne but Germain*, in the Latin as at the time of the Roman Empire. He spoke of the French as les *Gaulois*, He was deeply concerned about the permanence of peoples and the character of the nation." As the General would always say, the State may change but the nation remains the same. When the war ended was to be new beginning for France and Germany. Many will argue that after 1945, France pursued this policy of rapprochement with the former foe as only to neutralize Germany and in fact to keep the Federal Republic out of NATO. In the beginning there was natural caution towards a strong Germany—even if it was under the patronage of the U.S. But when de Gaulle returned to government in 1958, he was pragmatic and said that Germany has rearmed and was de facto in NATO.

In 1958, de Gaulle in a gesture to *Germania* extended his first invitation of state to Chancellor Konrad Adenauer. On 15 September, de Gaulle invited Adenauer to his home in Colombey des Eglise—a unique gesture for a foreign leader. They decided to see each other twice a year, a tradition of between Paris and Bonn ever since. In January 1963 the Franco/ German Treaty was signed between *Le Grand Charles* and *Der Alter* and thus opened the way for an extraordinary *entente* on the European geopolitical landscape. Relations between France and Germany, the former foes, remain a hallmark of de Gaulle's policy in the core of Europe.

As a member of NATO, France nonetheless developed its nuclear deterrent, the force de frappe; "De Gaulle was convinced that France must remain a great power. As one of the nuclear powers, the first A bomb of February 1960 was exploded in Sahara," recalls Allain Peyrefitte, a former Minister of Science. Le General tasked Peyrefitte for the development of the Hydrogen Bomb; he recalls, "The H Bomb was the specific direction of de Gaulle and I was in charge of the project. In January 1966 after his second election, de Gaulle told me that he wanted an H Bomb in two years because he shall not remain the whole term and he wants this achieved." Peyrefitte recalled, "De Gaulle told me 'if the H Bomb is achieved, before my departure nobody will dare suppress it. If it is not achieved before my departure nobody will dare finish the project.' I was tasked to accelerate the project; the scientific community said this could not happen until 1979. I told the General it was not possible; he did not want to know how it was possible but that it be done." The H Bomb was tested in 1968.

France's withdrawal from NATO's military structure in 1966 caused widespread consternation from Washington to London and Bonn. The General felt NATO's real power was held by the U.S.; he believed this was subordination and refused it. At the same time the French President was assuming iconoclastic political postures towards the Soviet Union, He supported the U.S. on the Berlin Blockade and U-2 crisis but spoke of Europe from the Urals to Atlantic. De Gaulle first used the term in a press conference of 1961. "In conversations with Ministers he spoke of Europe form Urals to Atlantic because he thought ancient peoples throughout Europe must cooperate but remain sovereign. It was an idea of confederation where everyone keeps his identity but cooperates," he added. Many people will criticize de Gaulle for not speaking of the ideological aspect of the Soviet Union even at a time of the chill winds of the cold war. Peyrefitte relates, "One day he told me, as his spokesman, that Russia will drink communism like a blotter drinks ink. I repeat this, today as it has not been mentioned since that day. I told this to the Quai d'Orsay, the Foreign Ministry, and they laughed, they said de Gaulle, does not understand there are no more Russians, but *Hommus Soviticus*, new Soviet man!"[10]

Almost forgotten too was the singularly important role France played during the October 1962 Cuban Missile Crisis. Former National Security Advisor Zbigniew Brzezinski recounts, "Several emissaries went to our principal allies. One of them was a tough-minded former Secretary of State, Dean Acheson whose mission was to brief President de Gaulle and to solicit French support in what could be a nuclear war involving not just the United States and the Soviet Union but the entire NATO Alliance and the Warsaw Pact." He continued, "The former Secretary of State briefed the French President and then said to him at the end of the briefing, I would now like to show you the evidence, the photographs that we have of Soviet missiles armed with nuclear weapons. The French President responded by saying, I do not wish to see the photographs. The word of the President of the United States is good enough for me. Please tell him that France stands with America." Dr. Brzezinski asked rhetorically, "Would any foreign leader today react the same way to an American emissary who would go abroad and say that country X is armed with weapons of mass destruction which threaten the United States? There's food for thought in that question."[11]

It took a Texan, President Lyndon B. Johnson to derail the delicate relationship with de Gaulle. Johnson, hardly known for finesse, soon was at loggerheads with the French. Here too there was a forgotten precedent. France had offered diplomatic recognition to the Texas Republic in 1837. Indeed the legation of the independent Texas Republic was situated on the stately Place Vendome in Paris. This did not deter France's Minister Chevalier de Bacourt from sneering, "This Republic of 150,000 inhabitants is a regular nest of bandits." A Consular official noted, "The United States seems a paradise to anyone coming from Texas, where one cannot leave the house without being armed to the teeth. The government is composed of brigands clothed in power."

Interestingly U.S. Ambassador to France Bohlen noted on the eve of the 1964 American Presidential elections in Memo noted the degree to which President Kennedy had finally come to understand de Gaulle. He was fearful that President Johnson "would not have the patience to undertake this task and would probably not reach the point of appreciating the complexity of the General." He added, "De Gaulle's personal and public politeness might very well mislead President Johnson into mistaking manners for substantial concessions."[12]

Indeed LBJ was hardly able to coexist with *Le General*. Later in March 1966 on the cusp of the NATO rupture, Secretary of State Dean Rusk advised "The election of President de Gaulle for another seven year term is a suitable time to review U.S. policy toward France. He is opposed to basic U.S. objectives, such as a strong NATO, a unified Europe and U.S. efforts to maintain freedom in South Vietnam. These strongly held personal views of President de Gaulle are unlikely to change. They are largely based on his messianic belief in the glory and importance of France, and are not subject to reasoned argument." Rusk's ruminations over de Gaulle and French policy have a decidedly familiar ring today. Still Rusk advised "We should lean over backwards to be polite and friendly to France, to President de Gaulle personally, and to all French government officials. Backbiting, recriminations, attempts at reprisals should be avoided no matter what the temptation."[13]

"We should continue quietly and firmly on our course, ignoring Gaullist objections, but always showing respect and friendship towards him and the French people, while awaiting the day when a more friendly and cooperative government comes to power in France," advised Rusk. Ambassador Bohlen hardly agreed, "I do not propose any polemics or name calling against France. To pretend, however, that our relations were normal, after what de Gaulle is apparently planning to do, in the hope of avoiding 'irritating' de Gaulle is illusory. In the first place what is there left to preserve after he has, in effect destroyed the French participation in NATO, which I had always assumed was a cornerstone of U.S. foreign policy?"[14]

The French withdrawal from NATO's military structure in 1966 presented the Atlantic Alliance with a serious physical jolt; NATO HQ was, after all, in Paris and France hosted an impressive infra-structural support network for the Alliance. Following de Gaulle's political pique, NATO moved its headquarters to Brussels and made Belgium a pivotal player in the Alliance. General Charles de Gaulle played to the crowds. His display of independence gained political support from all sides; yet few French wanted a formal break with the Alliance or an end to military American protection.

A 1967 poll after the pullout from the command structure saw that 54% wanted to retain NATO while only 12% wished total withdrawal from the Alliance. Still his policies soured what had been good relations with the USA. Richard Kuisel states, "Once de Gaulle became stridently anti-American, opinion followed. In 1965 when asked which country they considered to be 'the best friend of France,' French citizens ranked the U.S. a poor third behind West Germany and the United Kingdom. Approval of de Gaulle's adversarial stance towards the United States grew from about a third to half of the population."[15]

The post-NATO crisis gave the General a political bounce in the polls in 1966–67. Such events presaged Jacques Chirac's political postures during the Iraq War. By stirring the embers of anti-Americanism and playing to the crowds Chirac equally brought himself an effervescent bubble in the polls, but a costly political gain for the Elysee.

The history of 1966–67 also recalls other lessons in Franco/American relations. According to Kuisel, "By 1967 it was evident that within the Western Alliance Gaullist France was the principal obstacle to American policy. By then the American press and public were howling about French "ingratitude" and "arrogance." There were boycotts of French products by American stores and a motion in Congress for the returns of the remains of American soldiers buried in France. President Johnson's break with his predecessors style of entertainment in the White House, which featured French cuisine and wines, appeared to be part of this anti-French campaign."[16]

As an ironic postscript, despite his genuine popularity in 1966–67, by the following year, serious domestic unrest spearheaded by student riots brought an end to the de Gaulle era. By 1969, a referendum caused the General to step down in April.

Gaston Deferre, a Socialist candidate for President against the General opined, "Gaullism is based entirely on confidence in one man; and he refuses to define the policy he will follow. ...Gaullism will not survive de Gaulle." In one sense that was true, but in another the persistent if often unexceptional character acting by Jacques Chirac, illustrates that one profits politically by being the shadow of such a grand French figure.[17]

"Apart from his inflexibility the most remarkable element in his character was an apocalyptic or cataclysmic vision of the world and of his role in it," advises Brian Crozier. It was clearly Messianic. Still "de Gaulle could not live without drama, and when short of a natural crisis he would create one, the better to deal with it. It was thus with his two vetoes to Britain to join the European Common Market, or with his blows to military integration within NATO." Crozier stresses, "The General's ego was of suitably gigantic proportions...with the ego and a sense of doom, followed by salvation, went an "all or nothing attitude."[18]

"The end of the Cold War only reinforced French envy of America. They resent the global reach of America's power and Washington's presumption to speak in the name of the international community," opines Prof. Moisi. "In the short run, France's jealousy of America will be muted by the political constraints imposed on it by a united Europe, the other members of which do not share France's feelings. The French know all too well that their secret dream—to build a Europe that will challenge the United States—is the nightmare of their continental partners," he advises.[19]

The events of 2002–03 presented what would be described as déjà vu. Despite growing American disgust and distrust over the French intransigence on Iraq, George W. Bush, a Texan, was equally furious over Chirac's policies. The political formula pursued by Bush Administration officials translated into "*Punish France, Ignore Germany, Forgive Russia.*" Viewing the Iraq imbroglio in the Security Council, France played its cards deftly and decisively despite the clear diplomatic damage to relations with Washington. The point was not merely any defense of the odious regime in Baghdad, but the clear political calculation that the USA's unilateralism was an equally potent danger albeit one which only could be moderated by the multilateral prescriptions agreed to by the fifteen member Security Council. Thus in all power relationships the Paris government holds dear its right to *defer and demarche.*

Clearly American perceptions of France, even among younger generations who have fleetingly viewed history through the fog of social studies lectures, seem to harbor an innately arrogant view that the French somehow have never, at least since the glories of Napoleon, done much to defend themselves. De Gaulle's heroic role, albeit with the dose of political melodrama which was clearly needed after the occupation, is somehow incongruous with the American "view." Popular jokes among University students included; "How many French soldiers does it take to defend Paris?" The answer is "Nobody knows, it's never been done before!" This historically illiterate *humor* fuels the face-value myth that the French military has never defended Paris. Without quoting from the tomes of literature regarding the Battle of Verdun and many others, the stark but sanguinary answer rests with the Grim Reaper's final accounting in lives. The roster of the fallen can be found in horrifying detail in the smallest of graveyards and churches in France, Germany, Britain and Belgium.

By Armistice Day, 11 November 1918, when the guns finally fell silent for the first time since 1914, one and one half million French soldiers had been killed in the Great War, *defending Paris* if you will. Morts Pour la France! France's 1914 population of 40 million saw 7.5 million men mobilized and 1.4 million killed and another three million wounded. Britain mobilized 8.6 million men with nearly a million killed and 2.5 million wounded. Germany from its population of 68 million mobilized 11 million troops and lost 1.7 million killed with another 4.3 million wounded. And the USA whose military of 200,000 was miniscule in 1916 despite a population of 99 million saw a meteoric mobilization in 1917 reaching beyond four million soldiers. Of the American forces deployed to Europe, 124,000 were killed and another 231,000 wounded. All in all the Allied side saw 41 million men mobilized with 5.1 million dead and 12 million wounded. The Central powers (Germany, Austria/ Hungary, Turkey) saw 20 million mobilized with three million dead and 8.3 million wounded.[20]

The carnage on all sides during this *war to end all wars*, shadowed European calculations right until 1939, and without question set the stage for the humiliating fall of France in 1940. General Charles de Gaulle put France on the road to national recovery and psychological rehabilitation in the years following WWII. This does not minimize the militarily decisive role played by American, British, and Canadian arms, but equally should not minimize the singular role played by *Le General* in the postwar period. The prestige of modern France, and some would say pretensions, are rooted in this complex socio/political legacy and played out on the modern world stage by President Jacques Chirac who envisaged himself as the *dauphin* of de Gaulle. Though hardly of the stature or having the gravitas of *Le General*, Chirac cast himself as his living political legacy.

Viewing this European Union and France's role, What would de Gaulle have said of the Europe of 1992 or 2008, given his nervousness about the

Common Market? "Without doubt de Gaulle believed in sovereignty for defense, diplomacy and for currency. He thought at the same time France must be opened for competition with other countries. Thus, he would have agreed with the Market but surely not with a common European currency," Peyrefitte opined. France today is a vastly different country than in 1970 when the General died; yet he argues that the General's legacy for the 21st Century, remains that of a figure of permanence and foresight. "His figure is an example of will, energy, and of patriotism. This is valuable for the present and future. In 1950's, the political class was convinced that a united Europe would be ready in three or four years; he would say it is not an affair of three of four years but three or four centuries. Even if we have same money, economy, and unity, there will still be in the 21st century, French people, German people, and the other proud ancient peoples of Europe."[21]

De Gaulle's contrarian impulses remain a feature of French politics long after *Le General* was put to rest in Colembey-les-Deux-Eglises. In 1986, responding to Libyan support to terrorism in Europe, the Reagan Administration bombed Col. Qaddafi's headquarters. France vigorously opposed the over flight of American warplanes over her territory en route to Tripoli. The U.S. Air Force was thus forced to reroute its aircraft from Britain around the Iberian peninsula to attack Libya. The political backlash in America to the French blocking actions introduced a new tension between Washington and Paris simmered for a number of years.

FRANCE AND THE IRAQ WAR

A few days before Iraq invaded Kuwait, I recall visiting the offices of *Le Figaro* in Paris and reading a quite positive interview with Saddam Hussein; the article reflected the close political and commercial ties between Paris and Baghdad. Ironically not too long thereafter, French combat troops would be streaming to the Gulf to assist in the American effort to oust Saddam from Kuwait!

Fifteen years later and in the midst of the deep Franco/American divide over Iraq, the French Defense Minister Michele Alliot-Marie stated unapologetically "The relationship between France and the U.S. is the foundation of the trans-Atlantic relationship."[22]

The rocky relationship between America and France during the twelve years of Jacques Chirac's Presidency could change in style but not in substance. The political showdowns, which started with the Clinton Administration during the Balkan wars, would reach their zenith during Bush Administration and the Iraq war. While Chirac's flamboyant opposition to the Bush policies brought him a spurt of short term popularity, there's little doubt that they caused a deep and lingering rift in Franco/American relations. Naturally that pivotal moment of September 11th in an instant, changed the socio/ political landscape of so much of the world, and no less the core relationship between the USA and European Union. The predominant opinion holds that while the Al-Qaida terrorist attacks on America brought a near singular sense of trans-Atlantic solidarity, clearly the political fumbles and foibles of the Bush Administration in to the words of countless diplomatic sages, "squandered and lost that good will."

What is less appreciated is that *just prior to* September 11th, a widely discussed opinion poll by the Pew Center, found Europeans stridently critical of Bush policies. "George W. Bush is highly unpopular with the publics of the major nations of Western Europe. By wide margins, people in Germany, France, Great Britain and Italy all disapprove of his handling of international policy," cited the Global Attitudes Project.

When asked, "Do you approve or disapprove of the way George W. Bush is handling international policy," 65% of Germans disapproved, as did 59% of French, and 49% of British. More poignantly, when asked, "Which one describes George W. Bush?" 85% of French surveyed "He makes decisions based entirely on US interests" while only 8% admitted "He takes into account European interests when making decisions." Though France registered the largest criticism, 79% of British and 73% of Germans agreed with the assessment. Two key issues triggered opposition—the Kyoto Treaty on greenhouse gasses and scrapping the Anti Ballistic Missile (ABM) Treaty. The report added however, "A solid majority of Europeans believe that, whatever their view of Bush, the United States and Europe have not grown apart in recent years. Germans and Italians were most likely to see more common ground among the allies, but even among the British and French fewer than a quarter (24% and 20% respectively) believe differences between the United States and Europe have widened."[23] Significantly these comments were made on the eve of September 11th and long before the Iraq war.

During the Cold War after all there was a bi-partisan consensus in Washington to face off the threat from state players, the Soviet Union and Communist China. Moreover the American defense umbrella for Europe shielded an especially vulnerable West Germany from a frontal Soviet threat. During this period, while there certainly was much dissent, and differences in perception, the clear majority of Europeans—including the French—were focused on the Warsaw Pact as well as communist internal subversion. After the epic political events of 1989, and the subsequent collapse of the Soviet imperium, the direct military threat to Western Europe dramatically eased and thus too did the direct defense reliance on American arms. Psychologically most people could focus on a specific and formal threat from Moscow rather than from an amorphous mirage in the vastness of the Islamic world. Though France favored a more nuanced approach in dealing with the political permutations in the Islamic world, the U.S., especially the wake of September 11th, took the messianic view that the lure of democracy and economic betterment alone will prove sufficient to confront and confound the radicals. She moreover stresses the dangers from the *"hyper power,"* namely singular U.S. power. This concept, started by former Socialist Foreign Minister Vedrine carried into the nationalist Chirac government; namely the need to balance *the hyper power* instincts of the USA with alternative or competing poles of political power, presumably the European Union or perhaps People's China? The French seemed enamored with the multi polar geo-political structure and indeed with seducing many countries into the sphere of Paris, through the enchantment of neo-nationalism, anti-globalization, and of course anti-Americanism.

British Prime Minister Blair bluntly confronted this impulse during an landmark address to the U.S. Congress in July 2003: "There is no more dangerous theory in international politics today than that we need to balance the power of America with other competitor power. ..I believe any Alliance must start with America and Europe. If Europe and America are together, the others will work with us. If we split, the rest will play around, play us off, and nothing but mischief will be the result of it." Blair added poignantly, "To be a serious partner, Europe must take on and defeat the anti-Americanism that sometimes passes for its political discourse. What America must do is to show that this is a partnership, built on persuasion, not command."[24]

This point is well taken too as the perception among many Europeans, especially the French, remains that Washington wishes to remake the world, not only the Islamic world, into an American image and likeness. This is a strongly held view even among many of America's traditional friends. Dominique Moisi argues, "A consensus already exists among the French elite that even if France was right to condemn what in retrospect looks like U.S. adventurism in Iraq, Paris could have voiced its concerns in a less offensive way." He adds, "Now is the moment for Mr. Chirac to demonstrate that France is a responsible country, that it takes no pleasure in U.S. setbacks, and that it is not simply waiting for George W. Bush to be defeated in the Presidential elections."[25]

Though political permutations continued to bedevil Iraq policy between America and the French, the curious cultural war between the old friends confronts the contemporary era. France while loving to hate America, has shown little desire not to copy and devour its popular culture. Increasingly so, the USA, while taking habitually cheap swipes at the French, really could care less about the land of Lafayette, Napoleon and de Gaulle.

After forty years in the political arena with twelve years in the Presidency, Jacques Chirac announced he would not be a candidate in 2007. The American reaction, as much as many cared, was nearly all negative to the Chirac era which sadly had poisoned trans-Atlantic relations over the Iraq war. Domestically he equally failed to revive France's ailing economy, its deadweight high taxes and unemployment, nor solve its growing conflicts with home grown Islam. Still Chirac's step-down represented an end of an era in which the theatrical French president played the political superpower even if the backdrop chorus were the ex-colonies of the *Francophonie* and *Tiers Monde*.

"Anti-Americanism is the national faith of France," opined author and commentator Michel Gurfinkiel, adding with a touch of irony, "but the French are very relaxed about faith."[26]

WINDS OF POLITICAL CHANGE

The Presidential election in 2007 brought a new dynamic to the hexagon. Nicolas Sarkozy the standard bearer of the neo-Gaullist center-right and Seoglene Royal the doyenne of the *Socialist-lite* left represented a new postwar generation in French politics and a shattering of the old stereotypes. Sarkozy heir to the Gaullist mantle, is the son of immigrants, a Hungarian father and a Greek mother. Segolene Royal, the socialist who cast herself as *a left-wing Joan of Arc*, became the first woman to run for the presidency to reach the second round. Sarko and Sego dominated headlines for a year and became a long running political road show; both being smooth, packaged and airbrushed candidates *a la American*. Both represent the traditional Right/Left divide which dominates the political scene. Sarko was a protégé of President Jacques Chirac. Sego was a protégé of ex-Socialist president François Mitterand. But contrary to the past where ideology played a stronger role, France today despite being increasingly middle class and *bourgeois,* needs a strong dose of reality and leadership to revive a dispirited nation.

The passions of the Presidential election brought a plethora of political books. Publishing houses reported two million copies were sold with the best-sellers being centrist candidate Francois Bayrou *Project of Hope* (370,000 copies) Franz Olivier Giesbert *The Tragedy of the President* dealing with the darker side of the Chirac era (365,000), *Temonigage* Witness by Nicolas Sarkozy (245,000) Eric Besson's election eve expose *Who is Segolene Royal?* (60,000), and Segolene Royal's own manifesto Maintenant *Now* which sold a mere (11,000) copies.[27]

Without question France's economic malaise and domestic tranquility dominated the agenda. High taxes, rigid labor laws, the fastest rising public debt in Europe, and the constricting web of a generous welfare state served as an undertow to job creation and productivity. It's no secret that many entrepreneurial French have moved to Britain and the USA for better work conditions and the chance to keep more of their earnings; 52,000 French were registered to vote in the UK alone! During both rounds of the election, the French Consulate in New York maintained three separate polling stations in Manhattan to accommodate the large number of its citizens living in America.

During the campaign both candidates played a strong appeal to nationalism. Though foreign policy was not a key element in the elections, France's international role matters. Relations between France and the United States have been poor since before the Bush presidency. Clearly Jacques Chirac overplayed played the anti-American card in the wake of the Iraq war and had sadly created a serious rift in trans-Atlantic relations. Sarkozy has consistently stressed the importance of France's ties with Washington and he's known as being instinctively pro-American and should signify a marked improvement in the overall political atmosphere between Paris and Washington. Given France's powerful position on the UN Security Council and undeniable political clout in much of the developing world, he would usually favor the U.S. concerning many global issues. Sarkozy is above all a pragmatist, a realist, and a reformer but not the kind of romantic who would instinctively embrace the USA.

The extraordinary electoral triumph of conservative candidate Nicolas Sarkozy, raised hopes both inside France and among the country's key friends. Domestically Sarkozy offered a dynamic program to revitalize the languid economy and revamp the moribund social state. Internationally, he would revitalize the Franco/ American relationship. Sarko, as he is known, claimed a mandate. Indeed among the 86 percent nationwide turnout, he won 53 percent of the vote to Socialist opponent Segolene Royal's 47 percent. *Le Figaro* headlined "A Brilliant Victory." His UMP movement won the biggest electoral victory for the center-right since the days of Charles de Gaulle. He pledged, "The French have spoken and have chosen to make a break with the ideas, the customs and the behavior of the past." He added boldly, "I am thus going to restore the status of work, authority, standards, respect and merit." This conflicts with the Socialist view of the near sanctity of the welfare state.[28]

Sarko's success will be measured as much by his electoral majority as by the willingness of the minority to cooperate in his ambitious program for dynamic economic change. This willingness should not be assumed. The *Dirigisme* of a strong State whose entrenched social and economic power goes well beyond politics, serves as a dead weight to change. Sarkozy himself is pulled between the conflicting impulses of traditional Gallic protectionism and market competitiveness. Most French are wary of "Anglo-Saxon free enterprise." Sarkozy wants to bring a new dynamic to the commercial scene, yet he confronts a massive state sector; Electric de France (EDF), Gaz de France (GdF), and the Atomic power agency (Areva) all being in excess of 80 percent state owned.

While Nicolas Sarkozy is compared in many ways to Ronald Reagan or Margaret Thatcher, one should not be tempted to go quite so far; both Reagan and Thatcher worked in an Anglo-Saxon environment where social solidarity and work ethic are defined very differently than in France. France is proudly not Anglo Saxon and the mere mention of economic liberalism can cause Gallic sneers across the political spectrum. Still let us not forget that *laissez-faire* economics and even the word *entrepreneur* are French terms. France will define the renovation of the economic scene less in Thatcherite terms and more using the many French icons of economics to spur new growth in the world's sixth largest economy. More than a few French leaders and their Prime Ministers have fallen on the sword of social and economic reform— demonstrations and orchestrated strikes can shut down the country.

Importantly in the foreign policy arena, Sarkozy unabashedly reaffirmed the close ties with the United States. Concerning ties with America, he stated, "France will always be by their side when they need it, but I must also tell them that friendship means accepting that your friends may think differently." Thus Sarkozy did not offer the USA *carte blanche* support in Iraq but clearly aimed to improve the tenor and climate of the Franco/American relationship.

His successful campaign motto applied to his presidency, "Together all becomes possible." Despite being born after WWII, Nicolas Sarkozy embraced the historical iconography of Free France. During his majestic inaugural motorcade down the Champs de Elysees, he made a special stop at the statue of Charles de Gaulle and earlier honored youth in the French resistance youth shot by the Nazis in 1944. The aim was to seamlessly connect the generations his own and the today's youth with a classic "idea of France." Later on his inauguration day, Sarkozy visited Berlin to reaffirm Franco/German Amity; "For France, the Franco/German Amity is sacred. Never will it falter." He stated. "This represents a change in generations in France/German relations" opined *Le Monde*, " Indeed both Sarkozy and Angela Merkel started their political careers after the fall of the Berlin Wall and profited from a new Europe.[29]

Le Figaro editorialized, "A New Man…Nicholas Sarkozy is not only a new President, he's also a new man installed in the high functions of the State. Through his origins, what he says, through his style…The comparison is simple but it floats, yesterday, a perfume of the Kennedy's, a zest of glamour, a wind of modernity."[30]

Early in his tenure in a stunning diplomatic triumph President Sarkozy secured release of six Bulgarian nurses imprisoned for almost a decade in Libya. The President's wife Cecilia acted first as a secret emissary, and then negotiator, with Colonel Muammar Qaddafi to free the nurses and a doctor imprisoned in the North African nation on trumped-up charges. Dubbed "Super Sarko" by the French media, as a perfect finale Sarkozy himself turned up in Tripoli the Libyan capital for a lightening visit to do a little business with the Bedouin ruler. In a combination of diplomatic aplomb and commercial brashness, France's new President engineered a surprising political coup amid a characteristically maverick performance.

The influential *Le Figaro* advised, "To pull off this masterstroke, Sarkozy did not in any event hesitate in ushering in a new diplomacy, one both personal and conjugal. A 'Sarko method' that is well known on the national stage, combining audacity, discretion, pragmatism, and a good dose of communication." As Sarkozy often says, "*Baraka* (luck) is part of good governance." While characteristically quiet (some would say ineffective) European Union diplomacy droned on, Sarko the French action figure came to the rescue! The Presidential couple stole the spotlight and even trumped their own Foreign Ministry, the Quai D'Orsay. Moreover the deal removed a key impediment and opened the way for an overall normalization of relations between the European Union and Libya. Many EU diplomats were not amused by this brash maneuver.

SARKOZY IN AMERICA

Shortly thereafter, Nicholas Sarkozy visited New Hampshire for his summer holiday. Sarkozy's vacation diplomacy is focused on reinvigorating strained Franco/ American relations. It's all about going beyond political damage control in the period following the Iraq war and cementing closer ties with Washington. While later visiting the Bush summer residence on the Maine seacoast from his house in nearby New Hampshire, Sarkozy affirmed proudly, "It has been 250 years that France and the United States have been allies and friends." "Bush-Sarkozy : Climate of detente between France and the United States," headlined the leftist daily *Le Monde*, adding, "The French President desires 'more balanced relations' between the two countries."

Speaking of the seacoast Summit at the Bush home in Kennebunkport Maine, *Le Monde* added, "A sign of the rehabilitation France/American, was the lunch at Kennebunkport organized family style in his honor. This scenario would be unimaginable with Jacques Chirac after his 'betrayal' over Iraq." The Bush family (including George the Father and George W) hosted a lobster picnic and boating for the visiting French delegation.[31]

After the often tempestuous political ties between Paris and Washington during the Chirac era, the new President infused new optimism and confidence to Franco/ American relations. Nicholas Sarkozy is unapologetically pro-American and reflects a hoped for dynamism of a new France, not a brooding and embittered reaction to the rise of U.S. "hyper power," by willing to cozy up to Moscow and Beijing as a counterforce to American influence. It's clearly in the national interests of both France and the USA to overcome the frosty relations of recent years. France remains one of America's oldest allies, a vital member of the European Union, and a permanent member of the UN Security Council. Yet even during the strained personal ties between Jacques Chirac and George W. Bush, the USA and France were and still are cooperating on key international issues such as anti-terrorism, Lebanon, Afghanistan, Iran, and Darfur.

Significantly not long after the Bush/Sarkozy meeting, French Foreign Minister Bernard Kouchner paid a surprise but highly symbolic visit to Iraq. While offering solidarity with , "Iraq this great country, this friend of France," Kouchner also expressed the desire to "turn the page" on poor relations with the United States and look to the future. The trip came on the fourth anniversary of the terrorist truck bombing of the UN headquarters in Baghdad and the killing of Sergio Viera de Mello, UN special envoy, who was a personal friend of Kouchner's.[32]

As Pierre Rousselin editorialized in *Le Figaro*, "France no longer poses as a rival to the United States. It is no longer allowing itself to be locked into a role that is not its own; that of being the rallying point for all those who oppose America." He added, "Nicholas Sarkozy proclaims Franco/American friendship loud and clear, a friendship he believes does not entail any 'alignment.' On the contrary, it strengthens our ability to make suggestions."[33]

In a memorable address before the UN General Assembly, Sarkozy stated, "France remains loyal to its friends and to the values it shares with them. But loyalty is not the same as submission; loyalty is not a straightjacket. And France intends to put that loyalty to work in the service of opening up to others."[34]

Falling in love again. That's would best describe the theme and the sentiments of French President Nicolas Sarkozy's State Visit to Washington. Rekindling the Franco/American amity and stressing the transatlantic ties which were so recently tainted by animosity stemming from the Iraq war, the Sarkozy visit was not about damage control, but about stressing shared values, symbolism and aspirations.

"I came to Washington with a very simple message. I want to reconquer America's heart," Sarkozy said during a White House toast to President George W. Bush . He added, "I have come to tell you one thing—that is that France and the United States are friends, we are allies, always and forever." Significantly, President Bush brushed aside recent differences with France and said both countries were working together to solve global conflicts. "French and American troops are helping to defend a young democracy in Afghanistan. Our two nations support the democratic government of Lebanon," he said adding, "We agree that reconciliation and democracy in Iraq are vital to the future of the Middle East and our two nations condemn violations of human rights in Darfur, in Burma and around the world."

But it was President Sarkozy's magisterial and deeply emotional address before the joint session of the United States Congress which proved a political milestone which was cheered with standing ovations by both Democrat and Republican lawmakers. Relating heartfelt thanks for the sacrifices of American soldiers who fought and died in two world wars to preserve France's freedom, Sarkozy offered a special benediction, "I want to express the deep, sincere gratitude of the French people. I want to tell you that whenever an American soldier falls somewhere in the world, I think of what the American army did for France. I think of them and I am sad, as one is sad to lose a member of one's family." He added, "The men and women of my generation remember the Marshall Plan that allowed their fathers to rebuild a devastated Europe. They remember the Cold War, during which America again stood as the bulwark of the Free World against the threat of new tyranny....No one has the right to forget. Forgetting, for a person of my generation, would be tantamount to self-denial." Turning to current crises, he stressed "Let me tell you solemnly today: France will remain engaged in Afghanistan as long as it takes, because what's at stake in that country is the future of our values and that of the Atlantic Alliance. For me, failure is not an option. Terrorism will not win because democracies are not weak, because we are not afraid of this barbarism. America can count on France." In conclusion his speech ended with "Allow me to express one last conviction: Trust Europe. In this unstable, dangerous world, the United States of America needs a strong, determined Europe."[35]

France's left-leaning newspaper *Le Monde* described Sarkozy's address to the U.S. Congress as an "Ode to America." *Le Figaro* viewed the visit offering a very French angle, calling it "operation seduction." Later at Mt. Vernon, George Washington's home, the symbolism of historic Franco/American relations again shone forth. It was a Frenchmen, the Marquis de Lafayette, who was the first foreign dignitary, in 1824, to address a joint session of Congress. Lafayette who offered his services as a volunteer to help the American colonists fight the British, soon became Washington's friend and military confident and thus contributed to American independence.

The American press lacked the enthusiasm or at least chose not to put the Sarkozy visit to Washington as a diplomatic victory for the Bush Administration. Interestingly despite Sarkozy's dramatic reaffirmation of the Franco/American friendship, the media was lukewarm in its coverage. The *New York Times* buried the story in page A12, the *Washington Post* had a page two feature and a small page A4 story. Incomprehensively, neither the *New York Times*, the *Washington Post* or the *Wall Street Journal* published an editorial or an op-ed piece on this positive turnaround in relations with France. Clearly the Bush Administration looked to Nicolas Sarkozy as one of America's key and most vocal European allies, replacing Britain's Tony Blair. In the Summit's afterglow, Sarkozy's visit to Washington turned out to be a win-win diplomatic triumph for both sides but more importantly, a reaffirmation of the friendship with America's oldest ally.

During his last official visit to Europe, President Bush made a special stopover in France to meet with Sarkozy. *Le Figaro* headlined "Bush Celebrates Reconciliation," and stressed both the personal friendship between the two leaders and the strength of relations between the two countries. The visit highlighted further reconciliation between the U.S. and France. Bush later spoke with affection of France as "America's first friend."[36]

NOTES

1. Dennis Bark, Ed., *Reflections on Europe*, Dominique Moisi, "A European Triangle: France, Germany and the United Kingdom," (Stanford, CA: Hoover Institute, 1997) p. 74.
2. Herbert Luthy, "De Gaulle: Pose and Policy," *Foreign Affairs* Vol. 43 No 4, July 1965, p. 564.
3. Ibid., pp. 568–569.
4. Andre Fontaine, "What is French Policy?" *Foreign Affairs* Vol. 45 No 1 October 1966, p. 67.
5. Richard Kuisel, "Seducing the French; The Dilemma of Americanization." (Berkeley: University of California Press, 1997), pp. 134–135.
6. Brian Crozier, De Gaulle; The First Complete Biography (New York: Charles Scribner's Sons, 1973), p. 545.
7. Ibid., pp. 520–521.
8. Andre Fontaine, "What is French Policy?," p. 67 and Carl Amme, "NATO Without France," Stanford, CA: Hoover Institution, 1967, p. 156.
9. Jean-Luc Nothias, "Le Bilan des Essais Nucleaires Francais en Algerie," *Le Figaro*, 20 March 2007, p. 12.
10. Alain Peyrefitte Interview/Paris (August 1990).

11. Zbigniew Brzezinski, "A Must Read Speech," The American Prospect. Online 31 October 2003.
12. Foreign Relations of the United States, 1964–1968 Western Europe/Volume XII, (Washington D.C.: Government Printing Office, 2001), pp. 56–57.
13. Ibid., pp. 111–112.
14. Ibid., p. 114.
15. Kuisel, "Seducing the French," pp. 142–143.
16. Ibid., p. 140.
17. Gaston Deferre, "De Gaulle and After," *Foreign Affairs* Vol. 44 No 3 April 1966, pp. 435–439.
18. Crozier, "DeGaulle", pp.664–665.
19. Dominique Moisi, "The Trouble With France," *Foreign Affairs* Vol. 77, No. 3 May/June 1998, p. 97.
20. Charles F. Horne, Ed., Records of the Great War Vol. VII (New York: National Alumni, 1923).
21. Peyrefitte Interview.
22. Peter Spiegel and John Thornhill, "A Grand Vision for Europe through Parisian Eyes," *Financial Times* 16 February 2005, p. 3.
23. Pew Global Attitudes Project, "Bush Unpopular in Europe," Washington, D.C., 15 August 2001.
24. Tony Blair, "Prime Minister's Speech to the United States Congress," Number 10.gov.uk 18 July 2003.
25. Dominique Moisi, "Chirac Should Rebuild Trust with America," *Financial Times* 22 April 2004, p. 13.
26. Author Interview Mr. Gurfinkiel Paris 2007.
27. Mohammed Aissaoui, "La Politique est Entrée dans les Librairies," *Le Figaro*, 7 May 2007, p. 41.
28. "L'Eclatante Victoire," *Le Figaro*/Election Special 7 May 2007, pp. 1–3.
29. Henri de Bresson and Cecile Calla, "M Sarkozy et Madame Merkel d'Accord sur Urgence de Relancer L'Europe," *Le Monde* 18 May 2007, p. 8.
30. "Un Homme Neuf," *Le Figaro*, 17 May 2007, p. 15.
31. Christophe Jakubyszyn, "Sarkozy Chez Bush pour Restaurer le lien Franco-Americain," *Le Monde* 12/13 August 2007, pp. 1–4.
32. Visit to Iraq; Minister of Foreign and European Affairs/Bernard Kouchner, diplomatie.gouv.fr 19 August 2007.
33. Pierre Rousselin, "Diplomatie: Rupture et Continuite," *Le Figaro* online 28 August 2007.
34. French Mission to the United Nations/Address by Nicolas Sarkozy before the General Assembly 25 September 2007, p. 2.
35. French Embassy/Washington D.C./Address by President Nicolas Sarkozy before the Congress of the United States, 7 November 2007.
36. Alain Barluet, "Bush Celebre la Reconciliation entre Paris et Washington," *Le Figaro*. online, 13 June 2008.

Chapter Three

McWorld vs. France?

The French *hate* America. For many Americans, this remains a near scriptural statement of fact. *In fact*, it's a glaringly preposterous fiction when you consider that the French still visit America *en vacances*, and much prefer Florida and the Disney world complex, New York City, and of course California. Unless you consider a people who come to Florida beaches to do penance, or to Las Vegas hone their math skills, or perhaps to New York City to be bored by either Broadway Shows or the Metropolitan Museum.

   The French have been enchanted by America ever since Alexis de Tocqueville visited the early Republic with what is today described as *an attitude*, only then to be seduced and converted to near worship of the U.S. of the 1830's! His book *Democracy in America* stands as a poignant paean to Americans and our ways. On so many points his wisdom resonates as clearly today as it did 175 years ago.

   But for reasons I have yet to fathom the French in particular have found an odd enchantment with elements of the very culture they profess to hate, the TV, the movies, and the music. Forget the old adage that the French love Jerry Lewis, maybe a generation ago, but for well over a decade, I've seen posters for Eddie Murphy's latest flicks on train station platforms from Angers and Lyon, to kiosks in Paris. Add the latest action movies from the USA and you have the half the selections playing in *Le Cinema*. Hollywood's annual Oscar Night, a ritual I find profoundly boring and self-congratulatory, has long been a focus of the French media.

   This is certainly not to say that French Cinema does not have its own well-subsidized movies, which are often artfully produced, cerebral, and often actually quite good. The masterpiece *Indochine* with Catherine Deneuve proves the point. So does *La Vie en Rose,* the tragic story of Edith Piaf, which won a 2007 Oscar. Yet the box office receipts, the bottom-line, are based on what sells. There's little doubt that American movies make up the clear majority of the selections offered at cinemas across France.

An article speaking of the 2006 Cannes Film Festival, stated that for 2005, French production reached a new record with 240 films made of which 187 were of a French initiative. Indeed French movies comprised 37 percent of nationwide cinema attendance. Among the five principal European markets, French filmgoers are in the first row with cinema entrances, far ahead of UK and Germany.[1]

AMERICAN CINEMA AND CULTURE

While France produces more films than any other European country, and such movies retain a sizable minority market share even in the face of competition from giant American studios, the French filmmakers lobbied Brussels for an extension of the current subsidy system which allows the government to fund up to fifty percent of the cost of the movies. This *"L'exception culturelle"* exists under a special European Union exemption. Foreign critics believe among other things that the $650 million invested annually in the French film industry has created a dependency culture among filmmakers and a haughty disregard for audience tastes. Less known is that the National Center for Cinematography (CNC) receives a percentage of all box office receipts, even for foreign movies, which in turn subsidizes the production of French films.[2]

The cinema, a bastion of French culture, has long been under serious assault by America. *Paris Scope*, the entertainment weekly reports that in mid-August 2009, among the top ten films in France, eight were American. Up, Harry Potter and the Half-blood Prince, The Taking of Pelham 123, and Ice Age led the list. Among the grand cinemas of the Montparnasse, movie selections appear to offer nearly a royal flush by Hollywood. It's more than a summer romance, American films are box office hits year round. A year earlier such American blockbusters as Indiana Jones and the Royal City, Sex & the City, and Iron Man led the list.[3]

Yet the cultural condescension towards the American cinema is glaring. French film director Bertrand Tavernier warns, "If the technology is controlling us, it will transform us into stupid children, and in a way, part of the American cinema does just that." Phillipe Rogier author of L'Enemie Americain was even more caustic, "The French were not willing to accept the increase in American culture in their society." He told the BBC, *"The French would not call it a culture—it is a non-culture, a non-civilization, just a way of life."* Tavernier warns that American films are a "first step in an American takeover of France…the American understood that if they are forcing the people to see the film, the people who see the film will buy the product—they will buy hamburgers, Coca Cola, they will buy the clothes—an maybe they will buy the policy." He added, "They always understood that the first way to occupy a country was to impose their films."[4]

As early as 1927 the French government made a failed attempt to limit the number of American films shown in France. The quality daily *Le Figaro* concedes "The American Parade—the Grand Summer Offensive of American Movies." The article adds, "The French moviegoer is eclectic. They love the French cinema over all others. But Hollywood is in the summer, without question, the favorite child of the French public with the super productions of animation, action, and fantastic comedy with special effects and suspenseful dramas." Despite the French film industry being highly state subsided and filled with many artistic productions, the marketplace clearly favors the cinematic sensations and special effects from the USA. As *Le Figaro* admits, "with 89 percent of the market, American films reign supreme."[5]

Surf the radio airwaves of Paris and prepare yourself not for *retro* Piaf but for a crude and cacophonous assault of American Pop and Rock tunes, Rap music, and French-copycat Rap. Every American entertainer one would find in LA or New York is on the air here too—so I presume there's a market? Yet, instead of Spanish language and *salsa* programming as in New York or Dallas, there's Arabic and African Bi Bop! Of the more than 50 FM stations in the French capital, most echo American entertainment. Radio *France Info* and France *Culture*, while notable state subsidized exceptions, are under serious assault by forms of entertainment and cacophonous trash that mirror's LA's South Central or the Souk of Algiers more than the *City of Light*. Walk down a Parisian boulevard and see *Le Look American* with, T-shirted youth, which could as easily be in New York or Miami. I once thought the Chicago Bulls were somehow the patrons of the Paris *Metro* given the ubiquitous logo which seemed to be everywhere on people speaking the language of Moliere. Yes, and baseball a hats worn backwards on those whose ancestors once wore the cockade of Robespierre!

In many ways Paris is to France what New York is to America, a big, iconoclastic mélange of both riches and wretchedness. Homeless and beggars are common, one only ponders who with a massive social welfare schemes as France offers how so many have "fallen through the net," as the sociologists would glibly say. Yet only a Philistine could gaze upon Paris from simply hundreds of places and not be impressed by its greatness, grandeur, and scope.

The endless debate over McDonald's, or McDo as they are known, has become another feature of French life. While the ubiquitous hamburger chain is found through France, and most of Europe, the French at the same time act as if it somehow poses a personal culinary affront to each and every citizen of the Republic. Shall the arrival of the Seattle-based café group Starbucks in Paris produce the same red-hot emotions? In 1999, anti-McDo *activists,* more properly called hooligans, attacked the French-owned franchises causing great property damage. Jose Bove the farmer and self-styled Robin Hood has put McDo on his anti-globalization crusade and became a cult figure in the *protest circuit* at Davos and World Bank meetings. Actually the anti-McDo movement is a thinly veiled excuse not so much in defense of French culinary values, but for America-bashing. As one who has graced the Golden Arches far fewer times than *most* Frenchmen, I readily concede that McDonald's popularity in France and throughout Euroland rests less on its cuisine, (though the ingredients are all French) than on a product, presentation, and easy-lifestyle appeal. As with American movies, they attract.

A Frenchman Denis Hennequin is the President of McDonald's Europe and overseas a business empire of 6,400 restaurants of which 1,134 are in France. France is McDo's third largest market presence in the EU after Britain and Germany. More than ironically in 2005 McDonald's operating profit in France was second only to the United States.[6]

Euro Disney outside Paris has always elicited mixed emotions too. When we visited some years ago, I mused why Europe needs a *faux Disney castle* when the landscapes from the Loire to the Rhine offer so many authentic ones? Yet Disney is all about imagination and high tech diversions, so kids from France and throughout Euroland come for the unique entertainment magic. Though *Euro Disney* was never the theme park *extraordinaire* some would have fantasized, the complex still remains the number one tourist attraction in Euroland with over 200 million visitors since its opening in 1992. In 2007 while reaching a record 14.5 million visitors, as compared with the totally-French themed *Parc Asterix* which only drew 1.6 million guests in the same period, *Euro Disney* is still losing money. But despite the cultural love/hate relationship, *Euro Disney* ranks as the biggest employer in the Paris region. As a matter of fact, Orlando, Florida, home of the Disney complex, attracts approximately 3.7 million international visitors annually –half of them from Western Europe. In 2006 170,000 French visited Miami a 25 percent jump over the previous year. Tourism officials state that Florida is in third position from French arrivals after New York and the West coast.[7]

And speaking of Florida and what could be called *Americanization*, I hesitate to recount the historical and architectural devastation of many French cities, and not from WWII. Such rich cultural jewels as Angers or Nantes are as horribly affected, as would be post-industrial towns. Exit the *Auto Route* at any medium sized French town and be prepared to pass outskirts or should one say the *environs* and be visually assaulted by billboards, malls, and a form of development that seems to have taken its cue from California or *Nouveau Jersey*. Long gone are the distinctive cream and mauve lettered road signs, replaced by a standardized Euro code. Surrendering the suburbs to a chock-a-block sprawl of fast food, furniture, and mega-market permutations on Home Depots and Wal-Marts, and one has the impression that France has willfully copied more than MacDo. Indeed the French mega-retailer Carrefour is second in size to America's Wal-Mart but *Zut Alors has twice as many stores and is present in twice as many foreign countries!*

If people so hated America and American pop culture, you would be hard pressed to notice it. As a matter of fact, as an American I often wonder myself at the oft particular French attraction to things American. *Vive la différence?*

A LOVE/HATE RELATIONSHIP?

Naturally there's the glaring contradiction and a *near sophomoric* political and social hostility to George W. Bush. President Bush has faced a drumbeat of vitriolic criticism from the European elitist press. This has subsequently trickled down to a wider public opinion who while hardly instinctively anti-American have become increasingly *reconditioned* to view North America with a renewed smugness and *moral hauteur*. Ironically, the Euros caught this *political malaise* from the American media, who after all were not only fawning pro-Clinton in much of their coverage, but perpetuated the myth that in Election 2000, Bush was *not legitimately elected*. The Euros media reflected the elitist American opinion and succumbed to the allegation that Election 2000 was *stolen by* Bush. Subsequently the American people got what they deserved, and Europe in turn had a dunce as an interlocutor in the White House.

My suspicion was confirmed by none other than a member of the elite editorial board of the French daily *Le Monde* who conceded "Bill Clinton always had a very positive image of Europe and George W. Bush never had this. But when it comes to Bush, something the Americans cannot forget is that the *Image of George W. Bush, the image we have is built by the American media*. We read the American media and French correspondents in America. We had a very negative image of George W. Bush, which did not change after September 11th. Yours changed because he became the Commander in Chief—this image of Americans as victims of terrorism of Sept 11 and Al Qaida changed." He nonetheless added, "There was a tremendous feeling of solidarity with America but the image of Bush did not change. So we are still with what we read in the *New York Times* and the *Washington Post*." *Bien sur*, Indeed so![8]

Put bluntly, the condescending American views of George Bush by the Upper West Side and West Coast liberals had now permeated most of Western Europe. What had once been an ill defined smugness, turned into focused shrillness and distain. While many of the same criticism echoed during the Reagan years, the profound difference was that during the 1980's, the USA was still providing the military shield against the Soviets. Though the hard left opposed this view, the great middle classes reflected across the European political spectrum, accepted the close ties to Washington. While Ronald Reagan was certainly demonized by the chattering classes and the hard left of what was then the European Community, George W. Bush was deeply despised by the elites and a fair majority of ordinary citizens throughout the European Union. At the start of the Iraq War in 2003, French public opinion polls, the ubiquitous *sondages,* were not only presenting an "anti-war" message and critical of American policies, but more dangerously viewing the U.S. as a greater threat to world peace than Saddam! As dangerously a *Le Monde's* poll actually showed that one third of the French wished Saddam's Iraq to win the war, while another third supported the US. What I find most appalling is not whether they supported Washington or not, nor whether they were "against war," but that a sizable minority wished that Saddam Hussein's regime would triumph over the Anglo/Saxons, read Britain and America! So those well-educated and smug disciples of the *Liberty, Fraternity, Equality* and the *Rights of Man* wished to philosophically side with an Arab despot whose regime has made a vile mockery of the humanistic ideals the French apparently hold so dear.

DESPITE A SHARED HISTORY—RHETORIC RULES

Thus when vandals crudely desecrated a WWI British Commonwealth military cemetery in northern France, I'm reminded of the poignant memorial in Notre Dame of Paris to the supreme sacrifice of Commonwealth forces, from Britain, Canada, India, and South Africa—*one million of whom* died in France during the Great War. When Franco/ Muslims attack Jews on the streets of Paris, I recalled that sad plaque on the Isle St. Louis commemorating the inhabitants of Maison Halphen, among them 40 Jewish children deported in 1942 to the Nazi death camps. When editorial cartoons depict Uncle Sam as a boorish or naive warmonger, one remembers those unsophisticated American boys landing on Omaha beach on a June day in 1944. One could easily imagine that today's often cruel emotions have their psychological effect upon many young thugs who act out their frustrations in the twisted spirits of the times. Vile feelings often spur vile acts.

Yet, given the long and positive relationship between the USA and France, not to mention the American blood spilled in the defense of France in two World Wars, and treasure expended in her relief and rebuilding—such pro-Saddam sentiments can't simply be brushed off as voicing "another opinion," but as embracing a bitter, self-hating, and calcified view of the Western world. Significantly, I would surmise that many of such French supporters of Saddam equally distained France itself! Be certain of that! Opposing the Bush Administration as a "threat to world peace" comes naturally to many. No matter that Saddam's Iraq, was an aggressive dictatorship, the "peace movement," with Orwellian deft, clearly established the fact that Washington was the warmonger!

There was a triple theme—*Texan Cowboy, Environmental Disaster, and Illegitimate Election.* The Texan cowboy was viewed in the unrelentingly hostile and near childish coverage of Second Amendment and death penalty issues in American in French press. Environmental hostility reflected Washington not signing the Kyoto Climate Treaty. Then on the cusp of failure of diplomacy in Iraq, the UN's Chief Weapons Inspector Hans Blix told an MTV audience that he personally sees not signing the Kyoto Treaty as a reckless disaster more dangerous than Saddam's chemical and biological weapons. Such fueled an emerging schism in worldviews between the U.S. and the EU. The image of the USA as an environmental global villain, and the caricature of Uncle Sam in a top hat evoking the gilded age robber baron usually smoking a cigar, remains a crudely consistent theme in many European cartoons and editorials.

Indeed much of the European hostility towards the USA was not towards America *per se*, but to the Administration of George W. Bush. The smirky moral superiority had found a bountiful well spring in the Bush White House. For those European chattering classes who revel in an instinctive and ingrained smugness over the what is viewed as the somewhat simple if decent Americans, George W. nonetheless had emerged as an *icon of contempt* in the pantheon of a reviled Republican Administration. Though many of the same sentiments shadowed Ronald Reagan's Presidency, nonetheless Reagan's oratorical adroitness and personal panache could easily disarm both domestic and foreign critics in ways George Bush. simply couldn't.

Conversely on the eve of the Iraq war, New York's feisty former Mayor Ed Koch unambiguously slammed the French; "I hate the French government," he extolled on his radio show. Koch would end his program with the words "And Gaul must be defeated." The airwaves of America's talk shows spewed with a shrill anti-French near hysteria, which while often funny, was more often tasteless and downright wrong. Early in the crisis one WOR talk show put some context in the discussion with an interview of *Financial Times* columnist Gerard Baker; comment and humor was done to a cute background of typical French accordion music. Some shows brought balanced views while others reveled in pure anti-French jingoism. I often mused if America's *nouveau enemy* was not Old Western European France or Germany for that matter, would we be so quick to empty the quiver of stereotypical and satirical arrows at say Mexico or Cameroon? Somehow I doubt it.

France eagerly earned and indeed cultivated much of the opprobrium though her consistent and shortsighted political actions and *rhetorical rapiers* of Foreign Minister Dominique de Villepin. Equally the long stated political position that Paris government would use its powerful veto to block any second Security Council resolution authorizing military action against Saddam's Iraq, placed the Chirac government clearly at odds with Washington and in turn doomed any opportunity for a unified UN military response.

Major demonstrations against the impending conflict rocked Europe. Interestingly the largest manifestations were not in France. "Why this bias when the French were not more against the war in Iraq than the Germans, the British and the Spanish?" asked Patrice de Beer of *Le Monde's* editorial Board. "When people took to the streets you had a few hundred thousand in France, you had millions in Spain, millions in Germany, millions in Britain, and millions in Italy. And so the surprising thing for us is that *we* were almost single-handedly pinpointed by the British and the Americans![9]

On the governmental side the countdown to conflict in Iraq proved a testing ground both for the rhetorical anti-Americanism as well as France especially staking out a political position showing a Third Way. De Villepin's poor political judgment seemed to outdo itself at Institute of Strategic Studies (ISS) in London when *during the war* he did not say he favored the Anglo/American coalition to prevail over Saddam's forces. British tabloids such as the *Sun* were livid showing front page depictions of French President Jacques Chirac pictured as a "worm." To ensure, the message was understood across the *Manche*, the *Sun* published scathing bi-lingual editorials and distributed the newspaper gratis in Paris!

The rhetorical counter batteries of the Quai D'Orsay were quick to return fire across the Atlantic and the Channel. Foreign Minister de Villepin warned that many articles in the American and British press "lacked any basis in fact, which were lies, and we felt the need to explain ourselves."

The French claimed that the Bush White House has managed and "organized a disinformation campaign," against Paris. Had the Bush Administration even attempted this tactic, many of the U.S. news outlets would have instinctively taken the French side! Having served in the French Embassy in Washington during the 1980's, de Villepin may be aware that American news organizations are not government operated, controlled, or directed any more than Fleet Street editors in London answer to the Prime Minister. The French while genuinely shocked by Anglo/American broadsides against the position of the Chirac government concerning the Iraq war, may well take a glance at the pages of most of the Paris press to find an almost hysterically hostile attitude to London and Washington. French media contacts reminded me "It seems that the British needed a scapegoat to justify their war they had to redirect their anger against the French which is easy to do."

SLAYING THE HYPER-POWER

Much of this came from the French philosophical view that America has become the "Hyper-power" a phrase coined by Socialist Foreign Minister Vedrine and echoed by most of the Parisian political spectrum. Thus in the aftermath of the Cold War when America emerged as the "world's single superpower," France would offer the planet a political and philosophical counterweight. That French role has been self-anointed since the days of General de Gaulle, was often unquestioned, but evolved to the fore in the countdown to the Iraq war in 2002–2003. Yet speaking with a presumably unique moral sanctity was clearly not appreciated by all.

In his monumental book the *Anti-American Obsession*, French philosopher/ historian, Jean-Francois Revel bluntly admonishes his countrymen who often can't fathom the growing dislike of France, "Would you want me to tell you the truth without another cover up? The truth is that France has become one of the least favored countries of the planet. I have already spoken about her arrogance, her vanity. I would have to add the pretension of the governing class to teach the world a lesson. All the world, is not perhaps the right word. We don't want to teach a lesson to Saddam Hussein, Kim Jong-il, neither to Fidel Castro, or the Imams of the Islamic Republic of Iran, neither to the directors of China. We reserve our admonition and our distain to democracies, to Austrians, Italians, to Margaret Thatcher, Ronald Reagan, George W. Bush, and even Tony Blair who is insufficiently hostile to capitalism."[10]

ISLAM IN FRANCE

France's role of the keeper of a philosophical flame of global caring and solidarity with *Les Arabs* and the *Tiers Monde* are hardly new political trends in themselves, yet often represent new policy thrusts against an historic ally, the USA. The trend equally represents not so much the fruits of careful cultural lobbying of organizations such as the *Institute de la Monde Arab* (Institute of the Arab World) a well funded organization on the Left Bank practically in the shadow of Notre Dame, but an underlying feeling in France that close ties with the Arab World are clearly desirable for many reasons, cultural and commercial. Few will disagree that classical Arab civilizations represented in the great centers of learning with Cairo, Damascus, and Baghdad being most worthy of admiration and study. Nor can France turn from its important business markets from the Maghreb to the Persian Gulf. But this is not the central point.

Somehow I feel this has less to do with such practical issues as the flow of petroleum to France than keeping a quiet and unspoken *concordat* between the Elysees and the ethnic Arabs in France, "les Beurs." who happen to be a growing, radical, and restive minority. The Islamic Franco-Arab youths, often those split between both cultures and uncomfortable in each, present a dangerous political fault line running from Provence to Paris. Those second and third generation Algerian youth in the suburbs, the *banlieue,* of French cities, confront the vain political class with a combustible and confrontational element which can shatter the calm and concord which the country likes to envisage.

In Autumn 2001, a soccer match in Paris between the French team and Algeria brought catcalls and booing during the playing of the French national anthem, La *Marseillaise.* Such boorishness on the part of ethnic North African youth—mostly born and educated in France by the way—brought home a transparent but rarely mentioned reality; namely that France has a considerable and growing minority that which does not identify with the core culture of the host country—hardly les *Enfants de la patrie.* The popular slogan describing the tricolor flag's Bleu, Blanc, Rouge, has been replaced with the provocative banlieue jargon of the *new France* "Black, Blanc, Beur."

While not a "nation of immigrants" as is the USA, already by the 1920's there were three million foreigners in the country, a mélange of Armenians, Italians, Poles, and Russians, many of them political refugees. By the 1960's French industrial expansion attracted North Africans, Portuguese and Yugoslavs. By the 1970's people from ex-colonies in Africa as well as Brazilians streamed in.

One is reminded that even when *RMS Titanic* berthed at Cherbourg before its ill-fated voyage in 1912, many passengers embarking from France were from the Middle East and southern Europe. Among French Moslems today, a tendency has emerged to favor the less established Mosques such as those blossoming throughout the banlieue. In France the majority of Imams are self-proclaimed opening the door to more grassroots fundamentalism. Typically North African governments "send and pay" for mullahs to serve Muslim communities in Western Europe. In the past Moslem leaders once proudly earned and wore medals and decorations of the French Republic, have been increasingly marginalized by the radical youth. Moreover many of the new North African immigrants don't wish to identify with or assimilate into France or its culture, but view residence there as a place of safety, a source of income, and a grand subsidizer of their Islamic lifestyle in Europe.

"France, once a Western, White country with a Christian background, is morphing into a multicultural, multiethnic and multi-religious nation, with a strong Islamic element," states noted commentator Michel Gurfinkiel. He adds, "Like most other Western countries, and in spite of its nationalistic posturing, France has gathered large numbers of alien immigrants for decades, mostly from the third world : either citizens of the former colonies in North Africa, Sub-Saharan Africa, the Levant, the Indian Ocean, the Far East, or citizens of other Middle Eastern or tropical countries, or even « *cultural aliens* », i. e. French citizens from overseas territories in the West Indies, the Indian Ocean and Oceania, who settled, or were induced to settle, in France proper. In the long run, it has led to a dramatic demographic and societal transformation."[11]

Amir Taheri, an Iranian exile author advises, "France does have a problem with its Arab population. The North African minority, known as *beurs*, bear deep resentment about France's colonial past. It also regards itself as a victim of racial discrimination, much as do African Americans in the United States. The problem of the *beurs*, therefore, is social, cultural, and economic, not religious. Even if all *beurs* converted to Christianity or became atheists, they would still feel like victims, because they cannot get good jobs and are confined to the shanty-towns. There's even more to refute about the "subversiveness" of France's six million Muslims. Of these, for example, more than half have taken up French nationality and thus, one must presume, respect the principles on which the French republic is based. Another 1.5 million, mostly from Algeria and Morocco, are believed to have dual nationality. But there is no reason to believe that they wish to undermine the principles of French statehood."[12]

Interestingly while Arabs living in the USA tend to be more educated and have better lives, in Europe the opposite is true. "In general Muslims living in Europe, of which Arabs constitute a significant proportion, are poorer, less educated and in worse health than the rest of the population," writes Moises Anim. He adds, "The failure of Arabs in Europe is particularly worrisome, given that ten of the states or entities along Europe's eastern and southern borders, are home to nearly 250 million Muslims, most of them Arabs, with a birthrate double that of Europeans.[13]

The Great Mosque of Paris, a Tunisian-styled structure alongside the Botanical Gardens and near the old Roman Baths of Lutese, has long been a part of the cultural mosaic of this vibrant part of Left Bank Paris. I'm writing these words almost literally in the shadow of this edifice. Yet this Mosque, which dates to the 1920's remains part of the more "establishment" Moslem community. Today within French Islamic communities there are social rifts more of class and culture, than interpretation of the Koran. The *metis* culture of the ghetto and the call of *les integrists*—the fundamentalists—has become a curse to the mainstream Muslim community in France. It equally poses a threat to social tranquility and security within the hexagon itself. During the nervous deliberations over Iraq in Autumn 2002, a French diplomat at the UN confided to a network news correspondent that a key reason France does not wish to be seen as vigorously opposing Saddam concerns a possible *domestic political backlash* inside France itself!

A report by the French domestic intelligence services and leaked to *Le Monde* discovered that at least half of the 630 suburbs studied were populated by poor, young French of north African immigrant backgrounds. In what *Le Monde* editorialized as *SOS-Ghettos*, the *banlieue* had in effect become separate ethnic communities. The report warned the ghettoes, cut off from mainstream French society, could encourage radical Islam to take root. The intelligence service report deals with an extremely sensitive issue for France: just how bad the sense of alienation has become in the suburbs, among the French-born children of North African background. It concludes that the situation is actually worse than previously thought. Of these *banlieue*, at least half could already be called ghettoes, whose inhabitants felt rejected by, and were in fact rejecting, mainstream French society. Unemployment, crime and violence, as well as frequent anti-Western and anti-Semitic graffiti characterized these areas. The intelligence services concluded that many immigrants were rejecting French values and even the French language, following instead more traditional ways of life associated with their ethnic origin, including religious radicalization among young Muslims, and a backlash against young Muslim women who wore Western clothing.[14]

While between five and six million Muslims live in France, the largest number are of Algerian origin. Approximately one million are Moroccan, 400,000 Tunisian and at least 340,000 African. Interestingly the government estimates that twenty percent frequent the mosques. Moreover immigrants from outside the EU tend to live in the various "sensitive urban zones," where unemployment is rife and confrontation is viewed as a rite of passage. In October 2008, a Paris soccer match between the French team and rival Tunisia, saw booing and whistling during the *La Marseillaise*, prompting the French government to warn that such insults to the Republic at future matches will see the game stopped at once.[15]

Some French citizens have joined the ranks of jihadists. Many had links to having fought in Afghanistan, Bosnia or Chechnya. Pierre de Bousquet of the Ministry of the Interior (DST), warned, "The French *jihadist* is rougher, younger and more radicalized than a few years ago. The ease in which they are indoctrinated to serve as cannon fodder is worrisome." Still the French view the problem as facing an "adversary" rather than an enemy. "Our response is judicial, and not military," de Bousquet states, "To elevate the anti-terrorist fight to a war increases the risk as it gives the terrorist recognition."[16]

Following the Iraq war, attacks on Jewish institutions in France continued apace, as the Muslim youth vetted their pent up frustrations and anger not only at French society in general but at the traditional Jewish targets in particular. Following the burning down of a Jewish school in a Paris suburb, *Le Figaro* headlined "Chirac condemns anti-Semitism 'in the name of the Nation.'" Graffiti became common in Jewish cemeteries.

Writing in the *Jerusalem Post*, the brave and articulate Michel Gurfinkiel, editor in chief of the French weekly newsmagazine, *Valeurs Actuelles* stated:

> Life used to be easy for French Jews until very recently. The mere fact that so many Jews had gathered in one single country helped a lot. In 1939, there were about 350,000 Jews in France. By 1945, one third of them had perished (a comparatively low rate by Holocaust standards). Postwar arrivals from Eastern Europe and the refugee influx from Islamic countries brought about a new, younger community of about 700,000 souls, or close to 1 million, if one is to include the very assimilated Jews. A critical mass was thus reached, allowing for Jewish books, kosher food, Jewish education. French Jews were poised for a Golden Age. The fall, over the past three years, has been all the more breathtaking. The major reason for it is quite simple: The Jewish critical mass effect has clashed with a parallel critical mass effect—the rapid rise of a huge immigrant Islamic community, 10 or 12 times as strong as the Jewish community in numbers (estimates range from 6 to 8 million). In a perfect, ideal world, both groups could live together and integrate together into the larger French society.

Gurfinkiel explains how French Jews have experienced this clash since it began in October 2000: More than 20 synagogues and schools have been set on fire. Jewish children and Jewish teachers are routinely harassed at school. Rabbis are beaten or spat at in the street. And above all, the nation's elite has been strangely reluctant to admit there is something wrong going on. It took a year for the press to report seriously on this phenomenon. It took much more time for the government to respond. For any Jewish person with common sense and insight, the writing is on the wall."[17]

What commentator Michel Gurfinkiel describes as the Neo-French, form a now serious political bloc. He states, "Under French law, no census may be taken on the basis of race, ethnicity, religion or national origin. Still, it is widely estimated that :(a) about 10 million residents of metropolitan France, out of a total number of 63 million, i e. one resident out of six, have third world roots; (b) if one is to include the overseas territories, which are technically part of the same country under French law and international law, one should rather say that 13 million residents out of 66 million, ie. one resident out of 5, have third world roots ; (c) the immigrant or overseas communities are much younger and more prolific than the metropolitan communities : when it comes to the younger brackets of the global French population, they amount to 30 % of the total population at least, and in some cases, to 50 %."[18]

Today's *Gallia*, is alas, still divided into three parts; that of the conservative forces who coalesce around the De Gaulle legend and who say *La France* with a reverence expected from the pulpit of Chartres Cathedral; the collectivist France of Socialists or communists; the racial/religious mélange France where growing African/Islamic values are *officially accepted, but privately resented*. All three groups find their solidarity though an ethno "fundamentalism" as the path to preserve their identity.

The Gallia of the disaffected Banlieues exploded into the headlines and the French consciousness in October/November 2005 when gangs of mostly Arab and Africans rioted in the Paris suburb of Clichy sous Bois—before long a prairie fire of riots and ritualistic car burnings engulfed France from Paris to Provence. During a fifteen-day period, nearly 300 cities and towns were attacked by this Muslim rage towards "the system." The government's initial response to the violence was ham-handed and ineffective until a State of Emergency and curfews were imposed. Only then did the fires subside. Nicolas Sarkozy, the tough Interior Minister who was blamed by the rioters and some of the establishment for stoking the resentment by calling the rioters "scum and riffraff" nonetheless staked out his political position for the 2007 Presidential elections. The violence, called by many the French Intifada, confronted the State with the most serious challenges since the student street protests of 1968, had many causes—but at the end of the day highlighted the deep social, economic and religious rifts in France itself. It equally underlined the evolution of what many commentators see as *Eurabia,* a quasi-Islamic entity inside Western Europe. Still the troubles did not actually focus on Islam *per se* but a rather a hateful rage against the system—in this case the French Republic. The bonfires of the banliuees equally burned the cherished myth of multi-cultural France. Moreover the gangs of disaffected mostly Muslim youth, became the mob without a cause, set to the cacophonous cadence of

Gangsta Rap music and worshiping the cult of mindless violence as a way to gain "respect" and to protect one's "identity." Whether this group really sought social integration into the Republic remained questionable.

Quite naturally the French wish to keep close cultural and often political ties with former colonies and members of the French-speaking world, the *Francophonie*. This exceeds Britain's attachment to the Commonwealth. Linguistically too, one cannot really appreciate the French cultural attachment to their language which they view rather correctly as under assault from English, or should we be more precise, *Americans who speak English.* Globalization has English as its *lingua franca* quite the same as in different historical ages Latin and German were the pillars of science and learning. Comparable linguistic power would often parallel geographic empire or dominance of an institution or science. Latin and German were long mainstays of science. French and Italian, defined the arts and literature. English owes its near dominant role to the dual powers of the former British near-global empire and to American entrepreneurial skills developing a global business empire.

LANGUAGE AND GLOBALIZATION

The computer set the basic grammar for a global English usage while the internet spread English through cyberspace and through every exit of the information highway. "It's not really that France opposes globalization," advised Jean-Francois Revel but "France on the other hand would like to replace America as the leader of globalization!"

France will often decry America's "wild west" and essentially free market economic system, the French despite their education may have forgotten that while Adam Smith was a Scot, an almost equally important proponent of free market and libertarian ideas was the Frenchman Frederic Bastiat whose books *The Law* and the *Economic Harmonies* appeared in the 1850s. The books remain classic cases for political liberty and free enterprise. They would do well to read these books today. The French economy remains dependent on the still predominant role of the State.

Look at the French demography. With a population of 58 million, relatively high by West European standards, the numbers are boosted by a high birthrate among Muslim families. Approximately ten percent of France is Muslim. Such numbers have to be juxtaposed against a sharp decline among adherents of the Roman Catholic Church, the faith of the Daughter of the Church. In the past thirty years, the number of Catholic parishes has declined by half from 34,595 to 17,550 today.[19]

Though Pope John Paul II made a highly successful pilgrimage to Lourdes in southern France in Summer 2004, the reality remains that the once overwhelming part of the population, which considered itself Catholic and practicing, has fallen precipitously in the past twenty-five years. The Catholic Church moreover faces a severe shortage of priests; in 1980 there were 38,000, by 1995 the number fell to 28,000 while today the number has fallen drastically to 13,500. Given age, demography and retirement, it's expected that in a decade there will be 4,500 priests for a country of sixty million.[20]

Beyond a religious and ethnic composition, the key issue facing France is the cold hard statistical fact that too few people are working and paying taxes to support an ever-burgeoning older population. This situation is hardly unique, but poses a challenge of how to balance a graying population with fewer workers paying into social security systems. Longer lives and earlier retirement makes for an interesting dilemma. While most people across the European Union will concede this problem, few will offer the needed flexibility to allow their respective governments any givebacks from the benefit systems. The tight strictures of the welfare state will stifle growth and Entrepreneurship while at the same time proving a deadweight to the varied societies.

In a poignant essay in Dominique Moisi, the Deputy Director of the French Institute for International Relations concedes, "On the eve of the 21st century France faced four major challenges, which are together the sources of its melancholy. "The *First* is globalization, which is often blamed for the erosion of France's culture and its depressingly high levels of unemployment. The *second* is the unipolar nature of the international system, in which the United States leads and a once-proud France is grudgingly forced to follow. The *third* is the merger of Europe, which threatens to drown out France's voice. The *fourth,* and by far the toughest, challenge is France itself. The nation must overcome its economic, social, political, moral and cultural shortcomings if it is to successfully face its other challenges."[21]

These issues simmered well before the election of George W. Bush but were certainly exacerbated by a Republican in the White House. This was not that that Washington's policies were so substantially different, but their tone was decidedly less globalist and deferential to key European Union concerns especially on environmental matters. Following September 11th, the Bush Administration's determined defense and security policies moreover created an alarm among many countries who feared that the USA would pursue unilateral policy solutions to geopolitical issues. Such fears were focused on the Administration's policies towards the *Axis of Evil,* namely promoting regime change in Saddam's Iraq, Islamic Iran, and North Korea.

Washington's policies caused a deep political rift among traditional allies. France for one, substantially disagreed with the American intent towards Saddam's Iraq, and clearly disputed the Administration's unmistakable path to war with Baghdad. Though the concept of Iraqi disarmament though a UN inspections process was supported, there was painfully little enthusiasm in Paris for formal regime change, let along any military incursion into Iraq without a wider Security Council blessing. The essentially Anglo/ American nature of the diplomatic and subsequently military offensive against Saddam's Iraq, focused France to oppose the mission, to threaten use of its Security Council veto, and to try to rally a political counterforce to block military action in Iraq. The French initiative fundamentally failed and moreover caused serious political strains both across the Atlantic and the English Channel. Though President Jacques Chirac and his near theatrical Foreign Minister Dominique de Villepin enjoyed a substantial boost in popularity for their diplomatic choreography in opposing the war, the afterglow of the stunning American victory in "Operation Iraqi Freedom," tilted the balance back across the Atlantic. Before long the French settled back to more mundane issues of strikes and unpopular reforms. Chirac's popularity plummeted. Playing the modern *Sun King* was not a lasting role.

In the aftermath of the allied military victory in Iraq, and in the midst of debilitating domestic strikes in France itself, President Chirac attempted an *encore* performance through hosting the G-8 Summit in Evian. Still the superficial *bonhommie* between Presidents Chirac and Bush masked the deep undercurrent of mistrust between France and the United States. Moreover amid the mountain splendor and calm of the Evian setting, not far away in wealthy Geneva, anti-Summit protesters was trashing parts of that fashionable Swiss city. As the French police had forcibly closed access to the protesters, the demonstrations focused on nearby Geneva. The usual *Euro-mob* of anti-globalization and anti-war throngs which brought chaos to Genoa a few years earlier, were able to disrupt the holy grail of capitalism in Geneva while at the same time vetting their venom on America and capitalism in general.

Indeed, the Iraq conflict reactivated the traditional left and especially its militant Marxist and anarchist wings. On the official level, the confrontation with Saddam Hussein equally reinvigorated French policy and national standing. Jacques Chirac impulsively played the traditional Gaullist policy strains like a fiddle but hardly with the finesse of *Le General*. France, in its esteemed opinion, remained vindicated for its actions. "America's difficulties in occupying Iraq and Mr. Blair troubles over the alleged distortions of intelligence will only encourage France to stick to its line," advised Francois Heisbourg, Director of the Foundation for Strategic Research in Paris. "The sense of vindication in Paris is sustaining the romantic element in Mr. Chirac's foreign policy. It would be wrong to attribute his motivations over Iraq to cynical arrogance. Both Chirac and Blair were driven by the politics of conviction," he adds. "If a charge is to be leveled against French policy, it is a lack of realism and an excess of conviction. However, France will have to balance its romantic temptation with the realities of the post-war world," Heisbourg cautions.[22]

Romance aside, the French political class made a grave miscalculation over Iraq and suffered political and economic fallout vis-à-vis America for the medium term as a result. When asked how Jacques Chirac, a man of presumed political acumen, allowed this confrontation with Washington to get out of hand, Patrice de Beer of *Le Monde* opined, "The political price was international relations. He made a mess of relations of with the U.S. He made a mess of relations with Spain and Italy. Because he placed in the same basket the governments that were pro-American and the people who are for peace. He actually pushed public opinion towards their government because they felt insulted. In dealing with Eastern Europe, he acted the way people accuse the Americans of behaving towards Western Europe." De Beer added sarcastically, "What we can be un-happy with is that George W. Bush policies managed to have made Chirac more popular in France!"[23]

In the nervous aftermath of September 11th many overseas observers underestimated the Bush Administration's conviction and militant desire to preempt another terrorist attack as well as neutralize state patrons of global terror. Thus when the Chirac government actively opposed American initiatives on Iraq, Paris was placing itself on a philosophical par with America's enemies. While editorials disdainfully referred to the Franco/German opposition to the war as the *Axis of Weasel*, far stronger and scathing opprobrium was reserved for Paris and Berlin in the Pentagon, the National Security Council, and at the White House. Senior Pentagon official Richard Perle's acerbic statement that "France is no longer an American ally," was in the context of foreign policy statements almost as politically riveting as if he had announced a policy shift embracing Castro's Cuba. Perle added, "I have long thought that there were forces in France intent on reducing the American role in the world...very considerable damage has already been done to the Atlantic community, including NATO, by Germany and France."[24]

Secretary of State Colin Powell's criticism of France on Charlie Rose's PBS interview almost seemed friendly. Judging the political machinations of French policy at the UN prior to the Iraq war, Secretary Powell intoned, "I won't go any further than to say that it was a fascinating diplomatic experience. But now it's over and we have to take a look at the relationship. We have to look at all aspects of our relationship with France in light of this." When asked "will there be consequences for the French for standing up to the United States, Powell stated bluntly "Yes."[25]

Chapter Three

BOYCOTTS

While rhetorical salvos flew across the Atlantic between the politicians, the media gleefully magnifying the whole spectacle, it was on the commercial front that France suffered greater losses. French wine sales in the United States dipped dramatically. Naturally a strong EURO currency, greater product competition from American and Australian vineyards, and a seething tensions over the Chirac government actions in Iraq, has put French wine producers in the crosshairs of political disputes. Beyond boycotts and ritualistic dumping of Bordeaux into American streets to protest French policy, the deeper long-term damage exceeded the 20 percent sales dips in April and May of 2003. Still after sober reflection, the long-term results were not so jolting. American imports of French wine, the U.S. Department of Commerce shows that $809 million in 2001 jumped to $910 million in 2002, $1.1 billion in the pivotal crisis year 2003, then dropped to $1.02 billion in 2004 and rebounded to $1.1 in 2005 and $1.3 billion in 2006. Stated another way French wine exports since 2001 have surged nearly fifty percent despite boycotts![26]

Overall the damage goes well beyond wine and affects the entire spirit of Franco/ American relations. France remains the world's most popular tourist destination. According to the International Tourism Organization during 2002, 77 million people visited *La belle France*, far ahead of the 42 million visiting to the USA or 24 million to the United Kingdom. While Americans are not the largest number by any means, they are among the biggest spenders. A *Le Figaro* headline lamented, "French Tourism; the Summer of all Misfortunes." An article added that American tourists boycotted France for political reasons and the cost of an expensive Euro."

For the French, the commercial losses have been formidable yet the political damage in relations may be deeper. Facing the banes of the global recession, a weaker U.S. dollar, and indeed the prissy perceptions of many American towards France even after the Iraq war, it came as no surprise that American tourism to France dipped in 2003. In a genuinely ham-handed and near neurotic Public relations effort, the French government tourist office enlisted the persona of actor Woody Allen to pitch France to his fellow countrymen. This hackneyed ad campaign became the story rather than the product being sold. Instead, a simple but pastoral picture of an American military cemetery on 6 June or of the rugged expanse of the Normandy Coast with the simple word "Merci" would have been an attempt at a dignified makeup and classy comeback.

A barrage of global political and economic woes indeed impacted on French tourism; while total arrivals were off by two million in 2003, the number of American visitors declined by 20%.[27]

For those Americans who did visit France were faced with a historic heat wave, what the French call a *canicule*, baked the country like a soufflé. Though the French have created and perfected the world's fastest TGV trains, a bewildering array of mobile phone technology, and still bask in the proud shadow of the *Concorde* supersonic airliner, it appears that simple air conditioning is yet to be invented. Excluding some better hotels and supermarkets, which appear to have 375 varieties of yogurt, go to a bank, most shops, or the Metro and prepare to enter a stuffy and fetid sauna where even simple ventilation seems a futuristic concept. Paris sports a wonderful public transportation system, but take a ride on the super sleek green and white busses of the municipal RATP and ready yourself for *beaucoup* sweat and tears.

The old rationalization is that "well it never really gets that hot here." Though Parisian summers are not as bad as New York, they do regularly run in the 80's during the day, but not as bad at night. This heat wave raised temps in the 90's right up to 100F degrees, or from about 30–38C for the Euros. Basic ventilation and air conditioning is common sense, not a luxury frill. Nonetheless many French view air-conditioning as something "American" and thus not to be readily embraced. *Le Figaro* reported that the heat wave was the biggest since 1949. "France is overwhelmed by the heat," the newspaper conceded. The *canicule* was the most recent of the woes confronting France that summer. The weather *was* the news. The Paris government handled the crisis with all the finesse of clowns. President Jacques Chirac was *en vacances* in Quebec, and most Ministers were nowhere to be found. When the government met at Matignon towards the end of the crisis, they conceded that 5,000 of its citizens had perished from the intense heat. Later official estimates put the number at 14,500, mostly senior citizens! One could expect this in Romania or Russia, but *first world* France?

So in a sophisticated and medically advanced country like France, more than ten thousand people die in a heat wave? If this tragedy had happened in the USA, I'm certain French commentators would have had plenty to say about the uncaring nature of the American system, its lack of social solidarity, and the incompetent nature of its government in helping senior citizens. Thus when Hurricane Katrina slammed into the U.S. Gulf Coast and New Orleans in Summer 2005, the French were quick to find fault with the American relief efforts. Beyond the perfunctory round of Bush-bashing, Katrina represented a near singular natural crisis in American history. The French heat wave, while horrible, transpired in cities with running water, electric, and totally functioning public services. And 14,500 of the most vulnerable people nonetheless perished, far more than 1,000 during the Katrina catastrophe. Nonetheless, leading French commentators were still quick to offer advice on what they viewed as a kind of *American imperium in Iraq* as well as a post-Katrina incompetence at home.

Even a few years after the Iraq operation, the feathers had not settled between France and the USA. Viewing the growing distance between the two nations, the French when asked whether they have sympathy or antipathy towards America answered in September 2002; 39% held sympathy and 16% antipathy. But by June 2005 the number stood at 31% positive, 17% negative and 51% neither. In 2002, American views of France showed 50% favorable and 10% unfavorable. By 2005 that number had sunk to 35% favorable, and 25% unfavorable. Indeed, American responses towards France in 2002 saw fully 68 % viewing France as a partner and 18% as an adversary. By 2005, 44% viewed France as a partner and 45% as an adversary! For the French the numbers were equally negative with only 39% seeing America as a partner while 24% viewing at it as an adversary. Given the history of the 20th century, such statistics should cause serious pause in both Washington and Paris.[28]

"It is hard to define even what anti-Americanism means," intones the book *Sixty Million French Can't Be Wrong*. "Most of the French simply have mixed feelings about the United States. Some people are extremely welcoming of American ways but detest Americans. Others Admire America but hate Americanization…and some French just like American culture."[29]

Yet it is precisely that rivalry which has stoked the fires of pride and pomposity. The book *L'Arrogance Francaise* concedes bluntly, "With our sermons, our empty gestures and our poetic fights, we (the French) have pissed off the planet. Worse we make them laugh." Authors Romain Gubert and Emmanuel St. Martin add, "It's a sickness to which French people are addicted—believing that France must offer the world Light, Law and Liberty—that their leaders are the carriers of a universal message." And concerning Franco/American relations, the embers of mistrust were stoked by a French bestseller "L'Effroyable Imposture" (The Horrifying Fraud) which weaves a bizarre tale linking the U.S. government to the September 11th terrorist attacks on America.

Viewed from opposite sides of the Atlantic, both Franco-phobia and anti-Americanism are in a way, comforting and self-fulfilling prophesies and but perhaps really mirror reflections of two societies in an awkward love-hate relationship. So even after the political gales of the Iraq war, in the heart of Paris along the Seine, a statue to Thomas Jefferson was erected alongside the Pont Sulfrino. Jefferson, an early American Francophile, was an Ambassador long ago, but still a represents the intellectual and philosophical force which unites these two civilizations of the Old and New World.

Commemorating the fifth anniversary of the September 11th terrorist attacks, Nicolas Sarkozy French Minister of the Interior visited New York to express his solidarity with America. After making visits to local firehouses and awarding New York Police Commissioner Ray Kelly France's *Legion of Honneur* medal, Sarkozy visited Washington to meet with President Bush. Later in an address before the French American Foundation, he criticized France's contentious trans-Atlantic relations. He made the case for modesty as compared to an "arrogant France" then imploring, "Never more should we make of our disagreements a crisis.... It is not reasonable to embarrass our allies or to give the impression in rejoicing in their difficulties."[30]

At commemorations marking the 65th anniversary of the D-Day landings in Normandy, Sarkozy paid homage to the Americans "We owe you our freedom. France will never forget. It's on this spot which ties together our unfaltering friendship between the United States and France." He also listed the other allies aiding France in the war, "The British, Canadians, the Poles and the Czech aviators."[31]

NOTES

1. "Avant les Paillettes de Cannes, la dure Realite des Chiffres du Cinema," *Le Monde. online* 16 May 2006.
2. FilmFrance.net (2009), Enguerand Renault, "Frequentation record pour le cinema en Julliet," *Le Figaro*, 13 August 2009, p. 10.
3. *Paris Scope* 12 August 2009 pp. 80–81 and "Les Meilleures entrees en France," *Le Monde* 4 June 2008, p. 24.
4. "French Hit out at U.S. Cinema," *BBC News* online 19 February 2003.
5. Lena Lutaud, "La Deferlante Americaine," *Le Figaro*, 30 July 2007, pp. 21–23.
6. AboutMcDonalds.com/Media and mcdonalds.fr. 2009.
7. U.S. Department of Commerce online, *Le Figaro* 28 September 2007, p. B8 and Aurelie Devos "Les Parcs de Loisirs a l'abri de la Morosite Touristique," *Les Echos* 22/23 August 2008, p. 13.
8. Interview *Le Monde* Paris August 2003.
9. Interview *Le Monde* Paris August 2003.
10. Jean-Francois Revel. "L'Obsession Anti-Americaine," (Paris : PLON, 2002). pp. 88–89.
11. Michel Gurfinkiel, "The Gaza War and the Rise of the Neo-French," Michelgurfinkiel.com, 18 March 2009.
12. Amir Taheri, "Chirac and the Muslims," NRO online 19 December 2003.
13. Moises Naim, "Arabs in Foreign Lands," *Foreign Policy* May/June 2005, p. 95.
14. Piotr Smolar, "Les RG s'Alarment d'un 'Repli Communautaire' dans les Banlieues," *Le Monde* 5 July 2004, p. 1.

15. Stephanie Le Bars, "L'Islam Francais vote pour Renouvler ses Instances Representatives," *Le Monde*, 8 June 2008, p. 8. , Cecilia Gabizon, "Siffler la Marseillaise, C'est Obligatoire," *Le Figaro* online 16 October 2008.

16. "Le Djihadist Francais est plus Fruste, plus Jeune, plus Radical," *Le Monde*, 24 May 2005, p. 9.

17. Michel Gurfinkiel, "French Devolution," *The Jerusalem Post* 2 January 2004, p. 11. 22.

18. Gurfinkiel, "Rise of the Neo-French, 18 March 2009.

19. Elie Marechal, "En Trente Ans, la France a Perdu la moitie de ses Paroisses," *Le Figaro* 20–21 September 2003, p. 11.

20. Jean Sevillia, "Generation Jean-Paul II," *Le Figaro Magazine* 13 August 2004, p. 23.

21. Dominique Moisi, "The Trouble with France," *Foreign Affairs* Vol. 77, No 3 May/June 1998, pp. 94–95.

22. Francois Heisbourg, "Chirac Should Be More Cynical," *Financial Times* 4 June 2003.

23. Interview *Le Monde* Paris Aug 2003.

24. Martin Walker, "Pentagon Adviser; France 'No Longer Ally,'" *UPI* 4 February 2003.

25. U.S. Department of State Interview, Colin Powell 22 April 2003.

26. U.S. Department of Commerce/ International Trade Data 2007.

27. Judith Veil, "La France a Perdu 2 Millions de Tourists," *Le Figaro online*, 25 February 2004, p. 1.

28. Laurent Zecchini, "Francais et Americains gardent une Vision Negative les uns des Autres," *Le Monde* 18 June 2005, p. 3.

29. Jean-Benoit Nadau and Julie Barlow. "Sixty Million Frenchmen Can't Be Wrong." (London: Robson Books, 2004), p. 289.

30. Corine Lesnes, "Nicolas Sarkozy s'Aligne sur George Bush sur le Moyen-Orient," *Le Monde* 14 September 2006, p. 4.

31. "Sarkozy a Obama: Nous Vous Devons Notre Liberte," *Le Figaro.fr*, 7 June 2009.

Chapter Four

Pipelines, Pershings, and Protests—Germany and the U.S.

In the serious German weekly *Die Zeit*, a front page cartoon depicted former President George W. Bush dressed in cowboy garb, holding a cigar, and seen confidently crashing through the Saloon doors of Berlin's improvised Brandenburg Gate. In another issue, the cowboy theme continues with a cartoon of the globe with a ten-gallon hat atop it. Yet another, shows Bush his eyes totally covered by a big cowboy Stetson emblazoned with the crest Central Intelligence Agency. Other papers were not quite so diplomatic.

German/American ties, clearly one of Washington's key commercial and strategic relationships, reached their nadir during the Presidency of George W. Bush. What had begun as an intrinsically mistrustful chemistry between Social Democratic Chancellor Gerhard Schroeder and the newly elected Republican President over issues like the Kyoto Treaty and the exercise of American power, soon deteriorated into a downward political spiral. The notable exception to this trend was the firm and genuine solidarity Schroeder offered to the USA in the wake of the September 11th attacks on America.

Under the headline "Time for a Pullback in Europe?" an article in *U.S. News & World Report* stated, the President "has laid down the challenge: Allies can co-operate with the U.S. or compete—*but not both*. For NATO it's a crucial time....What concerns the President is that the European Community has been acting as a political and economic rival to the U.S. rather than its partner." In the President's words, "The Europeans cannot have it both ways. They cannot have the United States' participation and cooperation on the security front and then proceed to have confrontation and even hostility on the political fronts." Former President Richard M. Nixon was correct, especially in light of Congressional opposition to keeping forces in Europe which then numbered over 300,000. A generation later, the showdown over Iraq revived the same political fault-lines within the Atlantic Alliance.[1]

Chapter Four

FROM COLD WAR TO THAW

Nowhere were the security strains more apparent than in West Germany where despite a Social Democratic government in power in Bonn, few serious people questioned the need for a continuing American security posture to offset a growing Soviet/Warsaw Pact military threat. Words like *commitment and credibility* came into any discussion of cutting or trimming U.S. troop levels. At the same time, Germany's Chancellor Willy Brandt pressed for a wide ranging détente program not only with the Soviets, but especially with Poland. A clear commitment to expand a breadth of commercial relationships with the USSR and former East Bloc was a key element in Bonn's polity.

In another *U.S. News* article "Can Alliance Unity Survive?" the magazine states, "Rarely, if ever, have the strains of been worse. The U.S. is counting on fear of Russian power to prevent the partnership from unraveling." Adding "An unprecedented revolt against American leadership has plunged the Western Alliance into what many view as the most serious crisis in its 31 year history…On one crucial issue after another, allies in Western Europe and Japan are challenging the line dictated by the Carter Administration, on punishing Russia for its invasion of Afghanistan, sanctions against Iran to force the release of 53 American hostages, and negotiations for Mid-east peace."[2]

Issues like sanctions on the Soviets, a boycott of the 1980 Moscow Olympics, and complaints about President Jimmy Carter's leadership were part of the mix. *"Among Western Europeans there is a near universal contempt for the President's handling of foreign policy in general and alliance relations in particular. They complain for chronic vacillation and amateurish diplomacy which constantly leave them in the lurch."*[3]

It becomes glaringly apparent is that the recent cross-Atlantic strains between America and key West European partners were *hardly unique nor novel*. What became known as the Pipeline Issue dominated the trans-Atlantic agenda in the Carter and early Reagan Administrations. Given Germany's considerable dependence on foreign energy sources, the Bonn government considered a natural gas pipeline project with the Soviet Union. The logic was based on supply diversification and price. In fact France, Belgium, and Italy among others had joined in the plan which would bring 10–12 billion cubic meters of gas to Germany from an gross annual amount of 40–55 billion cubic meters. By the mid-1980's, according to Bonn government data, total deliveries of Soviet gas to Germany would be 24 billion cubic meters.

In fact the 3,700 mile pipeline from Siberia's Yamal peninsula to the terminus in Bavaria would see the biggest import deal in German industrial history. "While Bonn has given its approval, the deal is not to the liking of Big Brother in Washington" advised *Der Spiegel* sarcastically, adding, that the Americans were particularly concerned that, "What was worse the Europeans would become subject to blackmail through arbitrary turning on and off of the gas tap." *Der Spiegel* added, "If the gas plans were implemented, the Russians as early as 1984 would deliver twice as much to the Bavarian border as at present. With 24 billion cubic meters annually, the Soviet Union would be supplying 30 percent of the natural gas needed in the FRG." While major industrial forms like Mannesmann waxed triumphant, *Der Spiegel* added brusquely, "Only Ronald Reagan, it appears, might still spoil the deal of the gas, money and steel managers."[4]

President Ronald Reagan was inaugurated days later in Washington D.C. During the early months of his Administration, the President and U.S. Congressional leaders warned West Germany not to proceed with the pipeline, which Washington said would expose Europe to energy blackmail. During the Ottawa Economic Summit, the U.S. pressed its case. According to a study presented by the Chase Manhattan Bank, by 1990, "the USSR would be supplying 35 percent of Western Europe's gas requirements," thus making most of NATO increasingly dependent on the USSR.[5]

Indeed the Reagan Administration worked studiously on plans to persuade the Europeans to drop the pipeline project, which the Administration felt would create a significant reliance on Soviet energy and could pose a security threat in times of crisis. Thus there's less a touch of irony that a quarter century later, that dependency seemed a given. Germany was importing 40 percent of its gas, France 20 percent, and Italy 35 percent. The economic rapprochement was balanced by an uncomfortable relationship with the Russian government of Vladimir Putin. A study Pipelines, Politics and Power opined, "Russia is the world's largest gas producer. The EU is the world's biggest gas market. The EU gets over 40 percent of its gas imports from Russia... Russia is also the source of almost a third of the EU's oil and a quarter of its coal imports."[6]

The EU's energy dependence gives Moscow enormous geopolitical clout which can act as a tool for political influence. Tragically in January 2009, the a Russian natural gas pricing showdown with Ukraine, caused the collateral damage of energy supply shortages in a number of European Union states downstream.

Back in the early 1980's the U.S. was still suffering the aftershocks of the Carter Administration's diplomatic ineptness in dealing with the Europeans. For Europe and especially West Germany, initial impressions of Ronald Reagan were likely rooted in significant political underestimation. Not only would Reagan quickly establish himself as a formidable player, but would become the rhetorical and moral rallying point for Western Europe's diplomatic and defense opposition to the Soviet Union. For Germany the practical results of the Reagan Presidency were an enhanced NATO alliance, and a reinvigorated moral and political relationship with Washington which created the conditions for the epic political events in 1989.

In the early 1980's a unique political constellation emerged in Washington, London and Bonn. This *Triple Entente* of Ronald Reagan, Margaret Thatcher, and Helmut Kohl were to form the nexus for Western Europe's philosophical counter offensive to the Soviets. This unique and judicious combination combined a strong defense with a robust diplomatic posture. During this extraordinary period, the unexpected appointment of a Polish Cardinal as Pope John Paul II, brought an renewed optimism to the Catholic Churches in the Soviet-ruled East Bloc. Political rumblings inside communist Poland signaled the enduring weakness of the Soviet system, Reagan judiciously used the wedge of support for both the independent trade union Solidarity and for the Catholic Church to pry open the doors for political freedom in Poland. Though the battle of ideas actively confronted the Soviets during the Reagan Presidency, Moscow likewise redoubled its political efforts in Western Europe. Given her importance, Germany became a key target for political and espionage active measures. Nowhere was this more apparent than in Soviet support for the "peace movement" and opposition to the planned installation of Pershing missiles. The decision to deploy the Pershing medium range nuclear missiles was made during the Carter Administration in April 1979. The Pershing II's were to counter the Soviet multiple warhead SS-20's, which were *already in place*. Given that the Pershings were slated for deployment in German soil, the debate naturally focused on Germany.

As Germany's official Defense *White Paper* stated in 1979, "The Federal Government welcomes the unambiguous commitment to NATO and Europe by the President of the United States and his Administration...the United States has every right to expect the European parties to the Alliance to make reasonable contribution for fair burden sharing." The document added, "Western Europe is in many ways reliant upon the United States, the Europeans need the protection afforded by the nuclear deterrent of the U.S., a factor irreplaceable by any other." The White paper added, however that the *Bundeswehr* provides in Central Europe 50% of the NATO land forces, 50 % of ground based air defense, 30% of the combat aircraft, and in the Baltic 70% of the naval forces.[7]

While the Federal Republic of Germany was indeed pulling its own weight on the conventional front, the politically sensitive issue of deploying nuclear weapons, namely the Pershing, would create a *maelstrom* for Chancellor Helmut Schmidt. Yet the Chancellor's defense decisions, while most certainly judicious, could not meet the litmus test from the political left-of his own ruling SPD party.

Dr. Karl Kaiser, Director of the German Society for Foreign Affairs set the strategic stage: "The German dilemma is well known: in the event of war, Germany would have been the battlefield of the two opposing alliances and therefore, would have been more affected than any other country." Writing in *NATO Review* Dr. Kaiser added, "Consequently, preventing war has always been the steadfast goal of German policy. But one could only prevent war by being prepared for fighting it. Deterrence was an imperative for the Alliance, but even more so for German policy. Deterrence through nuclear weapons was part of this equation, but at the same time Germans did not want nuclear weapons to assume a war-fighting function. This created a schizophrenic attitude to nuclear weapons which profoundly disturbed German domestic politics for many years." He advised, "These developments came to a head in the late 1970's with NATO's *double-track* decision, when then Chancellor Helmut Schmidt, facing the protest of a vociferous minority, stood firm and paid the highest political price for his perseverance, he lost office. It was Chancellor Helmut Kohl who actually implemented the policy."[8]

In the early 1980's a rising tide of anti-Americanism portrayed President Reagan as a near singular threat to world peace. Germany's peace movement, a loose alliance of communists, pacifists, and ecologists marched to the tune of a nuclear free Europe, no NATO deployment of the Pershing missiles, and basically disarmament at any price. Ronald Reagan emerged as the political *bete noir* threatening European peace, a crude caricature painted both by Soviet *agit/-prop* and Europe's gullible political groupies.

Events in Poland as well as the planned deployment of the Pershings proved a raw nerve for the Soviet Politburo. Historian Timothy Garton Ash recalls, "It is so difficult to transport yourself back into the fears of that time. Because it did not actually happen, we somehow feel that it could never have happened. Yet, as I write this I have before me the official record of what the East German leader, Erich Honecker, told the Polish Politburo member Stefen Olszowski on November 20, 1980: 'We do not favor blood shed. That is the last resort. But even this last resort must be applied when the Workers and Peasants power must be defended. That was our experience in 1953 and it was also the case during the 1956 events in Hungary and in 1968 in Czechoslovakia." Dr. Ash adds, "There was also in the West, a larger fear that seems even more incredible today. This was the fear that in the heightened tension of the so-called Second Cold War—Reagan versus Brezhnev, American Cruise missiles against Soviet SS-20's—the Polish revolution might light the fuse for a nuclear war... This was the time of the huge peace demos in Bonn, London and Amsterdam. People put stickers on their cars saying It's five minutes to midnight."[9]

To that backdrop an eclectic united front of organizations formed and wittingly or otherwise, prepared for political action in Moscow's "Peace

Offensive." The movement seemed to be riding the waves of the ruling SPD floundering in election setbacks and party infighting. The SPD's congress in Munich in 1982 graphically illustrated Schmidt's dilemma as his party's far-left attacked the Chancellor's policies from within the hall, while outside a constant tempo of demonstrations outside rocked the Bavarian capital. What was increasingly apparent was the open collaboration of the German Communist Party (DKP) and various shades of crimson camp followers whose common aim was disarmament. While the ecologist Greens had often exhibited public anguish over the widespread communist penetration of their movement, such penetration remained the tip of the iceberg. Gerhard Boeden, Director of Germany's General Criminal Office, (BKA) stated, "Most of the participants want nothing to do with the enemies of the democratic state; but they don't know to what large extent these peace demonstrations are initiated, organized, and financed by members of the Soviet-controlled German communist party." Coinciding with the call of the Moscow-directed World Peace Council, nearly the entire communist and hard-left political spectrum organized Easter Marches throughout the Federal Republic. In Munich, a bizarre assembly of communists, pacifists, ecologists, and members of Chancellor's Schmidt's own Young Socialists marched to the tempo of the East Bloc's Easter Tune. Groups such as the DKP, German Cuban Friendship League, and the Women's International League for Peace and Freedom, participated in a day-long events culminating appropriately at the Circus Krone, a place favored by Hitler for political speeches.

Having personally witnessed many of these demonstrations and the professional *agit/prop* in Germany during this unsettled period, it was quite clear that there was a hidden hand directing much of the agenda if not the actual events. While the "peace movement" often reached a level of street theatre and presented its politics via colorful rock concert venues, the majority of West German's opposed the vocal minority who banged on the tin drum of political rancor. In fact this silent majority of Germans stood solidly behind the U.S. and NATO alliance. A public opinion poll released by the Emnid Institute, an affiliate of the Gallup organization, showed that 73 percent of Germans, "have a positive opinion" of the U.S. fully 77 percent "have a bad opinion of the Soviet Union." The poll revealed the complexity of the situation in Europe in the early 1980's. Of the citizens of seven countries surveyed—Germans professed the best opinion for the U.S., considerably better than British or French sentiments. Still if one viewed the raucous "peace" demonstrations it was clearly the vocal anti-American minority which captured attention. As the *Welt am Sonntag* newspaper wrote, "Anti-Americanism does not exist with the people but with the media, politicians, and the demonstrators. The paper adds that such feelings are acting slowly like poison to erode the U.S./German relationship. "So long as anti-Americanism reports appear in the mass media, so long as anti-American crybabies rant in the streets, so long as anti-American films appear, this danger continues."[10]

On the eve of Ronald Reagan's visit to Germany, huge pro-American political rallies, organized by the then-opposition Christian Democratic Union and its sister party the Christian Social Union (CDU/CSU) were held in Bonn and Munich. Demonstrators in the June rallies were said to number 170,000 and reflected what would be described as the "silent majority." While Chancellor Schmidt was personally irked by the rallies which clearly indicated the German/American relationship would be closer under the CDU opposition, the events clearly underscored a growing political chasm which Schmidt himself could not breach.

President Ronald Reagan in an historic address to the German Parliament, the *Bundestag,* viewed the relationship; "I don't believe that any reasonable observer can deny that there is a threat to both peace and freedom today. It is as stark as the gash of a border that separates the German people. We are menaced by a power that openly condemns our values and answers our restraint with a relentless military buildup."

"*Deterrence has kept that peace, and we must continue to take the steps necessary to make deterrence credible.* ...Alliance security depends on a fully credible conventional defense to which all Allies contribute." President Reagan added, "Some Americans think that Europeans are too little concerned for their own security. Some would unilaterally reduce the number of American troops deployed in Europe. And in Europe itself, we hear the idea that the American presence, rather than contributing to peace, either has no deterrent value or actually increases the risk that out Allies may be attacked." These arguments both ignore the history and the reality of the transatlantic coalition. Let me assure you that the American commitment to Europe remains steady and strong. Europe's shores are our shores, Europe's borders are our borders. And we will stand with you in defense of our heritage of liberty and dignity."[11]

Indeed the defense debate which riveted Germany would turn on many issues, yet the *sturm und drang* which plagued Schmidt's ruling SPD government, cleared after a September 1982 parliamentary vote of no confidence in the *Bundestag.* With the surprise election of Helmut Kohl, it appeared that German/American relations would have smoother sailing. Helmut Kohl's Christian Democratic (CDU/CSU/FDP) coalition government, at least temporarily, had cleared the highly charged political atmosphere. The new Bonn government allowed the opportunity for a fresh start in unambiguous ties with Washington. From the standpoint of the "peace movement," the Kohl coalition presented a red flag which would be challenged by white heat political emotions through demonstrations, disobedience, and disorder.

Yet as Stuttgart's Mayor Manfred Rommel wrote, "Most Germans feel friendship for the United States and think that the North Atlantic Treaty Organization is absolutely necessary. But they have no great aversion to the Russians—not withstanding the events in Poland and Afghanistan." Yet, many Germans still have a bad conscience about Hitler's invasion of the Soviet Union in 1941, and they wish to heal the past history between the two countries. He added, "This is why German reactions to Soviet misbehavior are often much more weaker than Americans expect them to be. It also explains why breaking off or reducing economic and cultural relations between West Germany and the Soviet Union is not popular even among steadfast NATO supporters."[12]

During the Cold War two trends defined West German opinion; one side (the majority) viewed the USA as a military protector against the Soviets. Communist crackdowns on freedom movements in East Berlin (1953), Hungary (1956), and Czechoslovakia (1968) provided ample objective evidence of the need for close American ties. Anti-Americanism was reaction of the vocal left-wing minority, which saw Washington's role in Vietnam (1960's), and Central America (1980's), and Pershing Missile deployment (1979–83) as its political rallying point. Thus, in a sense, the continuing Soviet threat kept Germany pro-American.

National elections were slated for 6 March 1983. In the run-up to the vote, I recall a near frenzied attempt by the peace movement and their political comrades to create the impression that a CDU victory would seal Germany's fate for America's impending nuclear showdown with the Soviets. The phrase *Schlagfeld Deutschland* "Battlefield Germany," was presented as a likely outcome. The mood was decidedly nervous.

In late February the Green Party sponsored a Nuremberg Tribunal Against First Strike and Mass Destruction Weapons in East and West. Staged in the city's *Meistersinger Hall* the pseudo-judicial program presented a classic piece of political polemics and leftwing propaganda in which experts from Germany and the USA made a case, and a Jury reached a verdict which was as pre-destined as night follows day. The Green Party's Petra Kelly along with a few former generals who had vociferously traded their NATO uniforms for the garb of the World Peace Council, as well as Americans such as Daniel Ellsberg, CIA turncoat Philip Agee, and ex-priest Daniel Berrigan, were among the presenters. The United States and German governments stood as the accused.[13]

In the anxious days before the Federal elections, it appeared that while Kohl's Christian Democrats would win, the fear lurked that the hard left may then resort to violence. The Rhine was foggy that March morning in Cologne, seemingly reflecting the national mood, and what could well have been the national future. Skies soon cleared. When election returns came into the Bonn press center that Sunday evening, both the CDU and CSU trounced the SPD opposition, though the counterculture Greens had made some surprising gains. Helmut's Kohl's CDU and Bavarian CSU had won a resounding electoral victory with 49% of the vote. Their coalition partners the Free Democrats (FDP) gained 7%. Overall voter turnout for the election was a momentous 89 percent!

That evening election parties in Bonn's *Adenauer Haus* witnessed an exuberant and almost giddy lifting of the gloom—not only had Kohl's coalition won but with the largest percentages since Konrad Adenauer in the 1950's. Nearby at the FDP headquarters more well-heeled liberals were toasting economic prosperity on the horizon. In another sense the Greens won too—their national party gaining just over 5% with 27 seats in the Federal Bundestag. Though not part of the new government, the Green party would build upon its already formidable standing throughout the State governments in Germany.

Helmut Kohl's election was a genuine turning point for Germany and NATO. While the Bonn government would continue to pursue its unambiguous commitment to West European defense, there were now fewer political restraints and caveats. Moreover, the fortuitous combination of Ronald Reagan, Margaret Thatcher, and Helmut Kohl, saw a unique political *triumvirate* not only dedicated to preserving the *defensive status quo*, but expanding the breadth of freedom in the Soviet Bloc. Kohl and Reagan spoke the same political language. Thatcher enunciated the case yet more elegantly. The Polish Pope John Paul II acted as spiritual vicar.

President Reagan visited Berlin in June 1987. Speaking at the Brandenburg Gate, the President issued his bold and riveting challenge to the reformist Soviet President, "Mr. Gorbachev, tear down this wall!" Even the optimists among us would have never dreamt that before too long, the infamous Berlin Wall would come down. As Eastern Europe rocked with pro-democracy demonstrations in the Autumn of 1989, the Kremlin's dominos began to fall. Poland, Hungary, Czechoslovakia, and the dour East German communists. The ill-named German Democratic Republic (GDR) was buffeted by a growing series of people power protests against the People's Republic. When the *Joshua Trumpet* sounded on 9 November, the Berlin Wall came tumbling down.

For Reagan and Kohl, standing firm in the 1980's had its political price but in the long run paid an unimaginable strategic divided—the final collapse of the Soviet *imperium* in the East Bloc and later the disintegration of the Soviet Union itself. The Revolutions of 1989, one of the 20ths century's defining moments, equally served as political midwife to German reunification in peace and freedom. That reunification came on 3 October 1990. Helmut Kohl would go on to win three more national elections and remain Chancellor until 1998.

Chapter Four

THE CLASS OF 1968

A noted German political figure once told me with a tinge of delighted irony, "The first word I knew in English was a four letter word." With perfect timing, he then quickly assured me that the word was "CARE" as in the ubiquitous humanitarian food packages which were a fortunate feature of the post-1945 era. Thus following the defeat of the Third Reich, Germans had become accustomed to the food from CARE packages, the "raison bombers" of the Berlin Airlift, and a benign if not shortage-ridden American occupation. As they say, this was a "generational thing," and indeed the German post-war politicians, of all persuasions, fondly remembered and recalled the role played by the USA in rebuilding Germany's cities, economy and political system. All parties can be proud of that achievement. Today's politicians are not cut from the same fabric. For many of them, their first word in English was a four letter word too; and probably the same expletive that they hurled at the USA during their formative years in the 1960's and 1970's. Those people the angry adolescents of the West German economic miracle, whose political views were formed between the hammer of anti-Vietnam war protests and the anvil of anti-NATO Peace rallies, became part and parcel of the German government.

It's extraordinarily ironic that former *radikals* the youngest of whom protested American involvement in Central America in the 1980's, later often sat center stage during the Schroeder government. Throughout the gilded government offices and halls of the European Union, there's much of the same. For this generation, the call *Aux Barricades* no longer meant rock throwing, marches under the crimson banners, or pseudo-scholarly sit ins at the University, but far more powerful direct actions in places like the UN Security Council, NATO, and the corridors of power. Beyond the obvious political ramifications in their own countries, one does not have to be too creative to assume that some of their old smoldering resentments towards the USA were rekindled by the Bush Administration and the War on Terror.

This is certainly not to say that *all* students of the *fashionable* left in the 1960's and 1970's are instinctively anti-American—happily, and not so surprisingly, many have changed their political colors and opinions. Many have not. All are older, not necessarily wiser, but have nearly universally traded in tie-dyes for silk Italian ties, and sandals for polished shoes, and VW minibusses for *Business Class*. They no longer smash windows but attend Summits in fashionable locales looking out at Alpine or tropical vistas. Indeed much of the political class in key Western European countries, comes from the instinctive political left and sometimes the radical left. To assume that this did play a part in the near knee jerk political anti-Americanism is to have overlooked an important point.

Germany is perhaps the best example, where Chancellor Gerhard Schroeder's SPD/Green government brought together a fractious coalition of Socialists of all stripes and ecology-minded pacifists. Viewing the socio/political philosophy of the SPD government in Berlin as juxtaposed to the Bush Administration in Washington was to witness a fundamentally different *weltanschauung* or worldview. Looking at the political players of many European governments, one could logically conclude that such ideological roots played no small role in the trans-Atlantic divide. Gerhard Schroeder, once the leader of his Social Democratic Party's Young Socialists (Jusos) presented a prime example. Long a proud member of the "Generation of 68" Schroeder wrote in 1979, "Yes, I am Marxist." These lines written in a Lutheran publication, were decidedly banal given that Germany's Juso's were openly hard-left and usually not even very youthful.

Better known was Foreign Minister Joshka Fischer. Long before his tenure in the ecology-oriented Green Party, Fischer had literally fought on the barricades during the early 1970's in Frankfurt, the epicenter of radical left-politics and violence. Fisher did not come from the traditional University circles but from street politics. Known as a street fighter and a bully, Fischer's exploits in demonstrations, provocations and violence, and his philosophical support for but never membership in the notorious Baader-Meinhof Gang/Red Army Faction, placed him in, should we say, more *activist* politics.

Fischer rose in prominence as a key figure "in anti-American, anti-liberal, neo-Marxist, revolutionary German radical left of the generation of 1968. This was the left which supported the Baader-Meinhof Gang,"[14] wrote the late Michael Kelly.

Otto Schily, the Interior Minister, in the Red/Green coalition was a young leftist lawyer "who marched in the ranks of the APO (anti parliamentary opposition) radicals and who was quite familiar with the Red Army Faction comrades. Significantly he participated in a Green Party's Nuremberg "Tribunal Against the First Strike and Mass Destructive Weapons in East and West," a sham trial of the American and West German governments.[15]

Other members of the Berlin government such as Environment Minister Jurgen Trittin spent his early formative political years in the Communist Bund (KB) and wrote in the party newspaper Worker's Struggle (Arbeiterkampf) before germinating into a political Green. The rather sordid political list goes on.[16]

Thus in this context, is it so really surprising that in such a key ally as Germany, during the Schroeder government, the Chancellor, the Foreign Minister, and the Interior Minister emerged from the tumultuous political *zeitgeist* of

1968 as critics of the Bush Administration? Even though Joshka Fischer to his credit moderated many of his positions to a far less confrontational posture towards the USA, the underlying tensions between Bush and the SPD/Green government in Berlin should not have been viewed in isolation. Germany's generation of leadership in the Social Democrat/Green government was far less attached emotionally to the U.S. than their predecessors. Yet as a diplomat stated, "With the collapse of communism, German reunification, and the growing political maturity of the EU, especially eastern enlargement, the rules have changed for good." Bonds between the two were already fraying before Iraq added the *Financial Times*, and "the election of George W. Bush marked a jolt for Germany after the close understanding between Bill Clinton and Chancellor Gerhard Schroeder." In fact "environmental and trade policy, the International Criminal Court and the Israel/ Palestinian problem were all causes of friction. But none of them matched the quarrel over Iraq and Germany's decision to side with France and Russia at the UN in blocking U.S.-led military action."[17]

The leftist dynamic of Germany's fractious SPD/Green coalition government aside, the political disagreements with Washington actually went much deeper. "Can the West be saved?" questioned the conservative *Frankfurter Allgemeine Zeitung*. "Is the vast store of common interests, aims and values shared by Americans and Europeans still big enough to form a powerful, mutual alliance in the 21st century?" As the editorial added, "On this side of the Atlantic, Europeans have identified one person on whom they can pin 'guilt' for this estrangement. U.S. President George W. Bush faced a wave of animosity that goes far beyond the opposition once expressed to the late President Ronald Reagan." Yet the commentary by Klaus-Dieter Frankenburger warned that long before "January 20, 2001, the day that Bush took office. The roots of the political estrangement, and ultimately to the disagreement over Iraq, run back to November 11, 1989, when the Berlin Wall fell. This collapse and the subsequent implosion of the Soviet Union, robbed the United States and Europe of their mutual image of the enemy, an image that disciplined them and strategically united them. Once the Cold War ended, both partners headed in different directions."[18]

Dr. Josef Joffe writing in *Die Zeit* opined, "The Wall fell in 1989, the Soviet Union shattered in 1991, the last Russian soldiers left Central Europe in 1994. That was the end of the Alliance."[19]

BACK TO BERLIN

Fast forward to Berlin. Checkpoint Charlie, the border crossing where the sharp divisions of the Cold War literally came face to face along a forbidding stretch of the Fredrichstrasse, now has that almost giddy ambiance of a theme park. Camera toting tourists stroll in the shadow of the sign "You are now Leaving the American sector!" Twenty years after the Joshua Trumpet sounded and the Berlin Wall dividing the city into the West and East, tumbled into the ash heap of history, a free and reunited Berlin has been reborn, regaining not only its role as the proud capital of a united Germany but as importantly, a sense of normalcy. Echoes of President John F Kennedy's 1963 visit with its memorable "Ich bin ein Berliner" speech or President Ronald Reagan's memorable 1987 exhortation "Mr. Gorbachev, tear down this Wall!" are now etched into Berlin's memorable and tumultuous history.

Berlin today resembles a vast work in progress with ubiquitous construction cranes and building sites. It's readily apparent that since German re-unification in October 1990, that huge sums of government money has literally flooded into the former communist East Germany—so far $1.4 trillion and still about $100 billion annually!

The results have been decidedly mixed; while there are impressive infrastructural improvements, most revenue supports a vast pension and social welfare system for the former communist East. Still the unemployment rate in the East remains nearly 18 percent. Given Germany's overall anemic economic growth the current and unpopular Socialist government continues to tread water. The Brandenburg Gate, the fashionable Unter dem Linden Avenue, and the numerous museums and monuments situated in former East Berlin have re emerged as a draw for tourists. The bleak former *no man's land* rubble of the Potsdamer Platz, has risen like the phoenix with an array of superlative architectural projects and corporate offices rivaling New York's. But prosperity breeds a smugness which overlooks past sacrifice. While few Berliners would doubt the singularly positive role of the United States in the reconstruction and rehabilitation after the horrors of the Hitler regime, there's a moralistic *hauteur* towards current American foreign policy and especially the Bush Administration. Having visited divided Berlin, just-freed Berlin, and now normal Berlin, I must confess to still feeling a sense of awkward surrealism in so many places; and normalcy, too. Memories of the epic 1948–49 humanitarian mission of the Berlin Airlift, the enduring tragedy of the Wall, and the ghosts of both the Nazis and the communists remain, but are outshone by the city's extraordinary rebirth and prosperity.

The Schroeder era ended in a confusing political melodrama. Politicians were singing the Berlin Blues. Germany went into political limbo with the inconclusive outcome of national elections in September 2005. Though nearly all pundits predicted a major upset of the ruling socialists and a victory by conservative contender Angela Merkel, they were mistaken. The outcome of Berlin's future coalition government hung like a murky autumn morning mist. Given that European elections often have unclear outcomes in which the public must endure interminable reshuffling of the political card deck—this has never really been the case on the national level in postwar Germany save for a brief period in the 1960's.

Ironically the loser (Gerhard Schroeder) acted like a winner and the winner (Angela Merkel) appeared the loser. Sadly, the post-election performance of incumbent Chancellor Schroeder evoked a buffo demagogue more than the leader of the world's third largest economy and key member of the European Union. Germany's anemic economy, desperately in need of reform and renovation, continued to advance but locked in lower gear; shifting up to its true potential would need genuine political vision allowing for structural reforms of a static social state with 11.6% unemployment and entrenched disincentives to entrepreneurs. Even Germany's once golden and goliath corporate landscape had eroded—due to the high cost of unification, the mis-governance and naturally global strains. In 1985 fully seven of Europe's ten largest companies (Daimler Benz, Siemens, Allianz, Bayer, etc) were German. In 2005 *none* of the top ten included German firms, the places being held by French, Swiss and Spanish companies. The rankings reflect Europe's changing corporate landscape from manufacturing, engineering and chemicals to pharmaceuticals and telecommunications as well as Germany's decline.[20]

What Germany needs is to turn back on to the socio/economic *Autobahn* of high octane growth and prosperity, not the meek and cautious ride offered by most of the political class. Domestically Chancellor Schroeder played on economic scare tactics and class envy which he manipulated with near magical ease. Politically speaking, an introspective Germany would have floundered and become game for the cheap anti-American politics which Gerhard Schroeder and his Social Democrats played like a fiddle. Relations with the USA—a cornerstone of the post war democracy which allowed for the economic miracle and enduring prosperity, were been mortgaged by the left's posturing over the Iraq war.

QUO VADIS GERMANIA?

"What road will Germany take?" opined Dr. Mathias Dopfner, Chairman of the influential Springer Media group writing in the *Wall Street Journal*. "Will it continue on the path of Franco/German social protection, driving Germany and thus Europe into permanent economic crisis and foreign policy isolation? Or the path of Anglo/American deregulated economics, which will finally free up Germany's enormous potential and thus inspire all of Europe and tie it more strongly to the Western alliance?"[21]

The formation of a *Grand Coalition* government in 2005 represented a pyrrhic victory for Chancellor Angela Merkel. Though her Christian Democratic (CDU) party won the largest batch of seats in the *Bundestag* (Parliament) she sadly failed to gain the sufficient majority to form a government. Thus Merkel had to settle for a fractious coalition composed of the main opposition, the Social Democrats (SPD). Prof. Merkel, a former physicist having grown up in East Germany, became the first woman Chancellor in German history. The inconclusive results of the elections and the nervous shuffling of the deck of political cards by all parties, reflected a kind of *Italianization* of German politics—where a plethora of parties from the Left, Right, Center and the lunatic fringe, brought a near political paralysis to one of the world's largest economies. This did not bode well for the future of a country mired in economic malaise, double-digit unemployment, and marinated in a cheap form of anti-Americanism which was nurtured by Schroeder's government and which remains entrenched in parts of his SPD.

What did this mean for the core U.S./German relationship? Ties improved quickly. Chancellor Merkel visited Washington and stressed "shared values" of both countries. Still despite the better political atmospherics, the classic Cold War relationship Germany once had with the U.S. is past. Chancellor Merkel, after all from East Germany, holds less nostalgia for the emotional epoch of the Adenauer era or for that matter the *wirtshaftswunder* (post-war economic growth) of West Germany.

Yet, Merkel showed her mettle when she told the prestigious American Council on Germany meeting in New York, "In this day and age German-American relations can no longer be founded exclusively on the postwar experience." Yet she added, "As far as our economic relations are concerned, there is absolutely no cause for pessimism. Our bi-lateral trade is worth some $100 billion. Outside the European Union the United States is Germany's number one trading partner. Some 3,000 German companies provide jobs for nearly 750,000 Americans. The United States accounts for the largest share of foreign investment in Germany and provides over a half a million jobs there."[22]

Equally Merkel's Grand Coalition allowed for the revival of some impressive economic growth. Europe's largest economy, powered by the thrust of exports, saw a GDP growth of 2.6 percent in 2007, but soon weathered the gale of global recession. The reliance on exports makes the German economy particularly vulnerable to a recession. Exports count for 40 percent of GDP or five times as much as the United States. Indeed the automotive and machine tool sectors are hyper-sensitive to the global environment.

Under Chancellor Merkel's government, American companies have regained enthusiasm for investing and operating in Germany. The 6th annual

Business Barometer survey by the American Chamber of Commerce in Germany and the Boston Consulting Group showed that Germany's attractiveness for both business and investment is growing. The 2009 study viewed 61 firms in Germany with $140 billion in revenues. Despite economic woes and an uncertain future, Germany ranks as the most attractive location in Europe for American companies. As an investment destination, Germany leads Eastern Europe, the UK and France. In 2004, in contrast, 19 percent of firms saw Germany as attractive as opposed to 27 percent taking a negative opinion. These are among reasons Germany remains the world's leading exporter.[23]

Nonetheless, the Economic Crisis of 2008–2009 saw Germany pulled into the global whirlpool. Foreign Minister Frank Steinmeier, speaking before the UN at the onset of the crisis, warned "Recklessness, greed, and a lack of common sense among the players has set us back years. The long-term consequences cannot be assessed yet. ..there can be no future without rules and no player will be able to lay down the rules on their own. It will no longer be possible for any one country to act as if they were immune to undesirable developments."[24]

Regarding international security policy, Afghanistan or Iran for example, Germany operates very much in the shadow and moral restraints of her history, and thus closely within NATO. Volker Perthes director of the German Institute for International and Security Affairs views Berlin's dilemma. "A deeper reason for German reluctance to fight lies in its collective subconscious…the American re-education campaign after the war was successful," he said. As part of the re-education after WWII, the U.S. in particular required that school curricula, newspaper articles and popular culture promoted an anti-militaristic democratic awareness among the public. Karsten Voigt, the coordinator for German American relations adds, "After the last war the Americans wanted an especially peaceful German nation. Now they have it and are astonished and unhappy that their re-education campaign was so successful."[25]

Regarding the oft-cited "anti-Americanism," this is often actually symptomatic opposition to U.S. policies, rather than a blanket dislike or criticism of the American people or institutions. "It is not blind anti-Americanism but European preferences for soft power, multilateralism, and international justice," which are at the root there are conflicting visions with the United States, argues a German writer. While Washington's "Unilateralism" is often the bane of the Europeans, the numbers of hardcore anti-Americans are quite thin. "A relatively constant, deeply embedded anti-Americanism in Great Britain, Germany, France and Italy hovers at around ten percent. It fluctuates during transatlantic spats, rising as it did during the Suez Crisis of 1956, the Vietnam War, the 1980's Euro missile deployment, and most dramatically the Iraq war. But the same studies show that about a quarter of the populations consistently sympathetic to the U.S." As the article adds, "During the Cold War, the vast majority of Western Europeans favored a strong alliance with Washington." Moreover as political scientists Robert Keohane and Peter Katzenstein demonstrated, "negative European attitudes, even at their peaks, had no impact on European policy towards the U.S., or on transatlantic tourism, trade or consumer behavior."[26]

Germany's Grand Coalition rekindled positive relations with the USA and for the most part, reflected the politics of a mature democracy. Yet in national elections in September 2009, Chancellor Angela Merkel won an impressive mandate for political and economic change. Her conservative Christian Democratic Union (CDU/CSU) returned to power but with a new and preferred coalition partner, the pro-business Free Democrats (FDP). A coalition of choice replacing the former coalition of expediency, allowed the Chancellor to pursue realistic market-oriented policies on the domestic front and to strengthen the vital transatlantic relationship with the United States.

Longtime political commentator Theo Sommer stressed that "Germany will remain predictable and reliable." In a stirring and heartfelt tribute to the United States, Chancellor Merkel addressed a joint session of the U.S. Congress in Washington D.C. and outlined the post-war relationship between America and a politically free, and now united Germany. Commemorating the 20th anniversary of the fall of the Berlin Wall in November 1989, the Chancellor underscored the close political partnership between Germany and the United States. Citing the positive role played by American Presidents such as John F. Kennedy, Ronald Reagan and George Herbert Walker Bush, Angela Merkel stated, "We Germans know how much we owe you, our American friends. We as a Nation, and I personally, will never forget that."

Viewing Transatlantic Relations, Merkel conceded that while America and Europe had their share of disagreements, "I am deeply convinced that there is no better partner for Europe than America, and no better partner for America than Europe." She also stressed, "Germany and Europe will also in the future remain strong and dependable partners for America."[27]

NOTES

1. "Time for a Pullback in Europe?" *U.S. News & World Report*, 1 April 1974, pp. 15–18.
2. "Can Alliance Unity Survive?," *U.S. News & World Report*, 9 June 1980, p. 21.
3. Ibid., pp. 21–23.
4. "Extremely Faithful—Opposition to the German-Soviet Pipeline Gas Deal is Growing," *Der Spiegel* 19 January 1981, pp. 34–38.

5. "Can Reagan Derail Soviet-German Natural Gas Deal?," *Human Events*, 1 August 1981, p. 3.
6. Katinka Barysch, Ed. "Pipelines, Politics, and Power; the Future of EU-Russia Energy Relations," (London: Centre for European Reform, October 2008), p. 1.
7. White Paper 1979 Security of the Federal Republic of Germany and the Development of the Federal Armed Forces, Bonn; Ministry of Defense, 1979, pp. 19–24.
8. Karl Kaiser, "Forty Years of German Membership in NATO," *NATO Review*, July 1995, p. 4.
9. Timothy Garton Ash, "The File—A Personal History," (New York: Vintage Books, 1997), p. 153.
10. John J. Metzler, "Minority Anti-American Spirit Captures Attention in Germany," The Register, 2 May 1982, p. E. 12.
11. U.S. Department of State, Documents on Germany 1944–1985, (Washington, D.C.: GPO, 1985), pp. 1346–1348. For the inside story of Unity see "Germany Unified and Europe Transformed; A Study in Statecraft," by Philip Zelikow and Condoleezza Rice.
12. Manfred Rommel, "West German Turmoil," *New York Times*, 3 October 1982, p. E 17.
13. "Nuremberg Tribunal Against First Strike and Mass Destruction Weapons in East and West," The Green Party (Germany) February 18th to 20th 1983, pp. 11–16.
14. Michael Kelly, "A German Radical for Saddam," *Washington Post,* 14 February 2003.
15. "Nuremberg Tribunal," 1983.
16. Ansgar Graw, "Bumerang '68," *Die Welt* 6 January 2001, p. 10.
17. Haig Simonian, "Culture Shift Strains U.S.-German Relations," *Financial Times* 21 May 2003, p. 6.
18. Klaus Dieter Frankenburger, "Alliance Drifts in Current of Conflict," FAZ. net 14 June 2004.
19. Josef Joffe, "Gullivers Landung," *Die Zeit*, 3 June 2004, p. 1
20. Paul Betts, "Germany Loses Big Company Crown to Swiss," *Financial Times*, 23 November 2005, p. 25.
21. Mathias Dopfner, "Help Us, America," Reprinted from *The Wall Street Journal* © 3 March 2005, p. A12, Dow Jones & Company. All rights reserved.
22. Angela Merkel," Challenges to the Transatlantic Partnership," Address before the American Council on Germany 4 May 2006.
23. "Germany Rises to the Top in AmCham Business Barometer VI," Commerce Germany, February 2009, Vol. 7, Issue 1, p. 21, and Nicolas Kumanoff, "More Business, More Investment," *Atlantic Times* April 2008, p. 12.
24. German Mission to the UN/Address by Dr. Frank-Walter Steinmeier Minister of Foreign Affairs to the UN, 26 September 2008, p. 6.
25. Christian Kreutzer, "Germans to the Front?" *Atlantic Times* March 2008, p. 4.
26. Paul Hockenos, "Conflicting Visions," *Atlantic Times* May 2008, p. 4.
27. Theo Sommer, "She'll Be Back, for Sure," *Atlantic Times* September 2009, p. 3. and Speech by Dr. Angela Merkel, Chancellor of the Federal Republic of Germany, before the United States Congress, Washington D.C. November 3, 2009, Germany. info, pp. 2–6.

Chapter Five

War on Terror—Hands across the Seas?

The Grim Reaper visited New York on a picture perfect September morning. On September 11th 2001, with chilling and calculated coordination and brutal focused force, the hydra-headed monster of international terrorism methodically attacked sites in New York and Washington D.C. America came under attack.

What evoked the Japanese attack on Pearl Harbor in 1941, but without the formal calling card, saw an assault on America's financial and political capital in 2001. The destruction of the World Trade Center, a commercial symbol of America throughout the world and the attack on the Pentagon, and a planned crash into the White House, were decisive targets for those who harbor that special venom for the USA. The apocalyptic events stunned New York as if in a horror movie; hijacked airliners smashing into skyscrapers, the City on full terror alert, total shutdown of American airspace, and an evacuation of all sensitive sites such as the United Nations and Financial Markets. The burning World Trade Center towers presented a surrealistic spectacle. At first the twin towers looked like two giant smokestacks belching black smoke into the clear blue September sky. Before long the buildings buckled and collapsed. I witnessed this from a distance and saw one tower implode into a vast cloud of gloom and destruction.

"THE DAY THE WORLD CHANGED"

Those who lulled themselves into the wistful mantra "it can't happen here," were riveted by this catastrophic reality. The *Economist*'s somber cover stated "The Day the World Changed." In a message of solidarity by Pope John Paul; II to President George W. Bush, the Pontiff stated, "Shocked by the unspeakable horror of today's inhuman terrorist attacks against innocent people in different parts of the United States I hurry to express to you and your fellow citizens profound sorrow and my closeness of in prayer for the Nation at this dark and tragic moment." The following day in the General Audience in Vatican City, the Pope stressed unequivocally, "Yesterday was a dark day in the history of humanity, a terrible affront to human dignity."[1]

For those who looked the other way when terror struck in Israel, Northern Ireland, Spain, Turkey and so many places "somewhere else," the attacks on New York and Washington proved the stark price of pleasant indifference. What of the warnings? The October 2000 attack on the Navy's USS Cole, a sitting duck moored in Aden port and the earlier bombings on American embassies in East Africa, offered plentiful warnings. But for a generation an emasculated CIA, FBI, and City Police forces could not seriously monitor, track down, and bring such groups to justice until a formal crime had been committed. Anti-terrorist measures were politically orphaned for too long as the violent groups gained in sophistication, state support, and capability. During the 1990's moreover the Clinton Administration, mired in its own mirth as well as political scandals, took little time to seriously address the gathering storm clouds which were blocked out by the Wall Street stock market bubble. The attacks on New York and Washington proved a frightening wake up call.

President George W. Bush stressed that America must not only track down the perpetrators of these cowardly assaults against our freedom, but moreover not exclude those countries which allow the terrorists safe haven. The President warned these are "More than an acts of terror, they were acts of war." Paraphrasing the Reagan Doctrine towards terrorists "You can run but you can't hide," the U.S. applied the time honored counter-measures to preempt further attacks, not to react to its grisly aftermath. The security and political follow up would define the Bush presidency. An aggressive preemptive strategy would be employed in what George W. Bush characterized as a "Monumental struggle of good versus evil."

Global political solidarity and military support was quick in coming. The decision on September 12th to invoke article 5 of the NATO treaty stating that "an armed attack against one ally in Europe or North American shall be considered an attack against them all," remained the most profound expression of Alliance solidarity. "In the months since terrorists crashed hijacked airliners into the Pentagon and the World Trade Center, NATO allies and partners have lined up behind the United States in an unprecedented display of support and solidarity," wrote Christopher Bennett in *NATO Review*. He added, "Few of the Alliance's founding fathers could have imagined that the first invocation of Article 5 would come in the wake of an attack on the United States and not on a European Ally. However, all would surely have been impressed by the speed of response and degree of unity it represented."[2]

Shortly after the chilling and heinous attack against America by the hydra-headed monster of international terror, the UN Security Council acting with surprising speed, passed a resolution #1373, not only condemning the attacks but calling those who aid, support, or harbor those responsible to " be held accountable."[3]

It must be said that the UN had long opposed Afghanistan's Taliban regime through economic sanctions and had called for the handover of prime suspect Osama Bin Laden. Yet Afghanistan's ruling Taliban thugocracy continued to harbor Bin Laden's Al-Qaida terrorist network. Afghanistan which had been devastated by the Soviet invasion, followed by civil war, and then rule by Taliban's mad mullahs, remains a beckoning quicksand for any foreign force. Afghanistan's tribal and ethnic rivalries were wisely exploited by the U.S. to oust Taliban from "The Islamic Emirate of Afghanistan."

The complex ethnic quilt of warlords, tribal chieftains, and well funded foreign terrorist mercenaries turned Afghanistan into a heart of darkness. When Taliban thugs gleefully dynamited ancient Buddhist statues at Bayman, the world looked on in horror. This benighted regime was a curse on Afghanistan much as the Islamic radicals have been to Iran. The Bush Administration fully understood the depth of the challenge and that's why America did not shoot from the hip with ritualistic cruise missiles attacks into the desolate Afghan hills for the "feel good factor." A far bigger counterstrike was planned for the practitioners of terror and the mendacious regimes harboring them. But Winning takes a coalition. The Gulf War coalition brilliantly assembled by Secretary of State James Baker and President George Bush in 1990 fully understood the subtleties and complexities of the Arab world. While the U.S., Britain, and France bore the military brunt, the Coalition's "Group Photo" saw many Arab states opposing Saddam. Iraq could not play the "West against the Arab Brother" game. While NATO pledged its support for the USA in this counter terrorist battle through invoking Article 5, countries such as Britain, France, Germany, and Turkey came into political play. Subtle diplomacy not boastful bravado was the way to prepare the counterstrike.

Dr. Henry Kissinger advised wisely, "America and its allies must take care not to present this new policy as a clash of civilizations between the West and Islam—the battle is against a radical minority." In the aftermath of the attacks, President George W. Bush showed sensitivity in visiting a Mosque in Washington and stressing that Islam is not the enemy, but *fundamentalist Islam*. In essence the U.S. had to convince its allies that we are fighting fanatics who happen to be Muslim. Moderate Arab states such as Egypt and Jordan have had their share of experience with Islamic terror. In his call to arms of brilliant clarity, President George W. Bush outlined the struggle; "freedom and fear are at war." He added, "Whether we bring our enemies to justice, or justice to our enemies, justice will be done."[4]

An epic battle of global proportions had begun. Rightful retribution, not revenge, became the *modus operendi*. The Bush team went on the diplomatic offensive. America's new envoy at the United Nations, Ambassador John Negroponte, had a challenging and fruitful, first few weeks at his new post. And he hit the equivalent of a diplomatic Grand Slam Home run by getting a tough American-sponsored resolution unanimously adopted by the Security Council. Though no small feat, the stunning singular shock of September 11th, has provided the critical momentum for such a resolution. Resolution #1373 clearly and strongly mandated that *all* States shall refrain from supporting and providing safe haven and financial aid to terrorists. The document goes well beyond the Bin Laden network's home base in Afghanistan's Evil Emirate, to the wider web of terror extending from North Africa to South Asia.

CHARTING THE PATH

The Bush Administration carefully crafted a diplomatic framework to carry out the war on terror, starting from the Security Council which reaffirms "the inherent right of individual or collective self-defense," to the green light from the NATO Alliance for the same, and the individual statements of support from countries both in the Middle East and farther a field such as Japan and the Philippines. Importantly Philippine President Gloria Macapagal Arroyo offered key support stating that the Manila government (who has more than enough experience with Islamic fundamentalists) will "go every step of the way" with Washington, and offered the use of two former American military facilities of Clark AFB and Subic Bay.

Clearly the Administration poised its diplomatic ducks in a row and proceeded with the military counterstroke accordingly in a struggle which the President termed "a battle between good and evil." Countries such as Britain, France, and Russia knew only too well the unambiguous calling card of terror within their frontiers. British Prime Minister Tony Blair demanded Afghanistan's Taliban regime, "Surrender the terrorists or surrender power." In a passionate address to his Labor Party conference, Blair spoke of the "Moral power of a world acting as a community," and the need to stand up collectively against barbarism. Earlier New York's feisty Mayor Rudy Giuliani addressed the UN General Assembly's debate on terrorism. Rudy did not mince his words but bluntly told the gathered delegates that the atrocity which took place merely two miles away at the World Trade Center; "This is no time for further study or vague directives...There's no room for neutrality on the issue of terrorism. You're either with civilization or with terrorists." He implored, "On one side is democracy, the rule of law and respect for human life. On the other is tyranny, arbitrary execution, and mass murder."

General Assembly President Han Seung-soo of South Korea stated, "The fight against terrorists is an issue that transcends cultural and religious differences, while threatening people of all cultures and religious faiths." Han added, "We must never forget that terrorism is not a weapon wielded by one civilization against another, but rather an instrument of destruction through which small bands of criminals seek to undermine civilization itself." That's a crucial point for those who have been trying to paint the problem as a "Clash" between Christianity and Islam. Amb. John Negroponte stressed, "The war we wage is not a battle against Islam...we helped defend Muslims in Kuwait. We helped defend Muslims in Bosnia and Kosovo. We remain the single largest provider of humanitarian aid to Afghanistan."

Turkey's delegate Umit Pamir stated, "If there were any arguments that terrorists might have also had a defensible cause, September 11th must have put this forever to rest. There are no gray areas in the fight against terrorism; nor are there *good terrorists* and *bad terrorists*." Ambassador Pamir added significantly, "Through the tumultuous years of our fight against terrorism, the United States always stood, and at times singularly, by Turkey. Now, in their hour of need, Turkey firmly stands by the United States."

But this "gray area" haunted discussions, blurred moral distinctions, and eroded solidarity. Though the attacks were horrible, denizens of defeat were already spinning the yarn and "we must strive to find the gray area." Tragically the "gray areas" remained the searingly poignant memories of the smudgy gray smoke over the World Trade Center and lower Manhattan—*not a cloud of moral ambiguity*—but a gray cloud from this pyre of heinous political violence. In the immediate aftermath of the September 11th attacks on America, the global solidarity was extraordinary if not exceptional. Even the parapets of the French intellegencia *Le Monde* echoed the common theme "We are All Americans." For few fleeting weeks, the world stood in solidarity with the USA. The emotions, the psychological numbness, and the fearful expectations for the future solidified the global community in ways few events have during the past century. Within a week of the attacks French President Jacques Chirac was in America, first in Washington where he told a White House press conference, "I wanted to tell President Bush who is my friend, and then all the American people, first that France and the French people are totally supportive, that their solidarity is heartfelt...I wanted to tell them too that France is ready to consider *every means* that can be employed to make this fight against terrorism effective so that this *evil* of our times is truly eradicated."

Chapter Five

USA/EU UNITED

Yet later in New York, as the first overseas leader to visit since the attacks, Chirac told a UN press conference, "I should like to stress that the battle against terrorism has become an absolute priority in today's world...it can be waged effectively only in an *accepted international context*, and from this point of view, we must clearly recognize that the UN is the best body capable of getting everyone to work together." He added, "We must not confuse the fundamentalist, terrorist and fanatical groups with the Arab or Muslim worlds. That would be a cardinal error, would be profoundly unjust and above all result in us falling into the very trap set for us by the terrorists."[5]

Chirac whose impressive personal gesture in visiting the smoldering site of the World Trade Towers nonetheless was not giving George W. Bush a political *carte blanche* to eradicate what Chirac himself was calling *evil*.

The support from Germany was no less forthcoming. In the hours after the attacks Germany's Chancellor Gerhard Schroeder telegrammed President George W. Bush "My government staunchly condemns these acts of terrorism. The German people are at the side of the United States of America in this difficult hour. I wish to express my deep-felt condolences and complete solidarity to you and the American people. Out thoughts and prayers go out to the victims and their families."[6]

A week later, the German *Bundestag* in Berlin overwhelmingly passed a resolution of support for the USA, Chancellor Schroeder stated," "I said this is not just a war against the United States, but a war against the civilized world. I stand by those words. What we have here is not a 'clash of civilizations' but a struggle to protect civilization in this one world." Schroeder continued, "In the face of this unprecedented attack, Germany will give its *unreserved support* to the United States of America. Our statements of political and moral solidarity with the U.S. are at the present time more than just a matter of course. Here in Berlin, in particular, we Germans will never forget what the United States has done for us." The Chancellor added, "What we as Germans and Europeans wish to achieve is unreserved solidarity with the U.S. with respect to all necessary measures. The *Bundestag* resolution moreover expressed "emphatic support for the U.S. effort to build a worldwide coalition to fight terrorism."[7]

Shortly after the attacks, support came in so many ways, some of them quite unexpected. On the high seas the German naval vessel Lutjens was in the vicinity of the USS Winston Churchill. The German ship with its crew standing at attention in dress uniforms, raised an American flag to half-mast, and signaled "We stand by you." Months later the German naval Commander Michael Meding was honored at a Washington ceremony sponsored by Congressman Gil Gutknecht (R-MN) and Senator Richard Lugar (R-IN). Solidarity from Germany came in other substantive ways too. The German American Solidarity Fund, set up a public charity in the months after September 11th raised $8.5 million which was donated to disaster relief and to the families of fallen New York City firefighters. Separately $35 million was raised by German industry ad donated directly to American charities."[8]

Addressing a postponed session of the UN General Assembly, Germany's Foreign Minister stated, "11 September thrust a dangerous future upon the world. ...humanity has rarely been as united as it was on that terrible day two months ago. This unity was born of horror and compassion, but also of the realization that we can only successfully counter this new deadly threat if we combine our full force and energy. 11 September was a defining moment, a day which altered the direction of world politics. A new alliance was created. It must now be strengthened." Fischer stressed that the source of the attacks came from a Afghanistan's Taliban. He added, "As hard as this decision may be: without the use of military means this threat cannot be averted."[9]

Addressing the European Parliament in Strasbourg, Prof. Romano Prodi stated "Following the attacks on 11th September against our longstanding ally the United States, the European Union has publicly committed itself to do all it can to help bring to justice the perpetrators, organizers, and sponsors of these acts, and to hold accountable those hiding, supporting or harboring them." Prodi stated clearly, "We thus pledged our complete solidarity with the government and people of the United States. Over the days that followed, I was very satisfied to see this declaration of solidarity translated into swift and concerted European action."[10]

A Hungarian delegation led by Istvan Szent-Ivanyi, Chairman of the Parliamentary Foreign Affairs Committee visited New York in October. After a visit to Ground Zero in lower Manhattan, Szent-Ivanyi's comments delivered at the Hungarian Consulate eloquently illustrated the bonds of friendship between America and Hungary. During the Autumn of 2001, New York and indeed America basked in a warm glow of support and solidarity from Europe. During the first phase of the counterstrikes, against the Taliban in Afghanistan, the allies stood shoulder to shoulder with Washington. So one may ask, what then caused the deep political rift across the Atlantic? Why was there so much discord and genuine disagreement between many of America's traditional allies and the Bush Administration? Given the amazing levels of global goodwill in the aftermath of September 11th how could things have changed so radically?

The answer rested in Baghdad. Though the White House viewed the Saddam's regime as a *clear and present danger* to the world community, clearly many other countries did not share this conviction. This was not so much that the Europeans had really much political sympathy for the vilified Saddam, but that Iraq provided a good bottom line for business and trade. Moreover, given that Saddam was seen as "being in the box" from a tight UN sanctions regime, the perception in many capitals was that the issue had been resolved, albeit uncomfortably. Still in the anxious aftermath of September 11th the President took a pro-active posture. In well under a year, George W. Bush was transformed from the seemingly hesitant former Texas governor to a primetime U.S. President. His chief political instincts and virtues, and his team around him, especially Vice President Richard Cheney, Defense Secretary Donald Rumsfeld, and National Security Advisor Condi Rice, kept George Bush both focused and firm. The challenge thrust upon Bush in the frightful hours of September 11th and the nervous weeks after, were in many ways more daunting than the situation facing FDR after the attack on Pearl Harbor. After all by December 7, 1941 war was already raging for a few years in the Far East and Europe; it was just a matter of time before a hesitant and neutral America would be dragged into the conflict. In the case of September 11th, the USA for far too long had convinced itself there were no war clouds on the horizon and moreover as the *world's sole superpower*, what could possibly happen? Despite its superpower standing, the U.S. was in the final analysis attacked by a mountain bandit with a cell phone, not by another country, but a shadowy terrorist organization.

DEFINING THE OBJECTIVES

Thus in his first and probably most important State of the Union address, President George W. Bush memorably defined an "*Axis of Evil*," and set out the road map for American victory in the War on Terror. Amid an enthusiastic reception from a joint session of Congress, the President outlined a plan of global action against terror while at the same time safeguarding American homeland security. Still by naming names, Iraq, Islamic Republic of Iran, and North Korea, Bush defined *formal state players,* specific rogue regimes that could be identified, destabilized, and perhaps decapitated.

Clearly George W. Bush had a tougher road to follow than did Franklin D. Roosevelt. Though December 7th remains a "day of infamy" nonetheless amid the global conflict, the actual attack was not a total shock. The War on Terror did not necessitate the massive troop and resource mobilization as did WWII, nor does the conflict have an obvious ebb and flow which could be charted by for example by the Battle of Midway or the D-Day landings in France. As the President stated from the onset, this is a conflict which shall have many battles and victories of which we will not know of publicly.

"Terror Inc" has few formal addresses, formal targets, formal armies, and formal state structures. Bluntly the enemy is not an easily definable entity. The President's speech was a forceful, eloquent, and a cogent reaffirmation of American goals in the conflict. Still the *"Axis of Evil"* implied that these regimes which had notably distinguished themselves as longtime state sponsors of terror and in turn were harboring those same terrorists who struck in New York and Washington.

The *Axis of Evil* slogan galvanized domestic support, but began to create nervous misgivings abroad over how Washington would proceed on the foreign policy front. The French were furious. Foreign Minister Hubert Vedrine (the Socialist predecessor to the more famous de Villepin) denounced Bush's *"simplistic"* and *"unilateralist views."* Vedrine stated that concerning the Middle East and globalization, the trans-Atlantic gulf has widened. "We are now menaced by a new simplicity which is to bring back all problems of the world to the one fight against terrorism. It is not serious. Europe should not fear in expressing itself. If we are not in agreement with American policy we should say so. We should say so."[11]

Weapons of Mass Destruction (WMD) entered the daily political lexicon at the United Nations and world capitals. Without question Iraq posed a quandary for all but the most skeptical critics of the Administration. Since the end of the Gulf War in 1991 Saddam had been squeezed by a tight economic sanctions regime, more than a dozen UN Security Council resolutions, but had *never been verified as disarmed* by international inspectors. Through the 1990's the Clinton Administration pushed and pressured to open the gates of Baghdad to genuine and intrusive inspections; there were many face offs and showdowns and military air strikes. *Saddam had failed to comply with seventeen UN Security Council resolutions*!

Robert Kagan, writing in Of Paradise and Power recalls, "The growing split between the United States and its allies on the Iraq question came into the open at the end of 1997, when the Clinton administration tried to increase the pressure on Baghdad to cooperate with UN arms inspectors, and France joined Russia and China in blocking the American proposals in the UN Security Council."[12]

THE ROAD TO BAGHDAD

George Shultz, President Ronald Reagan's Secretary of State advised, "By 1998 the situation was untenable. Saddam had made inspections impossible. President Clinton in February 1998, declared that Saddam would have to comply with UN resolutions or face American military force. Kofi Annan flew to Baghdad and returned with a new promise of cooperation from Saddam. But he did not cooperate." Secretary Shultz added, "Congress then passed the Iraq Liberation Act by a vote of 360 to 38 in the House of Representatives; the Senate gave its unanimous consent...it supported the renewed use of force against Saddam with the objective of changing the regime." In November the Security Council passed another resolution declaring Iraq to be in "flagrant violation" of all resolutions going back to 1991. Shultz stated, "President Clinton ordered American forces into action in December 1998—but the U.S. military operation was called off after only four days—apparently because President Clinton did not feel he could lead the country in war at a time when he was facing impeachment...so inspections stopped."[13]

Clinton justified massive air strikes on Baghdad in December 1998, as necessary to destroy Saddam's WMD projects. Though backed by the British, the attacks lacked support from the UN Security Council. WMD would haunt Bush from the beginning too. Since Saddam claimed no longer to possess the large caches of chemical and biological weapons he once held in his arsenal, why was he then so obstinate in not allowing UN inspectors to prove the point and then subsequently drop the crippling economic sanctions and global ostracism?

Suspend for a moment one's opinions, nationality and moral codes. Since Saddam no longer *had* the weapons, *why* then would the Iraqi dictator risk his life and regime to conceal *what he did not have*? In other words, if there was truly nothing to hide, Saddam could have confounded his enemies and still been in power. But though the Western Europeans along with the United States supported *continued and intrusive* UN weapons inspections, the European timeframe was longer and open-ended while Washington's was dictated by ominous shadows of September 11th. The American position was clearly dictated by a desire to depose Saddam whereas the Western European posture strove to control and manage the WMD imbroglio—with or without Saddam. Unlocking the Gates of Baghdad became the key—how would one figuratively reach the goal? Europe favored continued and endless UN inspections whereas the Bush Administration—fearing a delay and Saddam's subsequent use of those weapons—favored direct military action.

This proverbial fork on the Road to Baghdad, and that of two interpretations, naturally held political consequences for American relations with Western Europe. Nonetheless less than a year after the horrible September 11th attacks on America, the U.S. image abroad was eroding mostly in the Muslim world but in Europe too.

But beyond public perceptions concerning the USA, business and electoral decisions naturally framed the equation through much of Europe. Germany's Social Democratic Chancellor Gerhard Schroeder was fighting a tough uphill election campaign—a substantial part of Schroeder's Socialist support and that of his Green Party coalition partners, naturally viewed the impending Iraq conflict as American adventurism and George W. Bush as a cowboy. Some of Schroeder's rhetoric and that of his SPD party faithful on the campaign trail could only be described as crude anti-American rants.

"As early as September 2002, German Chancellor Gerhard Schroeder declared that Germany would not contribute to a military operation under any circumstances, even if the United Nations Security Council authorized such force," stated Congressman Doug Bereuter Chair of the House Subcommittee on Europe. He added, "That stance and Schroeder's anti-American rhetoric were clearly intended for domestic political consumption in a tight German election campaign. He did pull out a narrow electoral victory but at great cost to the U.S. German relationship." Congressman Bereuter adds, "More damaging to the transatlantic relationship was the position of French President Jacques Chirac. Where Schroeder opposed one aspect of U.S. policy, Chirac set himself in opposition to the United States itself." As the Congressman recalls, that in March 2003, the mood on Capitol Hill was perhaps best summarized by his own statement in hearings of the House International Relations Committee "If the French government politically treats (us) as an enemy, they cannot be regarded by us as a friendly government."[14]

Well before the Iraq conflict negative views of the U.S. were on the rise. A Pew Center Poll illustrated the issue, "Despite an initial outpouring of public sympathy for America following the September 11, 2001 terrorist attacks, discontent with the United States has grown around the world over the past two years." "The main lesson," Poll Director Andrew Kohut said "is that while there is a reserve of good will towards the United States, the post powerful country in the world has an increasing number of detractors." He added "The post-cold war reality was that "how old friends who need us less, like us less" especially in Europe. So in December 2002, more than a year after September 11th and before the fractious political showdowns in the United Nations before the Iraq war, the negative numbers were already growing. Favorable views of the U.S had declined in the U.K. from 83 to 75 percent and in Germany from 78 to 61 percent. Yet on the to thorny issue of Iraq, most surveyed that the main reason the U.S would go to war in Iraq was "because the U.S. wants to control Iraqi oil." That view was held by 44 percent in Britain, 54 percent in Germany, and 75 percent in France. As to believing "Saddam must be removed," 75 percent of the British, 63 percent of French, and 75 percent of the Germans agreed yet significant majorities opposed military action.[15]

France, seeking a more assertive foreign policy role would play a crucial role in the post-September 11th world. Dominique de Villepin, the new Foreign Minister inspired by lyricism and enthusiasm hoped to overtake the cynicism of Vedrine's policies. With its "new look" under Chirac came the view, argues Prof. Frederic Charillon, "The argument is that France counts in the world by making a strong position." Being heard does not signify being listened to—this is the birth of *Villepinism*, a triple diplomacy on all fronts. Originally the idea was to complement, not to rival with the United States but the Iraq crisis passed over that foundations. Of course, De Villepin inherited political handicaps; a growing isolation of France on the European ladder and marginalization on the international level.[16]

De Villepin would later counter these constraints by a powerfully proactive foreign policy in the Security Council. In his near theatrical style, the *debonair* Foreign Minister could rhetorically duel across the Security Council's horseshoe table as well as using use his keen wit as a rapier in any press conference. The Count of the Quai D'Orsy might have been a hero in France but he emerged as an almost type-cast Hollywood villain in the eyes of many Americans. In early 2003, the military standoff with Saddam actually turned out to be a showdown with key American allies, France and Germany among them. The political pyrotechnics which arced over UN Security Council meetings were not half as bad as the deep diplomatic fissures created between the American/ British/Spanish bloc and the Franco/German/Russian bloc. This politically titanic struggle in the Security Council concerning Iraq, did not merely concern a *vote* but a wider disparate *vision* between Washington and Paris. This vision, with its powerful supporting actors on each side, would bedevil trans-Atlantic relations well into the future.

In the immediate aftermath of the war, Germany's Joskha Fischer confidently told the weekly *Die Zeit* "Europe is a real Power." He said that the "Iraq war is in the past, and the peace in the Middle East in the Future" He was of course reflecting on the role played by Paris and Berlin. Yet speaking of post-war Iraq, he added cynically "the issue of legitimacy goes beyond the capabilities of the U.S."[17]

Former Secretary of State Shultz viewed the UN debate leading to the Iraq war in another way, "Instead of focus being kept on Iraq and Saddam, France induced others to regard the problem as one of restraining the U.S. , a position that seemed to emerge from France's aspirations for greater influence in Europe and elsewhere. By March of 2003 it was clear that French diplomacy had resulted in splitting NATO, the European Union, and the Security Council... and probably convincing Saddam that he would not face the use of force."[18]

POLITICAL FALLOUT

Beyond the political fallout between Washington and the West Europeans there was an economic knock-on effect too. American consumers, particularly outraged at what was perceived as French obstructionism to America's plans in Iraq, began to turn from politics to the pocketbook. Consumer attitudes soured towards French and German products out of a thinly veiled disgust with lack of those countries support for U.S. efforts in Iraq. In one poll two thirds were very much or somewhat less favorable to French products; nearly half said they would try to find a substitute for French products while 29 percent said they "would boycott or avoid" purchasing French products. Slightly more than half viewed German products less favorably, with 47 percent looking for a non-German replacement, and 19 percent would boycott German products.[19]

Naturally there were the cases of dumping French wine in the gutter or simply saying *non* to French viniculture. Though estimates vary wildly on the French wine boycott effect, the point was that people voted with their wallets. What was rarely mentioned was the deeper and unspoken fear of German executives in the USA that their products too—especially the auto industry, would suffer from boycotts. During the German election campaigns of 2002 where anti-American sentiments bubbled to the top of the ruling SPD party's rhetoric as well as during the run up to the Iraq war, German firms deeply feared a backlash from American consumers.

Ironically foreign direct investment by American firms into Europe soared in 2003 at the height of the American-led war against Iraq, in spite of the fears that transatlantic tensions during the period would have damaged trade and economic links. A study released by Daniel Hamilton and Joseph Quinlan at Johns Hopkins University show a considerable increase in American companies investing $87 billion into Europe in 2003, a jump from the $67 billion the previous year. The study shows that despite some retailers vowing retail revenge on French products, American investment in France during that period rose to $2.3 billion. Equally American companies invested $7 billion into Germany in 2003. France was one of the major investors in the USA too with $4.3 billion invested in 2003; The study adds, "Virulent anti-war sentiment across Europe did not prevent European forms from investing $36.9 billion in the U.S. in 2003, up from $26 billion the previous year. The spin off in jobs has been huge with European affiliates of U.S. companies employing (in 2001 figures) 3.2 million and U.S. affiliates of European companies employing more than 4.2 million U.S. workers."[20]

The point is that despite serious political differences and diplomatic rifts across the Atlantic, commerce unites and often overcomes politics. Despite the roiling waters of the Atlantic in the aftermath of the Iraq war, the French contrary to many opinions did not close the door on cooperation with the USA. Addressing his diplomatic corps at the Elysees Palace in late August, President Jacques Chirac restated the goals of French Diplomacy—"to affirm the rule of law in the international order; to ensure the success of European unification; to strengthen peace and security; to make globalization more democratic." While characteristically praising the political and defense architecture of the European Union, he stated clearly, "Let there be, in this respect, no misunderstanding. Transatlantic ties and the partnership between Europe and the United States, our primary ally, constitute a crucial element of world security. A stronger Europe means first and foremost a stronger Atlantic Alliance. It therefore makes no sense to see the European Union and NATO as rivals."[21]

Viewing trans-Atlantic solidarity in the war on terror in essence comes down to a dual definition; Europe and America remain in solidarity if terror is defined classically as the radical Al-Qaida bombings or IRA outrages for example. America and the Europeans have more than enough experience with non-state actors committing cross border crimes. Fanatical Islamic fundamentalists have surpassed and outgrown the Palestinian radicals of the 1970's. An editorial in the conservative French daily *Le Figaro* opined: "The war against Al-Qaida is justified. It is in the interest of the Europeans and the Americans. But the war in Iraq is not that, not at all the war against Al-Qaida....the invasion has resulted contrary to its official objectives; inflaming radical Islam; uniting opinions the Muslim world; weakening the West and dividing Europe."[22]

Many viewed the challenge as a wider clash of civilizations and religions. This was not only the issue of radical Islamic fundamentalism—which started to bloom and grow following Iran's revolution in 1979—but the myopia of Europe's political class to confront the wider issues. Thus there is far less accord when viewing State sponsored terrorism or the State refuge for terrorist groups. Europeans see Al-Qaida, Hezbollah, Hamas and a gaggle of Algerian fundamentalist groups as *the terrorists*, but are decidedly less comfortable in connecting the dots of support and the paymasters to places like Tehran, Tripoli or Baghdad. While the West Europeans are more than willing to treat the symptoms of terrorism, Washington was singularly willing to take pro-active measures to treat the problem. Well prior to 2001, and with the absence of a clear and militarily definable threat from the former Soviet Union, the USA had emerged as the pivotal geo-political power. The Clinton team through its triumphal rhetoric, less than subtle diplomacy, and commercial babbitry gave the impression of swagger not seriousness. Europeans had cause for concern, but hardly alarm, since the U.S. record in post-1945 Europe reconstruction remained in the eyes of the majority justifiably impressive.

As Robert Kagan argues in *Of Paradise and Power*, "Well before the Bush Administration proved so maladroit at reassuring even America's closest allies, other post-Cold War Administrations had faced mounting anxiety about America's growing dominance. In the 1990's while Bill Clinton and

Madeleine Albright were proudly dubbing the United States the 'indispensable nation,' French Foreign Ministers along with their Russian and Chinese counterparts were declaring the American unipolar led world to be 'unjust and dangerous.' Europeans complained about the 'arrogance' and 'bullying' of the Clinton Administration before, during and after the Kosovo war in 1999."[23]

Former National Security Advisor Zbigniew Brzezinski addressed the dilemma "We as a people have been accustomed to the notion that national security is the norm. Henceforth national *insecurity* will be the norm for America and that is an enduring reality. There is no returning to the era of a sovereign, separate national security for us." Global security therefore, has to be our objective, and global security means a recognition of the seamless web of expanding interdependence in the world which is in the American national security interest not to undermine by but to institutionalize." He warned "I fear that current American policy by focusing almost exclusively on terror, will increase the probability that global hatred for the United States will intensify, we see evidence of that, tragically since 9/11 and sporadic terrorist attacks on the U.S. may become a more frequent reality."[24]

In the aftermath of the September 11th attacks on America, Jean-Marie Colombani, Editor in Chief of *Le Monde* editorialized memorably "We are all Americans." A few years later in the *Wall Street Journal* he wrote "Are We Still all American?" in which he stressed the urgent need for Europe and the United States to rebuild their relationship in the wake of the Iraq war.

Indeed the view from some of America's closest Atlantic Alliance allies towards the USA was less reassuring. Such divisions were obvious during celebrations of the Centennial of the Anglo/French *Entente Cordiale*. Amid the fanfare of the events commemorating the Anglo/French alliance, were polls which reflected enduring popular perceptions of the friends across the Channel—The French are arrogant, the British are anti-European. Far more interesting, was the view of which people do you *trust the most and trust the least*. For the French, the Spanish are most trusted (85%), the Germans (84%), the British (51%) and the *Americans (34%)*. The French moreover hold a negative view of Britain at (47%), the Russians (56%) and *the Americans (64%)*! Nearly two-thirds holding a negative view of the U.S.! For the British the Spanish were most trusted with (73%), the Germans (69%), and the Americans at (66%). The French were only popular with 55% of the British. Negative views of America were held by 30% of U.K. respondents in this BVA/ICM poll. When a *Der Spiegel* poll asked Germans "With which country is it most important for Germany to have good relations?" The answer was heavily 41 percent favoring France, 25 percent with the USA, 14 percent with Russia, 10 percent with China, and a mere 5 percent with Britain.[25]

Chapter Five

FROM SOLIDARITY TO SARCASM

Putting this matter into blunt context, America had a genuine image problem in France. The political polemics of Iraq seemed to overtake shared history and shared hardships. Both 1917 and 1944 come to mind for those who choose to recall. It's thus little wonder that at the 2004 Cannes Film Festival and Michael Moore's "documentary" Fahrenheit 9/11, a near politically pornographic anti-Bush portrayal was so exceedingly popular. Moore's film won the coveted Golden Palm Award and was feted by the Euro trash glitterati who was genuinely captivated by this latest piece of cinematic *agit-prop*. An unprecedented twenty minute standing ovation for the portly pseudo-proletarian Moore proved the *piece de resistance* of the Cannes Festival. *Le Figaro* stated "Michael Moore Unveils the Political Palm!" A rash of conspiracy theories, that the horrors of September 11th were orchestrated by the American CIA or Israeli Mossad became the sordid grist of internet blogs. Charges that a secret cabal orchestrated the "Reichstag Fire" of September 11th soon gained currency beyond the usual crackpot circles.

Still realism beckons. One can no longer describe anti-Americanism as the exclusive preserve of the left or the kook fringe as it essentially was during the Cold War. Now the symptoms may be superficially similar but the problem goes far deeper, extending to the staid and generally conservative British publications such as the *Economist* and the *Financial Times*. Covers on the venerable *Economist* have sported anti-Bush themes from the memorable "Better Ways to Attack Bush" to the gripping and "Resign, Rumsfeld." Longtime *Financial Times* columnist Martin Wolf headlined, "The Savior of Democracy is run by a unilateral bully," and goes on to say "the world is too complex and dangerous for the pious simplicities and arrogant unilateralism of George W. Bush." We are not talking about the *Guardian* or *New Statesman*. The French and German press were far less forgiving.

As Gerard Baker opined, "Where did all the love for America Go?. That lovely morning Hate had its finest hour. Seconds later Love poured in...that single moment of terror, American had never been the victim of so much hate nor the object of so much Love." Yet in the midst of the Iraq war, Baker stated sadly "the world hates America a bit more than it did on September 10th 2001 and a lot more than it did on September 12th 2001. The net effect of the past two years has been, to give a significant boost to the America-haters."[26]

Still the post-Iraq conflict has not proven as seemingly one-sided as Washington's face off with France, Germany and Belgium appeared. Major West European countries beyond Britain have been militarily supportive to the American led coalition in Iraq. Such support and solidarity has been soft-peddled even by many Americans. During the 2004 Presidential Campaign

Democratic contender Senator John Kerry often derided those countries helping the USA in Iraq, ironically while at the same time calling for "multilateral policies which would encourage our allies to support us in Iraq." Though the Kerry campaign regularly called for America's Iraq policies to be blessed by the United Nations which would seemingly *ipso facto* bring support from America's traditional friends, the facts on the ground proved that the seemingly elusive allied support was there, albeit not in the numbers one could have hoped for.

A multinational military force was a key of the Bush Administration's effort in Iraq as to assure world opinion and the American people that this was not merely an Anglo/American effort. Besides the nearly 10,000 strong British contingent, Italy (3,000), Poland (2,500) the Netherlands (850), Denmark (500) were among NATO troop contributors. Australia, Japan and South Korea equally offered notable support.

Until Spain's conservative government was toppled in the aftermath of the 11 March terrorist bombings, Madrid had 1,300 troops in Iraq which were since withdrawn. Still a number of smaller European troop contingents serve in Iraq including those from Albania, the Baltic states, Slovakia and Ukraine. Though NATO's European fulcrum rests in the Franco/German core, sixteen other Atlantic Alliance members have made individual military troop commitments in Iraq. Italy and the singularly courageous leadership of Silvio Berlusconi's government had proven a notable major West European counter-weight to the trans-Atlantic diplomatic gloom. Not only has the Italian government, despite much domestic political opposition, been militarily supportive to the USA in Iraq but has provided the rhetorical cover for many of Washington's initiatives.

SHARED STRUGGLES

The 60th anniversary of the D Day landings in Normandy provided both the White House and the Elysee Palace the renewed opportunity to patch over if not reconcile profound differences in the Franco/American Alliance. Both George Bush and Jacques Chirac carefully choreographed comments at the commemorations. Speaking at the Normandy commemorations President Chirac stated, "France will never forget what it owes America, its steadfast friend and ally." He added emphatically, "Like all the countries of Europe, France is keenly aware that the Atlantic Alliance remains, in the face of new threats, a fundamental element of our collective security."[27]

Le Monde described the setting as "The Landings—A Day of Franco/American Reunions." Yet here's a poignant political opinion. "The solidarity between allies in the second world war and the homage paid yesterday to the heroes of D Day contrast sharply with the unprecedented estrangement between the U.S. Administration and many of its European and Asian partners," writes Francois Heisbourg, Director of the Paris-based Foundation for Strategic Research. He adds, "All the while, an American Rome is paying less and less heed to a European Athens. Under these circumstances, the choice for America's friends has become truly impossible. On the one hand we can stand with the current U.S. Administration: sending troops to Iraq under the NATO flag, supporting Mr. Bush's statements on the Israel Palestine issue... such a course would preserve the unity of the West, but it would also open the way for a Huntingtonian "clash of civilizations" between the Muslim East and an undifferentiated West."[28]

French philosopher Andre Glucksmann offered another view; "The right of people to be liberated from extreme despotism, the right to D Day, overcomes the usual respect for borders and the age-old principle of sovereignty...the landing in Normandy justifies the recent interventions in Kosovo, in Afghanistan, and in Iraq, even without Security Council authorization. For one decisive reason: the original legitimacy that presided over the creation of the United Nations prevails in authority over the ordinary jurisprudence of the institutions that have stemmed from it." He adds, "Can the United States still claim a right of interference, baptized in the bloodshed to liberate Europe? Yes...Because at its worst and at its best, the United States remains a democracy. And the most exemplary one."[29]

Glucksmann's words, and his peerage as a philosopher of the French Left, clearly illustrate the vexing political discord in Europe itself concerning issues of terrorism, Iraq, and the West's moral and military responsibilities in a world facing Islamic extremism.

Yet the very role of the NATO alliance has been questioned especially in the aftermath of Iraq. As the German journal *Internationale Politik* opined, "The trans-Atlantic alliance is no longer a given. During the Cold War, Europeans and Americans were joined together by a common threat and the protective shield that the United States held over Europe. But the stopgap solutions under ex-President Bush and simple 'Obamamania' can hardly provide a sustainable basis for successful joint action." The journal adds, "Blaming Bush for everything will not work for long, and we seem unable to get into our heads that the United States is no longer the 'European power' that it was during the Cold War. America's strategic interests now lie in the Pacific, the Middle East and South Asia." The article added, "Any country that wants to be taken seriously by the United States and valued as a reliable partner must be willing to do more than invoke a glorious past and common values. It must be prepared to deliver. Europe is not yet ready to do this. The result will inevitably be joint disappointment and the next transatlantic hangover."[30]

Defense Nationale of Paris added, "It is important to remember that Europeans are not *ipso facto* rejecting American support, which was so decisive for the European building during the Cold War. Instead, the focus is on political emancipation, a necessary emancipation from a form of strategic tutelage that is no longer required. What the European now wants is a renewal of the transatlantic relationship."[31]

The pressing threat of international piracy, especially in the perilous waters off Somalia and Yemen has united the USA and Europe. The pirate/terrorist threat to life, navigation and commerce presents a perfect case for a broadbrushed international response. Joint American efforts with key European Union states and Japan were well under way during the Bush Administration leading to a number of Security Council resolutions. Both resolutions #1811 and #1846 (2008) outlined the threat and the commitment of the international community to confront the Somali pirates. U.S. Navy ships and a serious commitment of European Union member navy vessels have joined ships from Canada, Japan, and South Korea to battle the buccaneers who attack both humanitarian aid cargo ships as well as tankers largely for the ransom. The EU force NAVFOR/Atalanta deploys five frigates and three supply ships in guarding the sea lanes off Somalia and Yemen. As in most such multinational operations, the key element remains not commitment but unclear rules of engagement when dealing with adversaries.[32]

Needles to say, Iraq should not have become the central issue for the American Administration, overshadowing and warping its multilateral relations. Clearly the U.S. must now reengage and revitalize its relations with Russia, with its European allies, and Latin America while at the same time maintaining a positive equilibrium with China, Japan, Taiwan and South Korea. Still given the past policy focus on Iraq, any precipitous withdrawal or perceived loss there would further radicalize sectors in all the neighboring Arab countries and have serious military reverberations in Afghanistan and Pakistan. The war on terror continues from fighting the Taliban in Afghanistan to the anti-pirate operations off East Africa and the global hunt for Al-Qaida. The United States and its European allies while rhetorically on the same page, are still expected to go off script when the going gets tough.

NOTES

1. "The Day the World Changed," the *Economist* newspaper Ltd. London, 15 September, 2001, p. 1 and Permanent Observer Mission of the Holy See to the United

Nations; "Texts of the Statements of His Holiness Pope John Paul II Concerning the Terrorist Attacks on the United States which took place on 11 September 2001," 15 October 2001, p. 1.

2. Christopher Bennett, "Aiding America," *NATO Review* Winter 2001/2002, p. 6.

3. United Nations Security Council Resolution #1373 (2001). Landmark resolution which aims to "prevent and suppress the financing of terrorist acts," provides wide-ranging measures against state sponsorship, finance, support or safe haven for terrorist groups.

4. George W. Bush, Address to a Joint Session of Congress and the American People, 20 September 2001, whitehouse.gov.

5. "Joint Press Briefing with President Jacques Chirac and President George W. Bush," Info-France, 18–19 September 2001, p. 1.

6. "German Leaders Express Condolences to the United States," Germany-Info 11 September 2001 and 20 September 2001.

7. Germany-Info 29 January 2002.

8. Germany-Info 29 January 2002.

9. Mission of Germany to the UN; Fischer Address to the General Assembly, 12 November 2001, pp. 1–2.

10. "Time for Real Solidarity," Statement by Romano Prodi, Europe. eu 24 October 2001.

11. Corine Lesnes, "Hubert Vedrine denounce le 'simplisme' et 'unilateralisme 'utilitaire' des Americains," *Le Monde* 8 February 2002, p. 3. see also "La France veut une relation 'de franchise' avec les Etats Unis,' interview with Dominique de Villepin, *Le Monde* 30 July, 2002, p. 2.

12. Robert Kagan, Paradise and Power, p. 44.

13. George Shultz, "An Essential War," Reprinted from the *Wall Street Journal* © 29 March 2004, p. A18, Dow Jones & Company. All rights reserved.

14. Douglas Bereuter and John Lis, "Broadening the Transatlantic Relationship," *Washington Quarterly* Vol. 27 No 1 (Winter) 2003–2004, pp. 148–149.

15. "What the World Thinks 2002," Pew Research Center for the People and the Press, Washington D.C., 4 December 2002.

16. Gaidz Minassian, "Villepinisme" contre "Vedrinisme," *Le Monde* 4 March 2003, p. 16.

17. Joschka Fischer Interview, "Europa ist eine echte Macht," *Die Zeit*, 8 May 2003.

18. Shultz, "An Essential War," 29 March 2004, p. A18.

19. Andrew Hill, "U.S. Opts for Homegrown Products," *Financial Times* 1 April 2003, p. 5.

20. Judy Dempsey, "FDI Soars Despite U.S.-Europe Strains," *Financial Times*, 9 June 2004, p. 4.

21. President of France/Address Jacques Chirac to the Ambassadors Conference/ Elysee Palace Paris 29 August 2003, pp. 1–3.

22. Jean de Belot, "Changer l'Europe," *Le Figaro*.online 16 March 2004.

23. Robert Kagan, Paradise and Power, pp. 116–117.

24. Zgibniew Brzezinski, "The Choice; Global Domination or Global Leadership?" Lecture Carnegie Council 25 March 2004.

25. Marie Guichoux, "La Confiance ne Regle pas Encore," *Liberation*, 5 April 2004, p. 6. and *Der Spiegel* 26 November 2007, p. 23.

26. Gerald Baker, "Where Did all the Love for America Go?" *Financial Times*, 11 September 2003.

27. Joshua Chaffin and James Harding, "Bush Hopes for Unity on Iraq at G8 Summit," *Financial Times*, 7 June 2004, p. 1.

28. Francois Heisbourg, "How Unilateralism is Changing Old Alliances," *Financial Times*, 7 June 2004, p. 13.

29. Andre Glucksmann, "Oui, l'Ami Americain," *Le Monde*, 6–7 June 2004, p. 13.

30. Eberhard Sandschneider, "The Importance of Being Europe," *Internationale Politik-Global Edition*, Vol.10, No. 1, Spring 2009.

31. Jean Dufourcq and Peter Faber, "Transatlantic Dialogue," *Defense Nationale* November 2006, p. 35.

32. United Nations/Security Council, "Report of the Secretary General pursuant to Security Council resolution 1846 (2008)," 16 March 2009 and EU/NAVFOR/Press Brussels, 15 April 2009.

UN Photo/Mark Garten. United Nations Security Council provided the forum for heated diplomatic exchanges in the countdown to the Iraq War. Although Saddam's Iraq was in open violation of more than a dozen resolutions, the Security Council failed to authorize direct military action against Iraq in March 2003.

UN Photo/ Mark Garten. U.S. Secretary of State Colin Powell yet-again explaining Washington's position on Iraq. Despite regular presentations before the Security Council, Sec. Powell never fully convinced the international community of the Bush Administration's case for war.

UN Photo/ Sophia Paris. French Foreign Minister Dominique de Villepin presented the prevailing West European diplomatic position. In American eyes, de Villepin played the suave villain who confronted Powell especially during the St. Valentine's Day massacre, the diplomatic showdown in the Security Council meeting 14th February 2003.

UN Photo/ Michelle Poirel. French President Jacques Chirac, presented himself as Europe's voice of conscience against the Iraq War. Chirac's policies, in vocal opposition to the Bush Administration, brought about a serious rift in relations between Paris and Washington.

Photo by John J. Metzler. Fahrenheit 9/11, Michael Moore's movie played prominently across Euroland in Summer 2004. Here the film is showing at Berlin's Delphi Cinema. Many critics view Fahrenheit as a classic political Agit/prop documentary.

Chapter Six

The Iraq War and the United Nations

St. Patrick's Day was an unusually warm day after a cold winter in New York. But a deep diplomatic chill, which prevailed in the corridors of diplomacy signaled the end of a bitter game between the Bush Administration and some members of the Security Council. It was on that day, that the State Department decided to withdraw its draft resolution authorizing the use of force against Iraq. There was a sense of deep resignation at the UN and a perceptible political seething over Bush's impending plans. "Now he gets the war he wants," was a particular refrain equally underlined by the fact that an *allegedly* illegitimate President will now get the chance to start a conflict to topple Saddam!

The Euro press who characteristically described *Dubya Bush* as a mindless Dunce equally viewed him as an illegitimately elected President. Robin Cook's bitter Parliamentary resignation speech from Tony Blair's government spilled the vitriol that chads in Florida determined this outcome in Iraq...Can you imagine! The smirking arrogance of a discredited member of the Labor Party trying to pull down Tony Blair by ranting and raving about Florida chads! Cook's ill-tempered remarks reflect an underlying theme that since Bush was not "legitimately elected," who is he to dare go to war without the *moral imprimatur* of the UN Security Council? Cook's caustic comments reflected an attack on the legitimacy of the Bush Administration much more than a criticism of its policy. Such hostile feelings remained just below the surface and were bitterly echoed by many diplomats and foreign correspondents alike.

Though the transatlantic rifts created during the autumn of 2002, the UN Security Council members worked feverously for a consensus resolution which would in effect, bring pressures on Iraq but with unanimous backing from the fifteen-member Security Council. It would be a long, lonely, and often tortuous road to Resolution #1441.[1]

Ireland as a non-permanent member of the Council brought its good offices to the fore. As a longtime EU member, a neutral state, and a close friend of the U.S., the Dublin government held a powerful if unappreciated position in the countdown to consensus. During the long weeks of closed sessions and behind the scenes bargaining, the Irish delegation pressed for a draft, which would essentially bridge the difference between the Anglo/American position and that of France/Russia and the others. While the Irish government clearly shared many of the American concerns over Saddam's regime, the Dublin government did not view the crisis with the same timetable as did Washington.

DIPLOMATIC DUCKS IN A ROW

When Security Council resolution 1441 passed in November, with unanimous backing from all fifteen members, the quiet but determined Irish contribution to consensus was probably not appreciated. Neither was the lingering sense of political déjà vu. After all for over a decade the Security Council was churning out resolutions concerning Iraq. Saddam's regime remained in unambiguous breach of a battery of international law. Equally military threats against Saddam were a regular feature of Anglo/American/Iraqi relations even after the Gulf War in 1991. U.S. and British warplanes enforced a no fly zone in both northern and southern Iraq. Crippling economic sanctions against Iraq were accomplishing little other than embitter the Iraqi civilian population and provide a rich source of revenue for a coterie of Saddam's black marketers.

Now at long last Saddam was being called to task to come clean on his elusive weapons of mass destruction of face the consequences—yet again. In his speech from the rostrum of the General Assembly on 12 September President Bush bluntly warned that the United Nations faces a difficult and defining moment, Bush called on assembled delegates to press the Iraqi regime to come clean on its hidden weapons of mass destruction. Citing a long lawyerly litany of broken UN Security Council resolutions which Iraq had disregarded, he told delegates that the grave and gathering danger from Baghdad's included biological, chemical and possibly nuclear weapons. By hiding such arms, "Saddam has made the case against himself."

"The conduct of the Iraqi regime is a threat to the authority of the United Nations and a threat to peace," the President stated, adding "Iraq has answered a decade of UN demands with a decade of defiance. All the world now faces a test and the United Nations a difficult and defining moment. Are

Security Council resolutions to be honored and enforced, or cast aside without consequence? Will the United Nations serve the purpose of its founding, or will it be irrelevant?"[2]

In cavernous UN General Assembly hall the President was not speaking to the choir but to the oft apostates; many who didn't view Saddam with any real sympathy but who quite often put the USA on the same moral and political pedestal. Yet, the diplomatic die had been cast. From mid-September the United States and its allies would pursue the path of diplomacy for one final resolution while at the same time preparing military forces for deployment to the Gulf. Almost as quickly as President Bush threw down the gauntlet, Baghdad made a seemingly concessionary counter move by announcing the unconditional return of UN weapons inspectors to Iraq. Under the looming shadow of an American military strike and facing intense diplomatic pressure from many Arab nations, Baghdad agreed to allow the unconditional return of UN weapons inspectors back into Iraq. The dramatic breakthrough came after discussions between UN Secretary General Kofi Annan and the visiting Iraqi Foreign Minister Naji Sabri. The White House reacted very cautiously to the developments knowing that Saddam was likely playing his well-honed tactical tricks to forestall both any new Security Council mandates as well as impending military action.

Well timed to throw Washington off guard, the move seemingly allowed the settlement of the long simmering crisis of international weapons inspectors. The UN inspectors had been withdrawn from Iraq just prior to the Clinton Administration's massive air raids in December 1998. Thus there had been no oversight to Saddam's weapons programs for four years; Iraq's apparent flexibility brought a new dynamic to the debate and held out a possibility that a looming crisis between Baghdad and Washington could be averted after all. Naturally this tactical concession would allow Saddam to stall for time, to encourage political divisions in the Council, and equally to play a well-honed hide and seek shell game with the inspectors once they arrived, months later.

While the UN arms inspectors booted out of Baghdad in 1998 could be set to return to resume their elusive quest for Saddam's weapons of mass destruction, there's little doubt that the Iraqi regime was playing to the gallery *showing apparent flexibility.*

At the same time, Washington was wise to go through the *charade* of the inspections knowing full well that Saddam will resort to bullying, blocking, and blustering but will then give the U.S. the *causus belli* to use military force. Though stalling tactics were part of Saddam's shopworn strategy to gain time, Iraq long-ago shifted and re-hid its weapons of mass destruction.

Arms inspections *per se* are a means to the goal of Baghdad's actual disarmament. And then there's the practical issue of the logistical time lag in re-starting the inspection process in itself.

But a new phase of the Iraq *GAME* had certainly begun. The U.S. was prudent not to jump the gun but to allow Saddam to let the inspectors in, to take the proverbial bait, and thus give the U.S. the time to choreograph the strategic buildup for offensive operations in early 2003. While the Bush Administration was preeminently wise to concentrate its efforts on securing a clear U.S. Congressional Mandate for future military options, wasting too much political capital for a new UN Security Council resolution was viewed as laborious and counter-productive. While the fifteen-member Council was predictably divided over Saddam's latest ploys, previous Council resolutions were already in place mandating an inspection regime. What the resolutions lacked was a *clear spelling out of the consequences* for Saddam's non-compliance.

The game-board was thus *SET*. The diplomatic divisions which re-emerged in the wake of the Iraqi offer to permit inspections were not unexpected and part and parcel of the very dynamism of working within a multilateral forum. As President George W. Bush warned, "If the UN Security Council does not deal with Iraq, we will."

Beyond the political calculus, there was the obvious but oft overlooked bottom line that Russian, French and People's Republic of China petroleum producers have and wish to have a yet wider stake in Iraqi oil production. *The Wall Street Journal* reported that companies which initialed deals with Iraq in the 1990's for major production after UN sanctions are lifted included Russia's Lukoil, France's ELF Aquitaine and Total, and Beijing's China's National Petroleum. Curiously, these countries reflected, should we say, held a "more open-minded view" of Iraq than did the USA. Concerning the Russian case, we're reminded of the close comradely ties between Baghdad and the former Soviet Union. In the run-up to the war, that friendship continued and this is not unusual. Yet one must ask Russia the rhetorical question; did it see its future business and trade relations revolving closer to the USA or with Iraq?

The Bush Administration was wise to play a tactical game of allowing the inspections to go forward, while preparing for the strategic military *Match*.

At the same time the USA pushed for a resolution demanding Iraqi disarmament backed up by the threat of severe consequences should Saddam not comply. The French offered a two step plan; formal return of the UN inspectors followed by the second resolution detailing the consequences should Saddam refuse. Indeed the arms inspections proved a double-edged sword for all parties. The root cause of the crippling economic sanctions imposed on Iraq by the Security Council a decade earlier, rested with Baghdad's noncompliance with full and transparent disarmament. UN inspection teams led by Rolf Ekeus, Richard Butler, and Hans Blix were focused on certificating of disarmament, which would in turn allow for the lifting of sanctions.

Thus Iraq had refused to come clean and be certified so. The UN had *to find* the elusive weapons or certify that there were none. Saddam claimed that all the proscribed weapons had been destroyed or accounted for, thus providing the conditions to lift sanctions. Nobody for a moment among the UN teams thought this to be true though estimates of the degree and extent of the hidden weapons varied widely. When UN weapons inspectors returned to Iraq, seeking out Saddam's weapons of mass destruction, the issue became what will the consequence be for the Baghdad regime should they revert to the old shell game of hiding, shifting, and blocking? Disarming Iraq would not be simple under the best of conditions, but one must presume that the conditions would be nebulous and perhaps openly confrontational and the final results inconclusive. That's where the problems started.

In early 2000, the Security Council tasked Hans Blix to lead the revived arms inspection teams United Nations Monitoring and, Verification and Inspection Commission (UNMOVIC). Blix, a former Swedish diplomat, follows in the footsteps of previous inspection team leaders including the focused and assertive fellow Swede Rolf Ekeus and the tough and tumble Aussie Richard Butler. A classic compromise candidate, Blix was the choice of Russia and France, over then weak American objections. Blix whose earlier tenure as Director of the UN's International Atomic Energy Agency (IAEA), witnessed what Washington viewed as a serious miscalculation of North Korea's nuclear program. Thus stigmatized as hardly the "tough guy" needed to direct the Iraqi operation, the mission revolved around both *mandate and macht*. At the time of his appointment, there were quietly expressed concerns that some members of the Council wish the teams not to find too much, or just enough, to satisfy critics and then sign off on Iraqi disarmament compliance? Naturally one must assume that anything of real value was long ago hidden in the vastness of a country that is bigger than California!

Importantly in a 12 September 2000 address to the General Assembly, Secretary of State Madeleine Albright stated, "We must also stand up to the campaign launched by Baghdad against the UN's authority and international law. Security Council resolution #1284 provides an effective plan for protecting world security through resumed weapons inspections and monitoring in Iraq." Albright stated bluntly, "Thus far, Baghdad has flatly refused to accept the resolution. The regime's strategy is to ignore the UN Charter obligations, and seek to preserve at all costs its capacity to produce the deadliest weapons humanity has ever known."³

Two years later, and in the wake of the 11 September attacks, the Bush Administration was pursuing an offensive strategy which would evolve into pre-emptive war. After achieving vital bi-partisan Congressional support for use of the military option against Saddam Hussein's Iraq, President George W. Bush had assembled another piece in the larger geo-political puzzle. Securing a tough new UN Security Council resolution, which would set a time frame for disarmament as well as outline the clear and unambiguous consequences for non-compliance became the next hurdle. Washington pressed for an ultimatum to Iraq; *identify, verify, and disarm*—OR ELSE. Other Council members took a more piecemeal and drawn out path towards disarmament. Given the players on the fifteen-member Council of which veto holding Russia, Communist China, and France hold a totally different *threat perception* than does the US or the UK. Diplomatic support for the U.S. attacking Iraq was *anything but* decisive; even major NATO allies were at best ambivalent or antagonistic towards any Anglo/American military operation, which is not specifically authorized by a Security Council resolution. The U.S. had played its diplomatic hand *maladroitly* while facing vocal opposition from France, Germany, and even Canada, by not making the right moves to assuage such concerns.

Ireland's delegate Richard Ryan in a speech a few weeks before the vote stated, "Ireland welcomed the fact that President Bush came to the United Nations and laid before us the concerns of his country regarding the threat posed by Iraq's failure to comply with its obligations under the Security Council resolutions. Iraq's failure to comply with its obligations has long presented a challenge to the United Nations and the Security Council." Stressing the importance of the impending inspections Ambassador Ryan added, "If Iraq, despite its recent communications, again fails to cooperate with inspectors, the Council must, as the Secretary General said, face its responsibilities." Ryan added, "The Resolution should make it clear that the Council will take any necessary decision to enforce compliance. Any such decision must be taken by the Security Council in full accordance with the Charter."⁴

On November 8th, the UN Security Council unanimously passed an American-sponsored resolution, demanding that Iraq *disarm or else*. The vote came after two months of intense diplomatic wrangling and in the aftermath of major mid-term election gains by President George W. Bush, and an earlier strong bi-partisan U.S. Congressional backing for military action against Iraq. The clear political *cause and effect* should be noted. President Bush called the vote *"a final test"* for Iraq. Saddam had calculated that diplomatic dithering would save him from the political *Armageddon* he so callously courted. For

President Bush, the line in the sand was soon be drawn around Saddam—either the truth *or* the consequences. That came through Resolution 1441. Thus after eight weeks of diplomatic dithering in what seemed like a garden maze of semantic and legal contradictions, Washington was finally able to finesse the resolution past the objections of Paris and Moscow. France and Russia feared that two earlier draft resolutions would have given the U.S. an immediate green light for war. Baghdad was confronted with a blunt ultimatum—list your weapons by December 8th, *then allow* unfettered international inspections, or face the military consequences.[5]

The French insistence on a two-stage process, allowed for some flexibility in the Security Council's deliberations but did not allow Saddam off the political hook. Yet, for Saddam this latest line in the sand appeared to be *yet another* ultimatum—the difference being that the White House would not take no for an answer and moreover was prepared for exactly the type of shell game and hide and seek tricks Iraq played with earlier rounds of arms inspections. National Security Advisor Condi Rice, warned Iraq that there will be "zero tolerance" for any breach of the agreement. Saddam faced the truth or the consequences—either provide full disclosure about his weapons of mass destruction or face the military consequences. French Foreign Minister Dominique de Villepin stated "The ball is now in Saddam's court." Indeed, French diplomats hailed the new resolution's text as focusing on Iraqi disarmament and weapons inspections rather than the original U.S. goal of regime change in Baghdad. Inspectors deployed into Iraq in late November 2002 to start an intrusive search policy. Saddam cooperated as to lull suspicions, and to derail the American military buildup in the Gulf. If Saddam appeared to blink, there was significant opinion in the Council, which would say, "well he complied, and the crisis is over." Saddam was a master in dividing the Security Council.

John Negroponte, the politically adroit American Ambassador to the UN warned Iraq, "non-compliance is no longer an option." Yet another challenge came from geography. In Iraq a country the size of California, it would appear easy to have hidden major components which would be searched out by a team of at most 100 inspectors.

In the impending showdown with George W. Bush, Saddam stood warned "Don't Mess with Texas." Colin Powell recalled, "1441 was a great diplomatic achievement for all the nations who joined together, the 15 nations who joined together and passed it. And it was a great win for the Administration, for President Bush. There were a lot of people who were speculating, well don't even go to the UN. Just go do it, just go to war by yourself. Well. It would not have been so easy." Secretary Powell added, And 1441 was a case where the President recognized that it was UN resolutions that were being violated, not just United States sensibilities. And so he took it to the UN and said "You have a problem. This regime, the Iraqi regime under Saddam Hussein, for the last 12 years has ignored this body. What are you going to do about it?"[6]

HINGE OF FATE

Despite passing the landmark resolution, the game was far from finished. Indeed #1441 mandated that the Iraqi authorities would submit declarations and equally that the UNMOVIC inspectors would produce regular progress reports—eagerly awaited diplomatic briefing sessions in which Dr. Hans Blix would assume an almost *Delphic role*—the UNMOVIC Oracle offering a verdict–usually equivocal—which would nonetheless be deciphered and viewed by all sides as supporting their position. Each of the Blix Reports, while highly technical and almost deliberately dull, provided a kind of weathervane showing as to whether storm clouds were gathering or clearing.

Having been present for each of the eagerly awaited presentations, and having experienced the electric eagerness for each and every word, one could say that the Blix reports provided what Churchill once called the *Hinge of Fate*. Except in this case there were no Churchillian persona but rather dour technocrats and nervous diplomats.

On 7 December, Saddam Hussein tried to stop the ticking clock on his regime's survival by providing the UN and international weapons inspectors with an exhaustive telephone book-type list detailing his presumably past programs of mass destruction—which of course he claimed not to have. Yet the whole point of the 12,000–page tome was saying there really is nothing, but since you want paper, we will give you a blizzard of facts and probably fantasy. At issue of course remained whether Baghdad's declaration was genuine, or complete. Naturally the Iraqis feel that with such a formidable document, people will be dazzled and dumb-founded by the sheer size.

The documents had all the veracity of a plagiarized college term paper—one of those suspiciously long and well presented papers, *which just don't seem right*, given the previous performance and record of the student. The logic was that if Saddam no longer has any weapons and says well, we have nothing but I can't give you a blank document. So Iraq then presents something so overwhelming and complicated that it causes enough confusion to buy time and perhaps sow division among Council members. The Security Council saw feathers fly after the U.S. gained early access to the material. The episode was genuinely the grist of a diplomatic caper. Originally the dossier after being flown from Baghdad to Cyprus and then Frankfurt, arrived at UN HQ in New York Sunday evening into the hands of Chief Arms Inspector Hans Blix. The material was supposed to first be analyzed and later distributed to members of the Security Council. Washington through a bit of *should we say friendly persuasion* got its hands on the cache first, through the assistance of the Colombian Ambassador who was December's president of the Council, and the tacit acquiescence of Blix, whisked one of two copies off to Washington late Sunday night, and later then distributed the photocopied tomes and CD-Roms to the other four permanent Council members-China, France, Russia and the United Kingdom.

Part of the problem rested with the dossier's data concerning nuclear matters—information which was presented to the Councils other permanent members, which happen to be declared nuclear powers and who quite frankly have the technical and scientific expertise to analyze the data presented. The ten other non-permanent members of the Council would, by previous arrangement, later receive a "sanitized version" of the dossier's nuclear information. Still many members, such as Syria, were not amused.

UN Secretary General Kofi Annan, was outraged, and privately said to be furious. American UN Ambassador John Negroponte later advised, "This is not a question of asserting some special privilege…it's more a question of drawing on the expertise of declared nuclear weapons states" which could in effect expedite the analysis of the enormous declaration. In fact the nuclear-related sections of the declaration alone contained 2,400 pages. The Russians backed him up; "the sole purpose of the exercise, is to make sure that non-proliferation treaties are respected. Nothing else is behind the process," added Ambassador Sergey Lavrov. By presenting the dossier and keeping to Security Council timetables, Baghdad was not in "material breach" of the #1441 resolution. As expected there was little new data, a possibly quite a lot of disinformation. It's not so much what Baghdad said, but what they failed to say. Saddam's sins of omission in other words.

Kofi Annan was clearly despondent. At his first press conference of 2003 he started with a nervously optimistic, "Good Morning Ladies and Gentlemen—and Happy New Year! We start the year with anxiety—anxiety over the prospect of war in Iraq, over nuclear proliferation in the Korean peninsula, and over what seems like violence without end in the Middle East.[7]

In an eagerly awaited update on UNMOVIC, Dr. Hans Blix overviewed the complex issues in an address to the Security Council on the 27th January "One of the three important questions before us today is how much might remain undeclared and intact from before 1991; and possibly, thereafter; the second questions is what, if anything, was illegally produced or procured after 1998, when the inspectors left; and the third question is how it can be prevented that any weapons of mass destruction be produced or procured in the future." Regarding the discovery of some 122mm chemical rockets in a bunker outside Baghdad, he made this famous statement, "Iraq states they were overlooked from 1991, from a batch of some 2,000 that were stored there during the Gulf War. That could be the case. *They could also be the tip of a submerged iceberg.* The discovery of a few rockets does not resolve, but rather points to the issue of several thousands of chemical rockets that are *unaccounted for*."[8]

Despite his tenure as UNMOVIC Chief Weapons Inspector on the eve of the Iraq War, Blix soon turned skeptic; in the post war phase he began to cast serious doubts as to whether Iraq still possessed the banned weapons. In comments to the press at his retirement in early June, Blix conceded that there are "lots of items are unaccounted for" but that "cosmetic inspections are worse than none." He joked that back home in Sweden he would continue to tend mushrooms and may extend his gardening to blueberries.

By the end of Summer he was sowing a bitter harvest. In a *BBC Radio* interview the Swede went to far as to say that the "culture of spin" dominated British arguments in the controversial debate. He compared the way Britain and America were sure Iraq had weapons of mass destruction to the way people in the Middle Ages were convinced witches existed and so found them where they looked. He argued that exaggeration, spin and hype damaged government credibility.[9]

In early February, diplomats gathered in New York for a vital Ministerial meeting of the UN Security Council, the outcome of which, could hinge *war or peace*. Eleven Foreign Ministers among them France, Germany and China, heard a presentation by Secretary of State Colin Powell, which was billed as offering *compelling new evidence* of Iraqi arms violations as well as breaches of the UN weapons inspection program. Powell's presentation to a *skeptical* audience sadly did not change many minds. Many observers, myself included, moreover felt that the Secretary of State, despite his elaborate *show and tell speech*, lacked genuine conviction. Powell clearly failed to hit the proverbial home run in the Security Council. Despite what Powell described as compelling evidence warranting immediate actions, France and Germany held to the tightly written inspection regime script of Security Council resolution #1441.

"For now the inspection regime, favored by resolution #1441 must be strengthened since it has not been explored to the end," intoned Dominique de Villepin adding, "Use of force can only be a final outcome. Why go to war if there still exists an unused space in resolution 1441." He added, "Consistent with the logic of this resolution, we must therefore move on to a new stage and further strengthen the inspections....we must choose to strengthen decisively the means of inspection."[10]

Joschka Fischer of Germany added, "The dangers of a military action are and its consequences are plain to see...on the basis of Resolution 1441 and in light of practical experience, we need to enhance the instruments of inspection and control. We need a tough regime of intensive inspections that can guarantee the full and lasting disarmament of Iraq's weapons of mass destruction."[11]

Britain's near singular European support for America's effort to disarm Iraq has of course rekindled the special Anglo/American relationship. Then came a vital letter of solidarity with Washington by seven additional European nations –notably Portugal and Spain as well as the Czech Republic, Denmark, Hungary, Italy, and Poland. Notably absent were what some *politicos* in Washington were calling, the *Axis of Appeasement,* France, Germany, and needless to say Russia. It was too easy to say cynically that for some countries to offer the USA political backing against Saddam cost little and was likely to gather much in reciprocal reward. Portugal and Spain, two NATO allies and tried and true friends, and the Danes who have chosen to remain great, and Italy supported the U.S. stance against Saddam. Equally for young, renewed democracies like the Czech Republic, Hungary, and Poland whose history has a special relationship with the bitter fruits of appeasement and sellout, the backing for America became all the more poignant and significant.

France's President Jacques Chirac who *did know better*, had played a policy of political pique against Washington while giving the impression that a pariah state such as Iraq can somehow be tolerated. France warned it may use its Security Council veto to block a new UN resolution. The Paris daily *Le Monde*, printed crude front-page cartoons depicting President Bush in caricatures, which would have made the old Soviet *Pravda* blush for their tub thumping anti-Americanism.

France while playing a very dangerous diplomatic game, had maneuvered herself into a near diplomatic Verdun which became catastrophic to her *long term interests*. Germany whose diplomacy, if one may politely call it that under Chancellor Gerhard Schroeder, was blindsided by his socialist government's reckless impulse that despite conceding Iraq is a rogue regime, it's the Bush Administration which was cast as the proverbial threat to world peace and not the Iraqi dictator. Put bluntly, to offset attention on a floundering economy, Schroeder played a cheap political game over Iraq, which did more to isolate and damage Germany's image than to solve any Middle Eastern problems. Schroeder's Iraq policy seemed to willfully belittle formerly smooth relations with the United States, the vital ally in Germany's post-war security and prosperity. Germany's postwar democratic culture with both Christian and Social Democratic Chancellors such as Konrad Adenauer, Helmut Schmidt, and Helmut Kohl possessed a political *gravitas* grossly overshadowing Gerhard Schroeder.

Ironically trans-Atlantic fulminations between Washington and the *Old Europe*—France and Germany, had sadly demonized the very democracies the U.S. helped create and nourish in the post-1945 era. While Washington argued with Paris and Berlin, the dictator in Baghdad had his last laugh. The double irony glared in that Germany, whose two year tenure on the UN Security Council coincided with these dramatic events, would have logically been viewed as being in Washington's corner in such deliberations. Now this NATO ally, sponsored since the early 1990's by the USA for a Permanent Council seat, was acting as anything but a partner. In the countdown to the Iraq war the US-German relationship suffered largely due to Gerhard Schroeder's political obstinacy and the Bush Administration's intransigence.

In Rome the morning of 14 February, Pope John Paul II granted an audience to Iraq's Tariq Aziz in the Vatican. "Peace is still possible in Iraq" headlined *L'Osservatore Romano*. The next day a special Vatican envoy met with Saddam in Baghdad to press for a peaceful solution to the crisis.[12]

ST. VALENTINE'S DAY MASSACRE

The Security Council meeting on Friday 14 February proved a diplomatic showdown, some would say a debacle for Washington. What I describe as The St. Valentine's Day Massacre saw the French ambush and then confront Colin Powell in the Council. It was crystal clear the political momentum was against the U.S. De Villepin was suavely playing the audience and was claiming to echo large anti-war majorities across Europe, West and East. A compilation of Euro polls published in Le Monde on St. Valentine's Day showed a stunning 90% against the war in the United Kingdom, 91% in Spain, 77% in France, 71% in Germany and 61% in Italy. Belgium, Greece, Hungary, Netherlands, Switzerland, and Turkey were all registering over 80% in opposition. Only Austria showed less than half the population opposed to the looming conflict.[13]

Chief UN Weapons Inspector Hans Blix presented a mixed verdict on Iraqi compliance with key disarmament resolutions in a report to the Security Council. Blix warned of serious questions regarding toxic stocks of anthrax and VX nerve agents, yet he did not produce a "smoking gun," nor startling new evidence of non-compliance. This played into the European position pressed by France that arms inspections must be expanded and toughened. Secretary of State Colin Powell, sarcastically spoke of Iraq playing tricks on the UN and warned bluntly that the inspections process could be endlessly strung out.

Praising the UN inspections regime in Iraq, French Foreign Minister Dominique de Villepin stated unapologetically "Real progress is beginning to be apparent…progress like this strengthens us in our conviction that inspections can be effective. But we must not shut our eyes to the amount of work that still remains; questions still have to be cleared up, verifications made, and instillations and equipment probably still have to be destroyed." He warned "No one can assert today that the path of war will be shorter than that of the inspections. No one can claim either that it might lead to a safer, more just stable world. For war is always the sanction of failure." He stressed "So let us allow the United Nations inspectors the time they need for their mission to succeed. Given this context, the use of force is not justified at this time. There is an alternative to war: disarming Iraq via inspections."[14]

German Foreign Minister Fischer added, "All possible options for resolving the Iraq crisis by peaceful means must be explored…there should be no automatism leading us to the use of military force."[15]

The diplomatic dust *may* have settled after the speeches in the Security Council but delegates remained *sharply split* on what to do next in Iraq. While Hans Blix offered little *new* evidence to support U.S. aims to topple Saddam's regime, his Report warned of serious questions regarding missing anthrax and VX agents. The Europeans pushed for wider weapons inspections. The U.S. and Britain in the meantime pressed for a new Security Council resolution to allow military action. Given the prevailing mood in the Council, such a move would have been blocked by a Russian or French veto.

Political chaos and diplomatic *angst* characterized those anguished days in the UN Security Council. As American and British diplomats pressed for retooling and refining their draft resolution on Iraqi disarmament, the entire exercise became shrouded by the bluntly threatened vetoes of France and Russia. A deep diplomatic funk prevailed in the corridors of diplomacy. And while President George W. Bush frantically lobbied leaders to swing uncommitted votes, from Africa to Mexico, the damoclean sword of a veto, made the draft resolution stillborn. On the one hand, the President was astute to push for the second resolution to attempt to broaden support for the looming war with Saddam and as importantly to provide needed political cover for British Prime Minister Tony Blair who was facing trials by fire in his own Parliament and in the court of public opinion. Thus the second draft resolution, then ricocheting around the United Nations had been tabled albeit with little support beyond its sponsors Britain, the U.S. and Spain.

Britain's Downing Street accused France of "poisoning the diplomatic process at the UN." Yet, the global atmosphere was becoming quite toxic too—huge anti-war (some would argue anti-American) demonstrations rocked European cities—London included. There was a strange political déjà vu if one recalled the *"peace movement"* of the early 1980's and this *movement,* which swept Western European cities on the verge of the Iraq war.

The same crowds, impressive organization, and simplistic message emerged. Some 750,000 marched in London, with large manifestations in Rome, Berlin, and in New York. "Don't Attack Iraq," and "Not in my Name," were among the slogans.

In the midst of lobbying, Secretary of State Powell visited the Council only to be rebuffed repeatedly, first after his Feb 5th *"Tell All Iraq Expose,"* then the St. Valentine's Day massacre when French Foreign Minister Dominique de Villepin unsheathed his diplomatic stiletto, followed by an early March Blix Weapons Report when the Secretary of State was again sandbagged by France, Germany, and Russia. Powell suffered his criticism well but one questioned his point in being a punching bag? Washington assiduously courted Angola, Cameroon, Chile, Guinea, Mexico, and Pakistan to convince "swing votes" to get the necessary nine for the resolution to pass. The strategic bottom line remains that the war to disarm Saddam was being dangerously delayed by the diplomatic dilly-dallying while American and British forces in the field were endangered in their mission by the approach of General Sandstorm. America played *guignol* to the political pique of Paris, the socialist smugness of Berlin, and the still-spinning weathervanes over the Kremlin towers in Moscow.

Interestingly Russia's retro/Soviet-style Foreign Minister Ivan Ivanov threatened to say "Nyet" and veto the resolution. President Vladimir Putin was not so rash. "For Putin, a tough stance for Russia is a risky plan," warned the *Moscow Times*, "It is unlikely Bush will step down from his threats to wage war against Iraq…without Russian approval of U.S. military action, U.S. officials have made it clear Russia risks being locked out of any role in a post-Hussein Iraq, including developing oil fields."

In early March, British Foreign Secretary Jack Straw stressed that only continued pressure on Saddam would bring results; "If the pressure on Saddam Hussein eases, cooperation will disappear. The fact is that he has given up only what he can get away with…Saddam trickles out concessions, calibrated exquisitely to the pressure he is under, and in a cynical attempt to divide the Council." Dominique de Villepin later countered bluntly, "As a permanent member of the Security Council, I will say it again; *France will not allow a resolution to pass that authorizes the automatic use of force."* [16]

Indeed President Jacques Chirac had near universal domestic support to wield the veto; from the socialist left to Le Pen's rightist National Front saying that France should have had the *honor* to cast its veto before Russia! *While France successfully defeated this resolution, the collateral political damage to Paris in its relationship with Washington should not be underestimated.*

Washington pressed for a "moral victory" through wooing and winning five of the six uncommitted votes on the Council—a costly game to achieve a pyrrhic political victory—would then anyway be defeated by the veto. Spain's Foreign Minister Ana Palacio advised that withdrawing the resolution may actually be wiser. In other words no vote, no veto, no embarrassment. This would in effect save the Anglo/American/Spanish draft from formal defeat, would avoid the humiliation of the loss, and essentially change the playing field. This entire charade caused serious political damage to trans-Atlantic relations, the standing of the UN Security Council, and played into the hands of Saddam. Washington was well advised to save further embarrassment and focus on the mission—the liberation of Iraq from Saddam.

The endgame could not have come quickly enough for Washington. A deep diplomatic *malaise* prevailed in the halls of diplomacy at the UN. There was a clear sense of resignation and diplomatic disequilibrium characterizing those anguished days. The issue became basically academic—the chance to grasp a diplomatic fig leaf in spite of what promised to be a political pie in the face in the form of a Franco/Russian veto. The Anglo/American Draft resolution was stillborn in Security Council

UNLEASHING THE FURY

The desultory diplomacy which characterized the final days before the military conflict illustrated that Saddam's primary game was keeping the clock running; conversely the Anglo/American coalition had run out of time given the impending weather. Secretary of State Colin Powell had been nearly pulled into the swirling vortex by the stillborn Security Council draft resolution but backed away from the UN impasse at the last moment. The Azores Summit signified a less than subtle transition to change the venue from a decidedly deadlocked UN Security Council to a concert of different players. Bush, Blair, Aznar and their host Barroso. On the eve of the conflict, the Azores Summit saw the leaders of the U.S., Britain, Spain, and the host Portugal not only agreed on the decisive next steps but did so in a clearly *Atlantic setting*. The imagery of Azores islands—vital crossroads in the mid-Atlantic—was part of the plan. So too was the historical imagery of the Anglo/Portuguese alliance, the oldest in the world.

Offensive military operations against Saddam's Iraq would commence soon thereafter. The United States and its allies unsheathed their terrible swift sword. The pounding and punishing air strikes—the Shock and Awe strategy—was unleashed on Saddam's regime. Soon thereafter ground operations would follow. The Marines and Army gained a lightning fast and decisive momentum and soon were at the gates of Baghdad. The sheer American force projection against an entrenched Iraqi enemy, defending its home country, and with numerous natural defenses, was an extraordinary military achievement. The U.S. forces advanced at dizzying levels, which would have astounded Gen. George Patton! Despite predictions of frightful casualties from "elite" defending Iraqi Republican Guard units and chemical weapons, the Allied forces soon crashed through the gates of Baghdad and toppled Saddam's statue, heralding a symbolic collapse of the Baa'th regime.

Still contrary to former Secretary of State James Baker's masterful coalition and alliance on the eve of the first Gulf War, Washington clearly had less diplomatic support this time round. While much was made of the over forty countries joining the coalition against Saddam, the poignant fact remains that save for a few such as Australia and Poland, not many were among the political "heavy hitters." The UN roiled with political passion. Australia's Ambassador John Dauth stated the case succinctly, "It is now time for the members of the Security Council to get beyond the acrimony, narrow political ambitions and separate agendas which have hamstrung the Council in recent months and seize the opportunity to make good of their responsibilities." Ambassador Dauth commented, "The Security Council's inability to agree how to deal with the threat posed by Iraq's weapons of mass destruction was a great disappointment to many nations…*let us be clear, the Council failed the international community. It failed to enforce its own resolutions.* The question for Council members today is whether they will allow this to gather pace, to become a trend towards impotence, or whether they can stop the Council sliding towards irrelevance and help Iraq get back on its feet after decades of abusive leadership."[17]

"There's an enormous amount of relativism among the political elites of Europe," a former President of a Nordic nation conceded to me privately, as some saw the American political posture of "you are with us or you are against us as quite simplistic." He added gravely, *"in a case like this there is not a real middle ground."*

In the aftermath of the war, the political gamesmanship continued unabated. It's a bit like a game of musical chairs round the table of the UN Security Council. Before the Iraq conflict, countries such as China, France, and Russia favored lifting Iraqi economic sanctions, while the USA opposed the move. Now with a new political tune playing in Baghdad, it became the U.S. who wished to lift the crippling embargo, while Russia said it's simply too soon. France conceded let's *suspend* the sanctions but not formally end them. The players had taken new places.

A myriad of international economic and transportation sanctions were slapped on Saddam's regime in response to Iraq's invasion of Kuwait in 1990. Since the end of the first Gulf War in 1991, the sanctions remained, pending Iraqi compliance and certifiable disarmament on weapons of mass destruction.

As the sanctions lingered, and a solution to Iraqi non-compliance fell by the wayside during the Clinton Administration, the general feeling emerged that the embargo's only real effect was causing a humanitarian disaster. In a sense that *was* true. Furthermore major Iraqi trading partners such as China, France, and Russia were loosing commercial contracts. Washington was characteristically placed in the role of the bad guy wearing the black hat and wanting to keep a noose round Saddam's neck through a tight international sanctions regime. Despite the embargo, or perhaps because of it, a flourishing a black market run by Saddam's political cronies thrived, often run through his socialist Baa'th Party which institutionalized corruption at the highest levels. The effects of the embargo were eased through the UN's *Oil for Food Program* a plan in which Iraqi petroleum sales paid for food and medicines. Oil for Food fed 60 percent of Iraqis. Equally, Baghdad earned $64 billion from oil sales since 1996 and in turn purchased humanitarian supplies.

Thus in the post-war period, the U.S. was right to press for fully lifting sanctions.

Naturally the sanctions gave the UN an undue control over Iraq's future—something the Bush Administration bristled at. Washington moreover felt that keeping the cumbersome Sanctions review Committee in the Security Council (Chaired by Germany) complicated the process of getting needed food, medicine, and supplies to Iraq. The *Oil for Food program*, while keeping the humanitarian pipeline open, encouraged a tightly scripted and rigid economic system, forcing a potentially rich country in low gear. It also became a clearing house for rife corruption, oiled with kickbacks and favors to individuals, governments and political parties.

Though Washington achieved its objectives on lifting sanctions, there was serious damage control needed in Europe. Colin Powell visited Germany in May. He was greeted by a thoughtful front-page editorial "Welcome Colin Powell," in the highly influential left-leaning *Die Zeit*. "It is good to see you in Germany, The war in Iraq is over. Sadly terrorism persists. Still, the memory of our trans-Atlantic disagreement will not linger forever." The editorial, penned by Michael Nauman advised, "In the long run, America's unilateralism in the war against terrorism could prove to be detrimental to the United States, and hence to its allies. On the other hand, Germany needs to understand that 'rogue states,' do exist and that something needs to be done about them."[18]

During the continuing political tempest in the Summer following the Iraq war, Tony Blair visited Washington and made a historic address to a joint session of Congress. "There has never been a time when the power of America was so necessary or so misunderstood."[19]

Later Blair faced widespread criticism from his own party and lingering shots from Blix over the nature of the British government's use and interpretation of intelligence. The weekend before the UN session a Berlin summit brought together Blair, Chirac, Schroeder discussed a harmonized approach to the Iraq. The 58th UN General Assembly, the first session since the Iraq war, literally started with a whirlwind, hurricane-like gusts and rain lashed UN headquarters in New York just an hour before the session's formal opening debate thus adding a foreboding *sturm und drang* atmosphere to the meeting.

Bush addressed the Assembly under the political shadow of the Iraq operation. First stressing the ongoing war on terror Bush stated, "By the victims they choose and by the means they use, the terrorists have clarified the struggle we are in. Between those who seek order and those who spread chaos; between those who work for peaceful change and those who adopt the methods of gangsters; between those who honor the rights of men and those who deliberately take the lives of men and women and children, without mercy or shame—Between these alternatives there is no neutral ground." The President warned, "All governments that support terror are complicit in a war against civilization." Concerning Iraq, Bush advised, "The primary goal of our coalition in Iraq is self-government for the people of Iraq, reached by orderly and democratic means…The success of a free Iraq will be watched and noted throughout the region. Millions will see that freedom, equality, and material progress are possible in the heart of the Middle East." He stressed, "Iraq as a dictatorship had great power to destabilize the Middle East. Iraq as a democracy will have great power to inspire the Middle East." [20]

EPILOGUE ON THE EUPHRATES

The Bush address to the Assembly received lukewarm response from many members of the world community still smarting from Washington's rebuke of the UN process on the eve of the Iraq conflict. A *Washington Post* editorial "A Failed Address," described the mood.[21]

Six months after the fall of Baghdad to the Americans, the diplomatic barometer continued to trend towards a tempest in trans-Atlantic relations.

French President Jacques Chirac led the political counter-attack against the U.S. Iraq policy stating; "The United Nations has just weathered one of the gravest trials in its history. The debate turned on respect for the Charter and the use of force. The war, embarked on without Security Council approval, has undermined the multilateral system." The President advised, "In a open world, no one can live in isolation, no one can act alone in the name of all, and no one can accept the anarchy of a society without rules There is no alternative to the United Nations…multilateralism is the key."[22]

Later at a press conference Chirac stressed that France and the U.S. "have common objectives in Iraq but also have a differences of opinion." He stated however, "the transfer of sovereignty to Iraq is essential," while Washington felt the transition process would be slower. Chirac however stressed the points of convergence with the USA namely on the issues of nuclear proliferation, the need fight crimes against humanity, and the traffic in human beings. Describing a 45 minute meeting with George W. Bush, the French President stressed despite having different points of view he "had spoken freely and in a friendly way with the U.S. President,...and never felt alienated from Bush, and never felt distant from his father."[23]

According to Guillaume Parmentier, former head of the CFE program at the French Institute for International Relations, "There is absolutely no French desire for American policy in Iraq to fail. American failure in Iraq could have wide repercussions on the stability of the greater Middle East, including North Africa, and this could have serious consequences for France, even domestically." Dr. Parmentier concedes, " In fact France's policy is not determined by a desire to counter the Americans, but by a deep seated mistrust, inspired by French history, of any excessive concentration of international power."[24]

A popular European view is found in Germany's *Der Spiegel* newsmagazine, "In fact Chirac's criticism of the American unilateralism has made the French president into a popular leader with a global following, as the ovations in the UN General Assembly demonstrated. The French head of state is the voice of resistance against the hegemonic USA, the custodian of international law, the spokesman of the broad but loosely knit coalition of nations uncomfortable with Bush's vendetta against "evil."[25]

Notably Germany's Gerhard Schroeder, whose SPD/Green government had been narrowly re-elected in 2002 on what could only be called crude anti-American campaign and a continuing opposition the Iraq war, trimmed his sails, as to avoid the dangerous political reefs which Chirac seems so comfortable sailing near. In a singularly important *New York Times* op-ed "Germany Will Share the Burden in Iraq," Chancellor Schroeder offered an olive branch to Bush, "Terrorism continues to be a very serious risk to security and stability in the world. With the fight against terrorism far from over, Germans and Americans stated united in the battle. Together we will prevail." He conceded bluntly "It is true that Germany and the United States disagreed on how best to deal with Saddam Hussein's regime. There is no point in continuing this debate. We should now look towards the future. We must work together to win the peace," he stressed but then added significantly, "In addition to its current military involvement in Afghanistan, the Balkans and elsewhere, Germany is willing to provide humanitarian aid, to assist in the civilian and economic reconstruction of Iraq, and to train the Iraqi security forces." He reaffirmed the core relationship of German-American relations, sentiments not often heard during his tenure, "Germany and the United States are linked by a profound friendship linked by common experiences and values...Today Germany is united, We Germans will never forget how the United States helped and supported us in rebuilding and reuniting our country....That Germany today is living a in a peaceful, prosperous and secure Europe is thanks in no small measure to America's friendship, farsightedness, and political determination, " Schroeder then advised, "However we must not forget that security in today's world cannot be guaranteed by one country going it alone; it can be achieved only through international cooperation."[26]

The article clearly illustrates the dichotomy of how many of the Europeans view the Iraq operation—namely that their close political ties with Washington do not offer an automatic European *carte blanche* for what is viewed as unilateral military action in places such as Iraq. Berlin's *Die Welt* headlined "Bush and Schroeder Don't Want any More Quarrels." A cordial meeting between Schroeder and Bush at the Waldorf Astoria Hotel in New York broke the sixteen month chill in relations between Berlin and Washington; Bush greeted the German Chancellor with the words "Gerhard, we should let the past lie and look to the future." Bush and Schroeder who had gone into the bi-lateral meeting with apprehensions, saw a sense of normalcy return to the relations.[27]

Addressing the UN General Assembly Schroeder reminded delegates that more than 9,000 German troops are currently deployed on international peace missions and that such deployments are clearly within the UN framework. He nonetheless stressed that "Only the UN can guarantee the legitimacy required to enable the people of Iraq to speedily rebuild their country under an independent, representative government." Yet, contrary to many former critics of the war, he offered, "Germany stands ready to support such a process by providing humanitarian, technical and economic assistance or also training for Iraqi security personnel."[28]

Russia's Vladimir Putin equally tempered earlier criticisms of U.S. Iraq policy but nonetheless clearly stated, "Despite strong differences about the ways of resolving the Iraqi crisis, the situation is ultimately coming back to the UN legal field. Here the position of Russia is consistent and clear: only direct participation of the United Nations in the reconstruction of Iraq will give its people an opportunity to independently decide their future."[29]

While little overt support for the Anglo/American policy on Iraq was enunciated from the rostrum of the General Assembly, important bi-lateral meetings on the margins of the debate gained quiet assurances from many states. Shortly thereafter in a decisive diplomatic victory for the U.S., the

United Nations Security Council voted unanimously to support an Anglo/American/Spanish resolution on Iraq's future. The outcome of the vote, which was decidedly unclear until the last moment, gave an international, if grudging, blessing to the coalition's continued occupation of Iraq. Though France, Germany, and Russia were not totally pleased with the resolution, a joint Franco/ German/Russian Statement conceded, "We and the sponsors share the same goals in Iraq i.e. to contribute to a swift stabilization of the conditions in Iraq, to support the political and economic reconstruction process and to promote the restoration of sovereignty of the Iraqi people through a government elected by them." Passing the UN resolution offered a political gain for Washington bringing wider political legitimacy for the Iraq operation and spreading the risk of the occupation.[30]

Despite the change in diplomatic tone, Washington was not to gain any significant military contributions from the West Europeans. Lingering bitterness from the earlier Iraq debates clouded relations and hampered the coalition in the first few years after the invasion. President Bush's State Visit to Britain in November 2003 proved a splendid but politically fractious occasion to highlight Anglo/American bonds of friendship and solidarity. In a strikingly brilliant address in London's Whitehall Palace, Bush warned, "the danger only increases with denial. Great responsibilities fall once again to the great democracies. We will face these threats with open eyes, and we will defeat them." In his *Three Pillar's* speech, Bush stressed; First "international organizations must be equal to the challenges facing our world" but that in the case of the UN "It's not enough to meet the dangers of the world with resolutions. We must meet those dangers with resolve." Second, "to restrain aggression and evil with force." The third pillar "is our commitment to the global expansion of democracy and the hopes and progress it brings as the alternative to instability, and hatred, and terror."[31]

The extraordinary capture of Saddam Hussein by American 4th Infantry units, brought early holiday cheer to the USA and chagrin to those who bought into the messianic myth of the fallen dictator. But beyond the political good fortune of catching the fallen Iraqi tyrant, the jarring psychological effect remains far deeper for Iraqis and the Arab "street" in general. Hopefully, the toppling of the ubiquitous Saddam statues would exorcise the ghost and the shadow of Saddam's hideous regime. As I wrote, "This cult of the personality must be defeated not only militarily as the American and British forces accomplished so splendidly, but smashed figuratively as the oppressed citizens of Baghdad did by toppling and smashing the statues, and thus the temporal political spell of Saddam—this *faux-golden Baal of Baghdad*." That said, there were still many Iraqis who feared the eventual return of the toppled ruler as if he would rise from the political dead. Smashing that myth and exorcising the legend are only part of the story it appears; as many Iraqis in the most genuine Orwellian twist, actually loved Big Brother!

Saddam was the idol of self-created legend—playing to an Arab aura he so carefully crafted. Given that his rule was portrayed as monumentally heroic, that's why discovery of this disheveled hobo was anything but heroic, but patently pathetic. Amb. Paul Bremer, the able American administrator of Iraq declared in Baghdad, "Ladies and Gentlemen, we got him! The tyrant is a prisoner." West European leaders put aside their differences to congratulate Washington.

Significantly Iraq's interim Foreign Minister Hoshyar Zebari presented a scathing criticism of the UN for "quibbling and failing to depose Saddam." Zebari told the Security Council, "Settling scores with the United States-led coalition should not be at the cost of helping to bring stability to the Iraqi people...Squabbling over political difference takes a back seat to the daily struggle for security, jobs, basic freedoms and all the rights the UN is chartered to uphold." He added in a scolding tone rarely heard in the Security Council, "The United Nations as an organization failed to help rescue the Iraqi people from a murderous tyranny that lasted over 35 years, and today we are unearthing thousands of victims in horrifying testament to that failure." The bluntly spoken Kurd implored, "The UN must not fail the Iraqi people again!"[32]

On the first anniversary of the dramatic events surrounding Iraq, Hans Blix returned to the United Nations—this time to promote his new book of recollections. Addressing UN correspondents during a rare March snowfall, Dr. Blix the dutiful if dour Swede recounted his lawyerly case over the elusive weapons of mass destruction. Highly equivocal he conceded that in 2002 he still presumed his inspection teams would find Saddam's proscribed weapons but he had "became more skeptical by January 2003."

In his book *Disarming Iraq*, Blix conceded, "Without a military buildup by the U.S in the summer of 2002, Iraq would probably not have accepted a resumption of inspections." Yet as to whether war was pre-planned or predetermined, he told correspondents. "Was it planned—well the military always plans. Was it predetermined, pre-planned yes, but predetermined, no. Think of a train, it moves forward, you have an engineer he can slow it, he can stop it, he can go to the siding depending what happens. Clinton stopped bombers that were already on their way to Iraq in 1998. But I still don't think it was predetermined."[33]

Blix wrote, "There were political and diplomatic controversies between the U.S. and the majority of UN member states, within NATO and among Europeans. Interestingly this was not a clash between great power as to whether Iraq should be disarmed, but about the method to achieve it. ...my conclusion was and remains, that the armed action that was taken was expected but not irrevocably predetermined." [34]

During the Cold War, the USA confronted disparate peoples of the Soviet Empire with the lure of Western values—either to regain them or to embrace them. This could easily apply to the Baltic states, Czechoslovakia, Hungary, or Poland—profoundly Christian European nations who had historically enjoyed better times and wanted to rejoin the flow of history in their European household. Though the post-Soviet era has nonetheless posed formidable challenges for the former East Bloc, the countries nonetheless are part of an essentially similar socio/political value system. Whether such political commonality applies to Islamic Afghanistan, Sudan, or Yemen is quite debatable.

Indeed in the U.S. there's a messianic political impulse, which is not well suited to confronting militant Islam. Moreover the *perception that unilateralism* shades a large portion of American strategic thinking has caused grating dissensions even among steadfast Cold War allies. This socio/political panacea may miss the wider challenge. Furthermore it often suffers coming from a one-dimensional view of Islam which is rooted in essentially western prescriptions for prosperity and political governance.

Significantly the Iraqi issue had clouded and often dominated the UN agenda since Saddam's forces invaded Kuwait in August 1990. The first war to oust Iraqi troops from Kuwait and the ensuing UN economic sanctions slapped in Iraq set the stage for what would become a decade long showdown with Saddam. A spate of UN Security Council resolutions followed, many of which centered on finding and destroying the elusive weapons of mass destruction. Saddam finally was ousted by military means in 2003.

In the post-war period, the diplomatic *froideur* continued concerning Iraq. Yet despite continuing rifts with France in the Security Council the U.S., Britain and Romania co-sponsored and passed, after four revisions, a resolution paving the way for full Iraqi sovereignty. The resolution, (#1546) unanimously supported by the fifteen-member council, marked a defining moment for Iraq. British Ambassador Sir Emyr Jones Parry stated, "The Security Council has powerfully endorsed the formation of a sovereign Interim Government which will assume full responsibility and authority for governing Iraq by 30 June. It is a crucial phase in Iraq's transition to full democracy."[35]

Lakhdar Brahimi, Special UN Envoy for Iraq wryly opined later, "The Americans came to the UN for a plan to end the occupation and pull out... The UN cannot say no to helping Iraq regain sovereignty and helping Iraq out of occupation."[36]

Le Monde editorialized "*A Victory for Bush*. President Bush used power to prevail in a unanimous vote that the UN approved a political plan for Iraq. Obtaining international legitimacy with the 15 members of the Security Council, including those countries opposed to American action in Iraq, . . . it is an indelible victory for George W. Bush...France climbed down."[37]

The multinational force mandate was renewed in 2007. Contrary to the prevailing misperception that the "UN never passed a resolution authorizing the multinational force in Iraq," the UN Security Council unanimously approved a resolution which while "determining the situation in Iraq continues to constitute a threat to peace and security...and acting under Chapter VII of the Charter of the United Nations, notes that the presence of the multinational force in Iraq is at the request of the government of Iraq." The resolution 1790 (2007) stipulated that this one year extension for the multinational forces is "for the last time."[38]

On the verge of the vote, Iraqi Ambassador Hamid al-Bayati stated, "My government while reaffirming the importance of the multinational forces role alongside our national forces in contributing to the efforts to establish security and the rule of law, requests that the Security Council consider extending the mandate in light of Iraq's achievement over the past few years." While calling for multinational mandate renewal "one last time," the Ambassador added, "It is also essential for the Iraqi government to be treated as an independent and fully sovereign state."[39]

Saddam's Iraq became the focus of three American Administrations, George Bush, Bill Clinton, and George W. Bush, and five Presidential American elections in 1992, 1996, 2000, 2004, and 2008. The shadow of the Iraqi dictator is yet to pass from Washington.

NOTES

1. UN Security Council Resolution #1441 (2002).
2. White House/President's Remarks at the UN 12 September 2002.
3. U.S. Mission to the UN/Speech by Secretary of State Madeleine Albright, 12 September 2000, p. 4.
4. Irish Mission to the UN/Statement by Ambassador Richard Ryan, 17 October 2002.
5. UNSC Resolution #1441 (2002) The resolution "*Deploring* the fact that Iraq has not provided an accurate, full, final and complete disclosure, as required by Resolution 687 (1991) of all aspects of its programs to develop weapons of mass destruction and ballistic missiles, as well as other nuclear programs; *Deploring* further that Iraq repeatedly obstructed immediate, unconditional, and unrestricted access to sites

designated by the United Nations Special Commission (UNSCOM) and International Atomic Energy Agency (IAEA); *Deploring* the absence since December 1998, in Iraq, of international monitoring, inspection, and verification as required by relevant resolutions, and Determined to secure full compliance with its decisions, . The resolution then Acting under the military enforcement clause Chapter VII of the Charter of the United Nations "*Decides* that Iraq has been and remains in material breach of its obligations under relevant resolutions" and provided a meticulous litany of information to the UN. The resolution paragraph 5 stated, *Decides* that Iraq shall provide UNMOVIC and IAEA with "immediate, unimpeded, unconditional, and unrestricted access to any and all, including underground areas, facilities, buildings, equipment records, and means of transport which they wish to inspect." Indeed Iraq obfuscation and constant cat and mouse antics in the follow up to this clear set of obligations put forth by the Security Council led to the final showdown. This was the operative resolution on which the Anglo/American Alliance based its legal right to attack Iraq. The famous "second resolution" of March 2003 was never approved.

6. Department of State/Colin Powell Interview with Charlie Rose, 22 April 2003.

7. UN Secretary General/Opening Statement Press Conference 14 January 2003.

8. UN Security Council 27 January 2003/An Update on Inspection. One of a number of weapons inspection Reports to the Security Council by Hans Blix. These Reports were eagerly awaited as Blix would chronicle his inspections and detail findings amid nuance of Baghdad's compliance. Blix assumed the role of a diplomatic oracle at Delphi as war and peace literally hung on his words. Among the more interesting were, 19 December 2002, 27 January 2003, 14 February 2003 (session of the infamous Franco/American face off in the Council), and 7 March 2003. Inspections in Iraq resumed on 27 November 2002—they had been blocked by the Baghdad government, in full violation of Security Council mandates since 1998.

9. "Blix Criticizes UK Iraq Dossier," *BBC News*.org 18 September 2003.

10. French Mission to the UN/ Address by Foreign Minister Dominique de Villepin 5 February 2003.

11. German Mission to the UN/Statement by Foreign Minister Joschka Fischer 5 February 2003.

12. "Peace is Still Possible in Iraq," *L'Osservatore Romano*/weekly 18 February 2003, p. 1.

13. "Les Europeens Majoritairement Opposes a une Guerre en Iraq," *Le Monde* 14 February 2003, p. 3.

14. French Mission to the UN/Address by Foreign Minister Dominique de Villepin 14 February 2003, pp. 2–4. Importantly the French *did not dispute* Saddam had the illegal WMD but remained committed to finding them through the ongoing inspections process not through military action.

15. German Mission to the UN/Statement by Foreign Minister Joschka Fischer, 14 February 2003, p.3. See also Secretary of State Colin Powell and UK Foreign Secretary Jack Straw, 14 February 2003.

16. United Kingdom Mission to the UN/Statement by Foreign Secretary Jack Straw, 7 March 2003, pp. 5–7 and French Mission to the UN'/Statement by Foreign Minister, 7 March 2003.

17. Australian Mission to the UN, 26 March 2003.
18. Michael Nauman, "Welcome Colin Powell," *Die Zeit* 15 May 2003, p. 1.
19. Tony Blair, "Prime Minister's Speech to United States Congress," *Number10. gov.uk* 18 July 2003.
20. White House/President's Remarks at the United Nations, 24 September 2003.
21. "A Failed Address" *Washington Post* 24 September 2003, p. A28.
22. French Mission to the UN/Address by President Jacques Chirac 23 September 2003.
23. French Mission to the UN/Jacques Chirac Press Conference, 23 September 2003.
24. Guillaume Parmentier, "Americans are Wrong to Vilify the French," *International Herald Tribune*, 20–21 September 2003, p. 6.
25. Romain Leick, "Kreuzzug der Ideale," *Der Spiegel* 6 October 2003, p. 138.
26. Gerhard Schroeder, "Germany Will Share the Burden in Iraq," *New York Times* 19 September 2003, p. A 27.
27. Ralf Beste and Gabor, Steingart, " I Understand, Gert," *Der Spiegel* 29 September 2003.
28. German Mission to the UN/Address by Chancellor Gerhard Schroeder 24 September 2003.
29. Russian Mission to the UN/Statement by President Vladimir Putin 25 September 2003.
30. United Nations Security Council Germany/Explanation of Vote 16 October 2003.
31. George W. Bush, "President Bush Discusses Iraq Policy at Whitehall Palace London," *whitehouse.gov* 19 November 2003.
32. United Nations Security Council S/PV 4883, 16 December 2003, pp. 4–5.
33. Press Conference/Hans Blix before the UN Correspondents Association 16 March 2004.
34. Hans Blix, "Disarming Iraq," (New York: Pantheon Books, 2004), p. 14.
35. United Kingdom Mission to the UN 8 June 2004, French Mission to the UN/ Security Council 8 June 2004.
36. Press Conference/Lakhdar Brahimi before the UN Correspondents Association 9 June 2004.
37. "A Victory for Bush," *Le Monde* 9 June 2004.
38. United Nations Security Council Resolution #1790 (2007) 18 December 2007.
39. Iraqi Mission to the UN/State of Extension of the Multinational Forces Mandate 18 December 2007, p. 7.

Chapter Seven

European Union Über Alles— The Old Versus the New Europe

At a reception at New York's *nouveau* Dahesh Museum, the European Union proudly celebrated its expansion. Amid the bubbly and jovial banter there was a genuine political effervescence celebrating an event which after all marked a historic union and resembled a symphony of states, nations and peoples playing together in near harmony. Years ago I recall interviewing Lithuania's President Vytautas Landsbergis who waxed poetic not only about his country's newly restored political freedoms, but who then described the role his country could play in the symphony of Europe. On May 1st 2004, the European Union welcomed ten new member states; mostly the former communist states such as Lithuania in Central Europe as well as two Mediterranean islands, Malta and Cyprus. Thus the EU population jumped by 74 million people up to 455 million—decidedly more than the USA and Canada combined.

EUROPE WHOLE AND FREE

Euroland is now a geographic and political reality from the Bay of Biscay to the steppes of Poland. Think of it—the traditional Euro core states of France, Belgium and Germany—now joined by the Baltic states, the Czech Republic, Hungary, Poland, Slovakia, Slovenia, Malta and Cyprus. Yet beyond the statistics of ten new member states and millions of citizens, the doubling the physical geography of the EU, the real change has been metaphysical. The historic nation states such as Estonia, Latvia, and Lithuania, forgotten and forsaken cantons of the former Soviet Empire, are not only independent and sovereign but actually part of both the NATO defense alliance as well as the political architecture of the European Union, two of the world's most exclusive clubs!

Europe's modern social, political, and monetary architecture, designed by the latter-day Leonardo Da Vinci's such as Schuman, De Gasperi, and Monnet emerged from the carnage and chaos of the Second World War. The original disciples of Europe were determined that never again would such a catastrophe befall the continent. Historian Niall Ferguson recalls the 19th century German historian Leopold von Ranke, "doyen of the study of statecraft, portrayed modern European history as an incessant struggle for mastery, in which a balance of power was possible only through recurrent conflict." These disciples along with the Apostles like Adenauer, began to figuratively and philosophically rebuild the edifice of Europe—brick by brick in the shattered cities, personal healing and reconciliation as in the national relationships, and institution by institution as in the structure for this new dream built on an old idea.

THE BUILDING BLOCKS

The American sponsored Marshall Plan helped rebuild the bricks and stones while the American military provided the security to shield them. The Marshall Plan's aid and assistance supported the foundation on which to build. Later NATO would provide the defensive shield. The institutions were no less important. First from the European Coal and Steel Community (1951), the landmark Treaty of Rome establishing the European Economic Community (1957), the Customs Union (1968) the European Monetary System (1979) the Schengen Agreement abolishing formal border controls (1990) and the Maastricht Treaty on economic and monetary union (1992), followed by the European Union single market (1993), and the changeover to the single currency Euro in 2002 were among the building blocks. Indeed the Europe of the Six in 1951 (Belgium, France, Italy, Luxembourg, the Netherlands and Federal Republic of Germany), was joined by the United Kingdom, Denmark and Ireland in 1973, Greece in 1981, and Portugal and Spain in 1986. Austria, Finland and Sweden joined in 1995, and ten new member countries among them the Baltic states, Czech Republic, Hungary, Cyprus, Malta, Poland, Slovakia and Slovenia in 2004. The EU-25 soon again gained two new members when Bulgaria and Romania gained admission in 2007.

Beyond this the national reconciliation was paramount. The extraordinary Franco/ German rapprochement, codified in the 1963 Elysée Treaty framed by de Gaulle and Adenauer was to be such a foundation of peace. Today the European Union—the Europe of the 27 nations—now has formally healed the political East/West rift resulting from the Cold War. From the collapse of communism in 1989 to EU membership took fifteen years. The admission process was a long and arduous road taking into account both criteria of working and free political institutions as well as a functioning market economy. The transitions in most countries were most difficult not for lack of trying but for an institutional and structural weight of the old static socialist systems.

Olli Rehn, the EU Minister for Enlargement told a Brussels audience, "This year marks a historic double-anniversary. 20 years ago, we saw the Berlin Wall come down and the democratic transformation intensify in Europe...we shall celebrate the 5th anniversary of the EU enlargement that peacefully reunified Eastern and Western Europe. Overall, EU enlargement has served as an anchor of stability and democracy and a driver of personal freedom and economic dynamism in Europe. It has brought about peaceful democratic change and extended the area of freedom and prosperity to almost 500 million people. Enlargement has increased our weight in the world, be it in international trade negotiations or when addressing issues of global nature, such as the climate change or development. It has substantially increased our crisis management capability, notably for peace-keeping missions."[1]

The EU's *Phare* program supported the countries to adapt to EU membership. The candidates states lacked the established political, economic and legal structures which would allow them to join the EU. "The *Phare* program was the Union's first concrete response to help the ex-communist countries make the transition to multi-party democracies and liberalized economies. Since its creation *Phare* has concentrated increasingly on projects to help ensure that the newcomers have the administrative ability to meet the rights and obligations of membership," states an EU document. Membership criteria dating from 1993 stresses that new members must have "stable institutions guaranteeing democracy, the rule of law, human rights and the protection of minorities." Equally the states must have "a functioning market economy that can cope with competitive pressures and market o forces within the Union; the ability to take on the obligations of membership, including support for the aims of the Union. The new members must have a public administration capable of applying and managing EU laws in practice." Indeed the EU rules and regulation are voluminous. The *acquis communautaire,* contains more than 80,000 pages of EU law and must be adopted as well as implemented! Naturally expansion has brought a series of economic benefits and challenges. Though GDP growth rates among the new countries tend to be much higher than the near anemic pre-enlargement group, the GDP per inhabitant is much lower. If we take Italy, France and Germany as the base mark of just over 100%, we find that new members vary from 35% in Latvia, to 57% in Hungary, and 74% in Slovenia.[2]

A skilled work force, lower wage costs, and privatizations have attracted foreign investment. But contrary to the prevailing perceptions, the new members have not diverted massive FDI flows away from the other fifteen EU members. A UN report advises, "Since the mid-1990's the FDI inflows of the 'accession 10' have accounted for a fraction of those to the European Union-15—a mere 3.5 percent in 2003 down from a high of 10.6 percent in 1995." In 1999, the new countries attracted $20 billion as compared with $476 billion to the 15; by 2002 the numbers for FDI in the new states was $21 billion as against $374 billion. Indeed the *combined* FDI for the ten new states in 2002 was the same as Spain's FDI that year.[3]

Naturally the ten new members each have individual attributes which can be turned to commercial advantage. The International Monetary Fund (IMF) states, two years after the memberships "The economic performance has been strong in the new EU members." Growth rates for the three Baltic states reached as high as 9 percent in 2006. Still there is a wide disparity between the core EU-15 (among them France, Germany and UK) with a 387 million population and $13.4 trillion GDP and the new EU-10 with a population of 102 million and a GDP of $866 billion.[4]

Many looked to Ireland whose membership in the European Community since 1973, and ensuing success story, is the grist of EU legend. "Ireland was the success story of the 1990's, ranking as the fastest growing economy in the European Union," states a report, "This strong performance has brought Ireland from among the laggards to a star performer. Fifteen years ago, Ireland was perceived as an economy in trouble; with slow growth, high inflation and high unemployment. Yet in the 1990's the Irish economy showed much stronger performance than any other EU economy, with annual double digit GDP growth rates. As a result unemployment fell form 17% in 1987 to just above 4.5% in 2003 and government debt shrank from 112% to just below one third of GDP" Before long Ireland joined Luxembourg as the EU's wealthiest countries. Ireland at long last has evolved from a regional economy into a modern and prosperous European country. By cutting taxes and encouraging foreign investment the Irish Celtic Tiger was able to exploit its access to the EU market and bring about a long-sought prosperity.[5]

Having witnessed the Celtic Tiger economy in both 1987 and 2003, the changes were dramatic. Ireland defines itself in a European Union mold rather than he old stereotypical insular and Anglophobic mode. Membership in the European Union has opened the proverbial horn of plenty for the Irish as the EU offers generous subsidies from for everything such as roads and agriculture. Yet it's the massive American and German foreign investment, attracted by generous tax breaks and a well educated work force which has been a major catalyst for change. The Central Bank of Ireland pegged GDP growth between 1993–2003 at an impressive 7.9%. Despite a strong *Euro* and high wages, Ireland remains an attractive place to invest and to reside.

Ireland had attracted record numbers of French, who seek to work in a society where jobs are more plentiful and taxes are lower. The only larger French "settlement" in the EU is in Great Britain. But economic prosperity had another side. By the 2000's costs had jumped accordingly with real estate prices at near London and New York levels. A pub ditty the Celtic Tiger Blues goes, "The buildings are all rising, and the rents are rising too." But after years of high growth and surging real estate costs, Ireland's economy has stalled seeing zero growth, higher inflation and unemployment at its highest since1999.

In the midst of the global recession, it's expected that Ireland's once vibrant economy will decline by 14 percent between 2008 and 2010. Dublin's Economic and Social Research Institute forecast a "dramatic slowdown" that the GDP decline would signal the largest loss activity in any industrialized country since the 1930. The once-booming Celtic Tiger economy was set to see a jump in unemployment from 7.7 percent in 2008, to 11.4 percent in mid 2009, to an average of 16.8 percent in 2010.[6]

THE SECURITY DIMENSION

The EU's security has been anchored in the Atlantic Alliance and *ipso facto* its close ties with the United States. Nonetheless the threat profile has been ever-changing—especially following 1989 as well as September 11th 2001.

Tensions among the allies concerning the threat, the perception of threat, and the response to the threat are not new whether dealing with the Kremlin or Al Qaida. Interestingly the early years of the Reagan Administration saw such rifts. While European members of NATO were enjoying a high level of post-war prosperity, they were not in the opinion of many Washington officials, pulling their weight in the military sphere. By 1979–1980, on the eve of the Reagan years, U.S. defense spending reached 5 percent of GDP; Germany stood at 3.4 percent, Italy at 2.1 and only Britain at 4.9 percent. Observers pointed out that by 1985–89 defense spending soon reached almost 6.2 percent of the U.S. gross domestic product; the NATO average was about half of Washington's burden. Nonetheless since 1962 when American forces in Europe numbered 434,000, the total by 1980 stood at 300,000. The U.S. still provided the lynchpin for Western Europe's security until the end of the Cold War.[7]

"Central to the future of the Atlantic Alliance and the Atlantic community is how America and Europe will define what is important in the future," writes Dr. Dennis Bark of Stanford. "Fifty years ago in the smoking ruins of Europe it was an Austrian Friedrich von Hayek, who was concerned with what he called "the principal ingredients of classical liberalism." Namely, "Those values on which European civilization was built...the sacredness of truth...the rules of moral decency...a common belief in the value of human freedom...an affirmative action towards democracy...opposition to all forms of totalitarianism, whether it be from the Right or from the Left."[8]

American reactions towards a united Europe have for the most part been ambivalent. Even among foreign policy elites, the European Union is often confused with the former Common Market or European Community. When there's been focus, it's usually in the realm of trade policy or the increasingly antagonistic political salvos across the Atlantic. European political integration continued as did the creation of the Euro as the common currency. Romano Prodi head of the European Commission, stated unambiguously that one of the EU's primary goals is to create "a *superpower* on the European continent that stands equal to the United States." But the real success story remains the intra-European economic integration itself. For example as a percentage of its total trade, 63 percent of Ireland's exports go within Europe; the percent is 65 percent for France, 65 percent for Germany, and 76 percent for Belgium. Among new EU members the export trend is higher with 79 percent of Poland's exports, 79 percent for Hungary, and fully 85 percent of the Czech Republic exports traded within the EU.[9]

"The rise of anti-Americanism, a form of irrationalism deliberately whipped by Messers Schroeder and Chirac, who believe it wins votes, is particularly tragic," writes historian Paul Johnson, "the early stages of the EU had their roots in admiration of the American way of doing things and gratitude for the manner in which the U.S. had saved Europe first from Nazism, then from the Soviet Empire—by the Marshall Plan in 1947 and the creation of NATO in 1949." Johnson adds, Europe's founding fathers—Monnet, Robert Schuman in France and Alcide de Gasperi in Italy and Konrad Adenauer in Germany, were all pro-American and anxious to make it possible for European populations to enjoy U.S. style living standards. Adenauer in particular assisted by his brilliant economics Minister Ludwig Erhardt, rebuilt Germany's industry and services, following the freest possible, this was the origin of the German economic miracle."[10]

NEW NATO, OLD EUROPE

In an extraordinary turn of political fate and fortunes, seven former communist countries have joined the North Atlantic Treaty Organization (NATO).

Given the context of post-war history, the accession of the Baltic countries and other ex-East Bloc states to NATO is nothing less than extraordinary. This followed the admission of ten countries into the European Union, moving the EU frontiers eastwards to Hungary and into the eastern Mediterranean. The enlargement of NATO to 26 member states, stands as an important symbolic step which has far more to do with *Euroland's* new political architecture than its security structure. NATO's new members; Bulgaria, Estonia, Latvia Lithuania, Romania, Slovakia, and Slovenia have gained the ultimate defense insurance policy and guarantees for prosperity. The new members fill out the map pieces offering geographic cohesiveness, lines of communication, and collective security to the continent.

Though new pieces of the *Euroland* political puzzle board have been added, nonetheless NATO's European center of gravity remains in France and Germany; to assume that new members have the military, political or economic clout to challenge the traditional power structure is preposterous. Politically though, as we witnessed through Bulgaria's strong support in the UN Security Council during the countdown to the Iraq war, this presents a clear gain. Wisely established by American leadership in 1949 as a defense treaty and bulwark against Soviet expansionism, NATO evolved into the most successful military alliance in history. It kept the peace which in turn allowed for unparalleled West European prosperity. Europe's economic renaissance would have never been possible in the wake of WWII had it not been for the firm bonds of the Atlantic Alliance, anchored in an American security commitment.

Yet part of the NATO expansion is more an affair of the heart than of the mind. In 1999, NATO first moved eastwards accepting the Czech Republic, Hungary and Poland. In one sense this was a belated *mea culpa* for FDR's political perfidy at Yalta in 1945 where the U.S. allowed these countries to fall into Stalin's communist sphere. The long forsaken Baltic states—Estonia, Latvia and Lithuania—once part of the Soviet Union, have joined the Atlantic Alliance, extending defense commitments to Russia's very doorstep. To have imagined that the Baltic would first regain their independence from Moscow, later reinforce their sovereignty through United Nations membership in 1991, and now to have been admitted to the NATO military alliance has shown an amazing political transformation. Both the new NATO and EU members, extend the frontiers of the Old Europe to new oft unstable borders and volatile geopolitical fault lines. Now NATO's frontiers face Ukraine, Belarus, and Russia itself. On the EU side, bringing the divided Greco/Turkish Mediterranean island of Cyprus extends the frontier to the doorstep of the Middle East and Malta places the EU off the shore of North Africa. Naturally in the wake of the Iraq war, there's been a genuine political rift between Washington and what former Secretary of Defense Donald Rumsfeld derisively described as the *"Old Europe,"* namely France, Germany, and Belgium. NATO's new members, what has approvingly been called the *"New Europe"* have a decidedly pro-American tilt. Sadly Rumsfeld's dangerously damaging quip concerning *Old and New Europe*, caused consternation among many pro-American figures in both France and Germany.

Spain's former Foreign Minister Ana Palacio trod bravely through Rumsfeld's rhetorical minefield. During a keynote speech at New York's Foreign Policy Association, she exclaimed "Europe is an unprecedented success story...What's more this new Europe is now beginning to resemble its old self, at long last embracing virtually all the countries that created it originally. Old Europe is a divided Europe. Old Europe is the Europe of the Berlin Wall. New Europe is the Europe that is now emerging in the European Union—the Europe of 25...and, if this is Europe, all this has been achieved with the incalculable and indispensable help of the United States." Palacio added, "Europe is a construction in law and based in law, which means that if something defines Europe, it's what lies behind the law that we are creating. And what lies behind that law we are creating are principles and values. Europe is democracy, the rule of law, the separation between state and church, and the free market economy. This is Europe. And, this, by the way, this is also the United States."[11]

Italian Prime Minister Romano Prodi waxed poetic before the UN General Assembly, "The challenge facing Europe today is not to become resigned to the world as it is, but to seek to improve it based on the values in which Europe believes: freedom, democracy, respect for others and peaceful coexistence. This is why we are adapting our founding treaties. This is why we are building a common foreign and defense policy. This is why we have invented a new citizenship—*European citizenship*—to which we are entitled by choosing to share certain values, not by virtue of kinship or nationality."[12]

Americans easily forget that today's political relations with Germany, France or Spain for that matter are no longer purely bilateral; that is Washington/Berlin, Washington/Paris, Washington/Madrid. Thus the close ties of the post-war era have been *superseded* by the epic events of 1989, as well as *subsumed* to what the Europeans regularly refer to as a *common European foreign policy*. This concept of Europe's foreign relations by consensus has often homogenized the policy positions throughout Europe's Ministries whether the *Auswarteges Amt*, the *Quai D'Orsay* or *La Farnesina*. The British Foreign Office for the most part has been a notable exception to this trend.

In the United Nations, for example, statements are usually presented by the current rotating President of the European Union so that one member, Sweden "speaking for the European Union" will put forward a position. Often then, the same official will interject, "and speaking in my capacity as the Foreign Minister of Sweden," add something which is specific to the policy of his country. The policies by consensus, a product of increasing European integration, are naturally different than Washington's bilateral ties with a particular European capital.

Indeed the Treaty on European Union, Title V outlines the provisions on a Common Foreign and Security Policy, "The Union and its member states shall define and implement a common foreign and security policy, governed by the provisions of this Title and covering all areas of foreign and security policy." The stated objectives are; safeguard the common values, fundamental interests, and independence of the Union; to strengthen the security of the Union and its member states in all ways; to preserve peace and strengthen international security in accordance with the principles of the United Nations Charter."[13]

Dr. Henry Kissinger opines, "In Europe, the national-state is giving up much of its sovereignty in favor of the European Union. One result of that transformation is that the national dedication that created the great period of European sacrifice and political construction has not been as easy to translate to the European structure." Addressing a forum of the prestigious Atlantic Council in Washington D.C., Kissinger added, "On the other hand, the national-state is no longer in the same position to conduct a global foreign policy as has been traditionally the case." He feels that this reality "explains some of the differences that have arisen between Europe and the United States in the past decade."[14]

Javier Solana, the EU High Representative for Foreign policy stated the case succinctly, "Indeed we are a global actor. With 25 member states, with over 450 million inhabitants, a quarter of the world's GNP, and around 40 % of the world's merchandise exports, and with the comprehensive array of instruments, economic, legal, diplomatic, military at our disposal, that claim is not an aspiration but a statement of fact." He added, "The origins and subsequent development of the EU mean that the prospects for shaping an effective foreign policy are both difficult and promising at the same time. Difficult because the EU was essentially set up to abolish foreign policy, in the traditional sense, among the member states, but also promising because the EU is an amazing economic and political success story."[15]

Naturally another political hurdle concerns the European Constitution. The framers have worked a number of years on a draft document in which the European Union would evolve towards a genuine United States of Europe. The constitutional treaty was drafted by a convention under the direction of former French President Giscard d'Estiang. European leaders reached a deal which steers the EU towards a more active role in foreign policy. The constitution became a massive legal document, lacking the elegance and clarity that its framers originally hoped would make it memorable tribute to the European dream. Despite the political class reaching a hard won accord in Brussels, this did not mean that the treaty would take effect; all 25 countries had to ratify the draft document either through parliamentary votes or through referendums over a two year period. Though some legislatures such as Austria, Germany and Hungary approved the arcane document, but national referendums would prove the constitution's demise.

Pope John Paul II as well as the governments of Poland and Ireland, and Spain prior to the Socialist electoral victory, had pressed for the document's Preamble to include a reference to Europe's Christian heritage. The politicians seeking to make the document as secular sounding as possible sadly sidelined this aspiration. Historian Paul Johnson lamented, "Europe has turned its back not only on the U.S. and the future of capitalism, but also on its own historic past. Europe was essentially a creation of the marriage between Greco-Roman culture and Christianity. Brussels, has in fact, repudiated both. There was no mention of Europe's Christian origins in the ill-fated Constitution."[16]

The proposed constitution fell by the political wayside, buffeted by a broad left/right political opposition, due in no small part "to the reluctance to hand over national sovereignty to central, remote and anonymous institutions over which people had no control," opined Walter Laqueur.[17]

Naturally in the realm of foreign policy, the embryonic powers of Maastricht and the new constitution would bring *Euroland* into a brave new world on a truly global scene. The common foreign policy will become a step closer. From an American viewpoint this offers a double-edged sword; Euro policy while often in broad agreement with Washington is just as apt to oppose the U.S. on many key geo-political issues. But as with so many carefully crafted plans, the complexity and arcane nature of the document saw a solid rejection by popular referendums in France and the Netherlands in mid 2005. The Euro skeptics gave their appallingly arrogant political class a true political Waterloo with a resounding vote of *Non and Nein!*

Despite the setbacks yet another version, the Lisbon Treaty was placed before the EU members. This document with its 346 pages of arcane articles, amendments and appendixes, was placed before national parliaments for approval. Only in Ireland did it face a national referendum where it fell on the sword of popular opinion, and some would say sovereignty. "Irish 'No' Curbs EU Hopes" headlined the *Financial Times*. "The European Union's ambitions to play a bigger role on the world stage were dealt a crushing blow, after Irish voters rejected a landmark EU Treaty on institutional reform." Indeed, "The Irish No delivers a hammer blow at the morale of the EU's political elites, who only three years ago, watched in despair as Dutch and French voters threw out a constitutional treaty that was the Lisbon Treaty's predecessor."[18] A year later Irish voters performed a dramatic turnaround approving the pact, opening the path to Europe's adoption of the Treaty and the appointment of an EU President and Foreign Minister.

In June 2009 Parliamentary elections, voters across the EU's 27 member states delivered significant gains for conservative and center right parties at the expense of the Socialists and left. The elections equally echoed a significant apathy within the EU, with turnout reaching fewer than half of eligible voters, reflecting the "malaise and disarray" on a number of issues ranging from the economy to enlargement. Jerzy Buzek, a former Polish Prime Minister, was elected President of the Parliament. He stated, "once his ambition had been to be a member of parliament in a free Poland, but now he was President of the European Parliament." He saw this as "a measure of how Europe can change." He also regarded it as "symbolic" for the other central and eastern European countries who joined the EU in 2004. "There is now no 'you' and 'us': we live in a shared Europe," he stated. In November Belgian Prime Minister Herman Van Rompuy and British Baroness Ashton become the Europe's first President and Foreign Minister.[19]

"For Europeans the problem of American hegemony is so vexing because there is so very little they can do about it," advises Robert Kagan. He adds, "European assaults on the legitimacy of American actions and American power, may be an effective if unconventional way of constraining and controlling the American superpower." Kagan opines, "Certainly 'legitimacy' is an asset the Europeans believe they have in abundance. It is their comparative advantage in the new geopolitical jostling with the United States."[20]

Thus within the context of *legitimacy,* and remembering their own histories, the *Euroland* countries look to their common foreign policy and to the benediction of the UN Security Council as *sine qua non.* "The U.S. foreign policy is light years away from the foreign policy orientation of the twenty-five member states that make up the European Union," writes Jeremy Rifkin, adding "These countries have increasingly shed the historical legacy of nation-state sovereignty in favor of working in consort, under international laws, to which they are bound. The European dream is one of inclusively, not autonomy. They seek to live in a world governed by consensus." Rifkin adds, "The sovereignty issue is one that ultimately divides the U.S. and EU, and an older American dream from the new dream shared among most Europeans.[21]

Given Europe's own sanguinary history of power politics, and precisely because of its consequences as ending only in 1945, there's a clear logic favoring consensus among democratic states. There's little question that the EU states are genuine democracies albeit for the most part, new ones. Though the

EU 27 have long historical pedigrees, only a handful—such as France, Great Britain and the Netherlands—had genuinely working parliamentary democracies predating the Second World War. Let us be frank. Some countries like the Czech Republic were old *nations*, with short lived democratic *state structures* (1919–1938), then interrupted by Nazi and communist *totalitarianism* for fifty years (1938–1989), only then to resume their natural place among *democratic* states after 1989. Others like post-1918 Poland and Hungary maintained quasi-democratic political structures before WWII, followed by communism until 1989. Spain weathered political authoritarianism until 1975 with the restoration of constitutional monarchy and democracy after the rule of General Franco. Even Greece the *"home of democracy"* could not seriously claim this system until the late 1970's when a series of military juntas stepped down!

The point is that while *Euroland* customarily speaks from the heights of what they view as a philosophical and political Olympus, its 27 individual member states have far less collective historical experience with working democracy than the USA or Canada. Thus while the modern incarnations of the EU governments hold a laudable and unassailable legitimacy, this for the most part remains a post-1945 or post-1989 phenomenon. Yet shaping foreign policy to fit a multilateral EU consensus is indeed challenging. Before the Iraq war, there were many divisions within Europe; the Franco/German/Belgian pact being clearly at loggerheads with the Anglo/Spanish/Italian alliance. This does not even include the deep rift between France and then candidate members of the EU such as Poland and the Baltics. Policy towards the Islamic Republic of Iran has proven equally divisive. Despite Iran's embryonic nuclear program, EU states eager to curry commercial favor in Tehran, have been politically timid towards confronting Iranian proliferation. Iran understands, as did Saddam's Iraq, that the lure of economic advantage for the EU shimmers like a *mirage*. Given the chance of petroleum and economic infrastructure contracts, the EU states have been easily divided.

Though all EU states are United Nations members in their own sovereign capacity, and many were in fact founders of the world body, the establishment of the EU's Common Foreign and Security Policy compels all countries to coordinate their activities. The EU Treaty requires them to uphold common positions so that their combined weight in UN committees and conferences. In the UN General Assembly, despite the majority of resolutions passing with consensus, the EU members usually vote with unanimity on the others. A six-month rotating Presidency among EU members puts a particular state in the role of coordination and representation of the Common Foreign and Security Policy. For example in the first half of 2004, Ireland assumed the role. During this six-month whirlwind tenure, the member state is not only the "face" of Europe but shall host conferences and provide physical venues for the EU's crucial decisions. Thus the EU/USA Summit in June 2004 was held in Dromoland Castle, reflecting the Irish presidency.

The EU common policy is especially vital in the fifteen member Security Council where there's increasing coordination to fit the Common Foreign Policy. Though Britain and France hold Permanent seats on the Council, other EU members have a rotating two-year tenure. During the Iraq war, for example, both Germany and Spain held such vital positions. Nonetheless the reality remained that France/Germany and Britain/Spain, were politically split before and following the conflict. Rebuilding frayed ties among European states in the Security Council became a focus following the Iraq war. Spain's pro-American position taken by the Aznar government, then critically viewed in France and Germany, still would have faced political hurdles had the Spanish election not produced the surprise Socialist victory. The unexpected election result, realigned Madrid's policy from a tilt to Washington and back to Paris.

Some years ago delegates floated the idea of a specifically European seat on the Council; yet with both Paris and London as permanent members, this idea did not fly. An Italian proposal that Italy would be granted a permanent Security Council seat failed to gain serious support. Reflecting the idea of "one Europe" the European public seems surprisingly receptive to the idea of a single EU seat on the UN Security Council replacing the French and British seats. Sixty percent agree Euro wide agree to this, along with 62 percent in France and 64 percent in Germany. Only Britain shows 37 percent approval with 55 percent disapproval. Curiously only 36 percent of American respondents support the single seat idea with 55 percent opposing the concept.[22]

Formalizing a permanent seat for Germany (and Japan) has long been seriously considered as part of wider Security Council enlargement. Though most delegates agree that the fifteen member council, whose last expansion was in 1966, does not adequately represent the size and diversity of the 192 member United Nations, the issue naturally comes down to the stark political calculus of which countries would be allowed. Germany and Japan, given their role in as key financial contributors to the UN system and their significant global commitments of economic development assistance, have been foremost among many contenders for permanent Security Council seats. Still given the Schroeder government's vocal opposition to the U.S. and Britain during the Iraq war, it appears that Berlin's candidacy, once championed by both Republican and Democratic Administrations, has gone into political limbo. Germany's tumultuous two-year tenure (2003–2004) on the Council coincided with the Iraq war and its fractious aftermath.

Germany seeks a permanent place at the Security Council table. "For forty years the composition of the Security Council has remained unchanged. I think it is high time to adapt it to the new global reality," stated German Foreign Minister Joschka Fischer before the UN General Assembly. "Just like Brazil, India, and Japan, Germany is ready to take on the responsibility associated with a permanent seat in the Security Council," he stressed.[23]

"The EU is the world's largest provider of official development assistance (ODA) totaling $36.5 billion in 2002... Indeed EU member states together are the largest financial contributor to the UN system. The EU-25 pay 38 percent of the UN's regular budget, more than two-fifths of UN peacekeeping operations and half of all UN member states contributions to UN funds and programs," states an EU policy document. The EU contribution of 38 percent contrasts with the U.S contribution of 22 percent and Japan's contribution of 19.5 percent. European Union official development assistance is quite impressive; of the $36.5 billion given in 2002, France ($5.5 billion), Germany ($5.3 billion), the United Kingdom ($5billion), and the Kingdom of the Netherlands ($3.3 billion) led the list. The EU stresses the role of economic development and have signed on to the UN Millennium Goals to reduce the proportion of people living in poverty and suffering from hunger.[24]

Peacekeeping and conflict prevention is equally a focus with the EU contributing 40 percent of the budget for a series of global missions. EU members are the major contributors too in the UN's regular assessed budget. France is assessed at 6.3% or $155 million, Germany at 8.6% or $157 million, Italy at 5% or $93 million, Spain at 3% or $54 million and the United Kingdom at 6.6% or $121 million. The USA, still the largest single donor has been assessed downwards to 22% or $453 million. Japan is slated at 16.6% or $304 million. Indeed the EU remains a major troop contributor to UN peacekeeping operations; in early 2004 some 5,145 served in various locales. Austria, Poland, Portugal and the United Kingdom were major troop contributors. Equally the EU remains the largest contributor to other Balkan missions under UN authority such as SFOR in Bosnia and KFOR in Kosovo. An EU document adds, "The objective of the EU's common foreign and security policy are, among other things, to strengthen the security of the Union in all ways and to 'preserve the peace and strengthen international security in accordance with the principles of the UN Charter." Support for human rights remains a core principle of EU policies as well. One of the objectives of the EU's foreign and security policy remains the development and consolidation of "democracy and the rule of law, and respect for human rights and fundamental freedoms."[25]

Within this context EU support for the International Criminal Court (ICC) and opposition to the death penalty remain key social policies. Moralizing over Iraq policy and the Kyoto Climate Treaty later center stage. For the European leaders, superpower status is derived from expanding cooperation rather than enlarging sovereignty. Rifkin writes, "it's not force of arms but negotiating skills and openness to dialogue and conflict resolution that are the distinguishing characteristics of this kind new kind of superpower. That's why 'process' is so important to the new politics. The essence of the European Dream is the overcoming of brute power and the establishment of moral conscience as the operating principle governing the affairs of the human family." He concedes, "Most Americans find such sentiments a bit gooey and unrealistic. Europeans say that the opposite is the case."[26]

Nonetheless the new European Dream has ancient roots, adds Rifkin, "In 1795, the German philosopher Immanuel Kant published an essay entitled *Perpetual Peace: A Philosophical Sketch*. Although it received little attention at the time, the piece was resurrected in the post-WWII era, and has become an almost biblical reference for the new European vanguard. Kant envisioned a 'state of perpetual peace' brought about by the creation of a 'world republic.' Kant believed that such a state would be possible once the nations of the world accepted representative forms of government."[27]

European politicians often retreat into sloganeering about Iraq and posturing over policy. Viewing the vital German/American security relationship, Jeffrey Gedmin of the Aspen Institute in Berlin opined, "The old security partnership is a different matter. Since the Cold War ended, Germans feel less dependent on the United States. Berlin's foreign policy priorities are today largely regional: enlarging the European Union (EU), making the euro a success, adopting a European constitution, keeping the Balkans stable. There's increasing prickliness across the political spectrum about American leadership and influence. Being "European" is in; being "transatlantic" is hardly chic, at least at the moment. There's another reality: Germany's capabilities are limited. It is a medium-sized country that spends meagerly on defense and faces serious economic challenges and a demographic crisis in the years ahead." Gedmin added, "Like France, the Federal Republic of Germany worked actively and energetically to undermine American policy. Are there limits to disagreement if we wish to have a functioning alliance in the future?" Indeed the tensions between some of Europe and Washington went beyond Iraq and the policies of the Bush Administration.[28]

This does not mean that EU/USA ties are as frayed as many observers presume. On the economic front alone, EU/USA trade and investment relationship remains the largest in the world; $2 billion a day crossing the Atlantic.

June 2004 proved a pivotal month in the USA/European Union ties. The 60th anniversary of allied D-Day landing in Normandy, the Sea Island Georgia G-8 Summit, the Dromoland Castle Summit, and the NATO Summit in

Istanbul were the scripted events which re-united the Americans and Europeans. Ironically the funeral commemorations of former President Ronald Reagan focused on the memory, if then controversial too, heritage of U.S./ European relations in the 1980's. The Dromoland Summit, hosted by the Irish Presidency, thus emerged as an important milestone. At a press conference, Irish Prime Minister Bertie Ahern eloquently underscored that "Trans-Atlantic relationship has been a core focus of the Irish Presidency…the EU and the U.S. have a common set of values and shared values."

Still despite the genuine support and encouragement to heal the trans-Atlantic rift offered by the Irish EU Presidency, even on the Emerald Island, long a safe refuge for American presidents in a political storm, the atmosphere had changed. The *overall image* of the USA remained under assault. One commentator opined that in the past, Irish/ American ties were seen through the prism of "JFK, and the Marshall Plan…today they are seen as George W. Bush, SUV's and the war in Iraq."

In the wake of the Summit, Portuguese Prime Minister Durao Barroso was confirmed as the President of the European Commission replacing Prof. Romano Prodi of Italy. The announcements marked the end of a simmering split between two political camps, one led by France and the other by Britain to appoint the singularly important European Union post. Premier Barroso, a center right political figure was a strong supporter of the U.S. in Iraq as compared with the center-left Prof. Prodi. Though a compromise candidate acceptable to both France and England, Portugal's Barroso did not bring the baggage of instinctive anti-Americanism nor a *Euro hauteur* into the equation. He moreover reflects the center-right orientation of the European Parliament and holds Atlanticist beliefs.

The NATO Summit in Istanbul, the historic Turkish metropolis spanning Europe and Asia, proved a pivotal political watershed. For Turkey, a secular Muslim state close military ally, the political payoff came up-front. President Bush (to the shock and pique especially of the French) called again for the eventual inclusion of the Turkish Republic in the European Union. Then, as NATO delegates apprehensively awaited the final two days countdown to the transfer of sovereignty from the coalition occupation to the Iraqis in Baghdad, the USA and Iraqi government, through a deft piece of political choreography, proceeded with the handover two days early. The surprise ceremony dumbfounded critics and totally threw the opposition and militants off guard.

Intriguingly in the countdown to the Iraq war in 2003, German intelligence agents inside Baghdad were apparently closely coordinating a covert information flow to the American side. Given that Germany's Schroeder government passionately opposed the war and the American and coalition effort, these explosive revelations published in the *New York Times* caused a fractious debate inside Germany itself. Clearly too, it appeared there was a deliberate intelligence leak to either embarrass Schroeder, or possibly vindicate him. Concerning the controversy stoked by the *New York Times*, veteran German editor Theo Sommer rhetorically asks, "Who in Washington is trying to throw spanners (monkey wrenches) into the German-American partnership—a partnership still in the process of recovering from the crisis caused by America's war of choice against Iraq? Who wants to undermine Germany's standing in the Arab world? Who is bent on discrediting the BND? But what is the purpose of those planting such information?"[29]

NATO naturally faces a changed mission but more especially a changed political atmosphere and perception. Despite political protestations to the contrary, NATO really has yet to define its mission in the post-Soviet world. *Defense National* of Paris adds, "Over the last 15 years, the Americans seriously underestimated the growing momentum behind the European project…its response to this process has therefore been flat-footed and sometimes confused."[30]

Another changed perception in the EU remains what is often portrayed as American *Globalization*. There are really two parts to this debate: one where the hard left and counterculture green radicals present globalization as one of the principal sins of the USA. The other entails an unofficial political opposition among certain EU governments who obliquely hint that globalization, American culture, and U.S. foreign policies are really all parts of the same mosaic. Prior to September 11th and the Iraq war, Anti-Globalism thus had become the *leitmotif* for anti-Americanism. It remains an uncritically worshipped totem for the political left.

As the brilliant French philosopher Jean-Francois Revel stated; "The simplistic article of Marxist faith that capitalism is absolute evil, and that it is incarnate in and directed by the United States, may be the most important principle shared by the current crop of anti-globalizers. America is the object of their loathing because for half-a century of more it has been the most prosperous and creative society on earth." Dr. Revel adds, "But ultimately it is something even bigger that the anti-globalizers want to destroy: liberal democracy and free-market economics." Writing in The American Enterprise, Revel recalls, "It was Europe that created the first world markets, as her capital, technologies, languages and peoples spread over every continent. She was the driving force in an international circulation of commodities, scientific knowledge, ideas and techniques. After the catastrophe of WWI, Europe drew back and turned in on herself. Her supremacy became a thing of the past." He advised, "After World War II, the United States became a powerful advocate in favor of free world commerce. If world economic activity at the turn of the millennium is now thoroughly global, capitalist, and U.S.-led, that has nothing to do with arrogance. The enfeebling of the European's position in the world is self-caused: they alone are responsible for their own heaped-up aberrations and follies over the first half of the past century. This weakening entailed the corresponding and virtually automatic rise of the United States. Strikingly, Americans continue to increase their lead, even since the consolidation of the European Union."[31]

Much of the obvious rhetoric and indeed less noticed sub-rosa simmering concerns the still appreciably different views of the *Old and New Europe*. The Franco/German powerhouse with its federalist views of European integration and rigidly regulated business environment, contrasts with the British-led free-market oriented bloc. Most of the new members of the EU members tilt towards Britain. One's *vision of Europe* equally offers endless possibilities for diverse political interpretations. The often tense relations between Paris and London belie often unseen undercurrents throughout the *Old and New* Europe. Much like the vital network of rivers throughout the continent, there exist rich and diverse socio/political political streams of thought which go beyond the banks of the Seine, the Loire and the Rhine.

Both what I view as the *Danubian Concert* embracing sovereign states such as Austria, Czech Republic, Hungary, Slovakia, and Slovenia as well as the *Baltic Accord* Estonia, Latvia, Lithuania and Poland—encompass a very different historical experience than the traditional EU core-countries. A powerful sense of nationalism, a recently re-established sovereignty, a distaste for strong central rule, and a willingness to embrace free markets characterize the region. A post-totalitarian trauma shadows many of these countries. Headlong experiments with market economics equally have indeed brought mixed lessons. Nonetheless, these historic nations cherish their regained freedoms.

The *Danubian and Baltic* states, both characterize and best illustrate the *New Europe*, a place where the political instincts and impulses for the most part remain pro-American and pro-market. This stands in juxtaposition to the *status quo* of the Franco/German/ Belgian *Old Europe* core. Some may be tempted to view the Baltic states as a modern version of the Hanseatic League, the Medieval mercantile arrangement among a loose confederation of city states, bound by commercial gain not formal political links. But contrary to the Hanseatic League where prosperous Germanic and Baltic port cities were united by the ties of trade and mercantilism, the New Europe goes well beyond a business compact. Though the EU's historic roots are firmly footed in the ideas of a common community of commerce, the Maastricht Treaty and proposed constitution are clearly formal political compacts. The EU remains not only *Euroland Ltd.* but Europe United. Thus viewing the EU as a hopelessly fragmented political grouping, misses the reality. Most of the new members see both EU and NATO membership as the ultimate business card and defense insurance policy. Though national sovereignty has been diluted, and economic policies harmonized, the political payoff emerges as membership in one of the world's richest, powerful and democratic suprastates. Given the geopolitical vulnerabilities of most of the new EU members, especially the Baltics and Poland, the pact seems well worth the price. The *Baltic Accord* looks to Washington as much as it does to Brussels as its political polestar.

As the Czech President Vaclav Klaus stated before the European Parliament in Brussels, "For us there was no alternative to the European Union membership…the citizens of the Czech Republic feel that the European integration has an important and needed mission and task." He warned however, "one or another institutional arrangement of the European Union is not an objective in itself; but a tool for achieving the real objectives. These are nothing but human freedom and such economic system that would bring prosperity. That system is the market economy." With recession stalking even the advanced economies, the IMF forecasts a -4.2 percent decline in the Eurozone in 2009 with a further 0.4 percent in 2010; the UK economy will decline 4.1 percent in 2009 and 0.4 percent in 2010. Germany's economy is expected to decline -5.6 percent in 2009 and fall another 1.0 percent in 2010. The critical U.S. economy will decline -2.8 percent in 2009 and 0.0 the following year. Capitalism is under assault.[32]

Nonetheless the European Union, and its single currency the Euro, will continue to evolve into one of the world's great commercial powers. Economically it has achieved super-power status. Politically though the *grand homogenization of sovereignty* continues among the members whose elected national leaders seem to evoke voting board members of *Euroland, Ltd.* Sovereignty on key issues appears to be subsumed into a vast compromise. Militarily, despite its capability to field military forces commensurate with its economic power, there's a philosophical and political unwillingness to genuinely do so. Here one finds the EU's impulsive recourse to the UN Security Council to provide the political benedictions for policy action.

DEMOGRAPHY OR WHERE ARE THE KIDS?

Given the collective carnage of the 20th century resulting from two world wars, few European states are willing to support a serious defense buildup. The reasons are predictable; the Soviet Union is gone, who is the enemy? The logic proceeds that any contemplated military intervention must first and foremost be directed towards humanitarian crises and carried out with the clear blessing of the U.N. There's also the unspoken demographic caveat that with populations falling or facing static growth, the very idea of a large armed forces and the ensuing risk of casualties from military interventions becomes politically untenable. Though the ten new EU members boosted the population to a seemingly robust 455 million, these numbers hold a hollow core as the population growth rates even in the new states (Baltics, Hungary, Czech Republic) are nearly nil.

Germany's post-war population averaged over a million babies annually peaking at 1.4 million in 1964; by the 1970's the numbers tumbled dramatically to average 812,000 in 1984 and dipped dramatically to 705,000 in 2004. In 2005 676,000 babies were born in Germany prompting Chancellor Angela Merkel to comment "without children our country has no future."[33]

Europe has become an ageing continent. That's a testament to the social systems, improved diets and health care, and but also a low birthrate. The impression that falling birthrates only plague Scandinavia, Germany and the Netherlands is false; those countries see little growth but neither does Italy, Spain, or Hungary. Only Ireland has a relatively stable birthrate. Islamic populations inside EU states moreover have risen dramatically. Indeed France's marginally higher birthrate does not reflect de Gaulle's nationalistic calls to cupid, or billboard signs "La France a besoin d'enfants," but from the domestic Muslim communities.

The Spanish birthrate is the lowest in Europe, lower than that of Italy or the Czech Republic, all of which have fallen to 1.2 children per woman. In Spain the birthrate is down to 1.07 children per woman. In 1950, for example, Spain had three times as many people as Morocco across the Strait of Gibraltar, says Buchanan, "By 2050, Morocco's population will be 50 percent larger." "Prosperity has strangled us" warns Dr. Pierpaolo Donati, a leading Catholic intellectual at the University of Bologna "Comfort is now the only thing anybody believes in. The ethic of sacrifice for a family, one of the basic ideas of human societies, has become a historical notion." Pundit Patrick Buchanan warns, "If the present fertility rates hold, Europe's population will decline to 207 million by the end of the 21st century, less than 30 percent of today's. The cradle of Western civilization will have become its grave." He adds wryly, "Americans in NATO will soon be defending a vast Leisure World."[34]

Tom Friedman a self-styled globalization guru of the *New York Times* describes Europe as "an assisted living facility staffed by Turkish nurses."[35]

Here are some sobering numbers to ponder. "The EU 27 population is projected to increase from 495 million on 1 January 2008 to 521 million in 2035, and thereafter gradually decline to 506 million in 2060," states Eurostat. As life expectancy grows and birth rates fall across *Euroland*, about one

Figure 7.1. Comparison of City Population Growth/Europe versus Developing World*

City	1955	1975	1995	2005	2015
Berlin	3.3 million	3.1 million	3.5 million	3.4 million	3.4 million
Bombay	3.4 million	7 million	14 million	18.2 million	22 million
Budapest	1.7 million	2 million	1.9 million	1.7 million	1.7 million
Istanbul	1.2 million	3.6 million	7.6 million	9.7 million	11 million
Jakarta	2 million	4.8 million	8.3 million	8.8 million	10.8 million
Karachi	1.4 million	4 million	8.5 million	11.5 million	14.8 million
London	8.3 million	7.5 million	7.9 million	8.5 million	8.6 million
Mexico City	3.8 million	10.7 million	16.8 million	18.7 million	20 million
Paris	6.8 million	8.5 million	9.5 million	9.8 million	10 million
Rome	2.1 million	3.3 million	3.4 million	3.3 million	3.3 million
Tehran	1.4 million	4.3 million	6.7 million	7.6 million	8.8 million
Vienna	2 million	2 million	2.1 million	2.2 million	2.4 million

*World Urbanization Prospects/The 2007 Revision, New York: United Nations, 2008.

third of the bloc's population could be over the age of 65 by 2050, a social shift with the potential to transform the lives of Europeans. Merely three years ago, just 16.5 percent of the inhabitants of the European Union's current 27 member states were over 65. The proportion is expected to grow to 18 percent by 2010, 25 percent by 2030 and 30 percent by 2050, according to recent forecasts from the Eurostat data agency. The number of residents over 65 surpassed those under 15 at the beginning of the decade. Currently, the EU's oldest" member states are Germany and Italy, where the proportion of over 65's is 20 percent. By 2060, it's projected that the United Kingdom will be the EU's most populous state with 77 million, France with 72 million, and Germany with 71 million.[36]

"Belgium's population is expected to age quickly with significant repercussions for public finance," warns the IMF, "By 2050, one out of four citizens will be older than 65, compared with one in six today, As a result, the total age related annual public bill will increase by almost 6 percentage points of GDP."[37]

Viewed another way the European population numbers are staggering—or should we say *underwhelming*. Take Italy with a population of 55 million in 1975, a quarter century later the numbers had gone to 57 million and by 2015 will settle back to the 1975 level! Germany with 79 million in 1975 inched to 82 million in 2002 and will remain static at 82 million by 2015. Hungary with 10.5 million in 1975 will have a million fewer people by 2015. The reasons quite simply are cascading fertility rates. Even Poland, once one of Europe's fastest growing populations with 38.6 million in 2002 will see a slight dip by 2015. As a matter of illustration Islamic states such as Iran saw its population rise from 33 million in 1975, then despite years of war, jumped to 68 million by 2002 and is expected to hit 81 million by 2015. Indonesia saw the same jump from 134 million in 1975, to 217 in 2002 to a projected 250 million by 2015. And to round the list Pakistan with 70 million in 1975 jumped to 150 million in 2002 and will likely reach 204 million by 2015.[38]

The UN State of the World Population Report 2008 is even more jarring; the Russian Federation's population stood at 142 million in 2008—by 2050 it is expected to tumble to 108 million; Ukraine stood at 46 million today will nosedive to 31 million in 2050; Hungary with 10 million in 2008 will slip to 8.5 million in 2050. Turkey on the other hand will see its population of 76 million rise to 99 million in 2050. Pakistan will go from 167 million today, to 292 million in 2050, and Bangladesh will leap from 161 million to 254 million.[39]

Russian President Vladimir Putin warned that demography presents a major problem for his country. Annual birth statistics are sobering; in 2007 Russia's had 2 million deaths and only 1.6 million births; Ukraine 763,000 deaths and 473,000 births, reflecting falling numbers since the collapse of the Soviet Union. But countries such as the Czech Republic, Poland, and Slovakia have a nearly equal number of deaths and births. Pakistan on the other hand has 3.7 million births versus one million deaths.[40]

Put bluntly, despite high living and health standards, and virtually no emigration, the populations of nearly every European country with the exception of France will decline, stay static, or grow in the most miniscule way in the next decade. High contraceptive use and widespread abortion policies have stunted population growth in once dynamic lands. France proves the exception largely due to generous maternity policies and benefits. "Due to this dynamism, France contributes itself to two-thirds of the children born throughout Europe…How to explain this mini baby boom which started in 2000 and has not stopped? There is today a veritable French family model. It is based on professional working woman, development of maternal nursery school from age 3. Thanks to this family policy not only do we prove that the work of women is not the enemy of birthrates, but we show quite the contrary."

"France is Europe's champion in birthrates; with a reproduction rate of two children per woman in 2006, she is with Ireland, the most fertile country in the European Union," lauds *Le Monde*. Yet half the children born in France are conceived out of wedlock. This nonetheless contrasts with the appallingly low birthrates of 1.33 children in the Czech Republic, 1.31 in Slovenia, and 1.27 in Poland who fall far below the 2.1 replacement rate. Italy with 1.35, Germany with 1.32 and Spain with 1.38 have been in decline for a decade.[41]

In Eastern Europe the situation is sadly compounded by plummeting birthrates, abortion, and the lure of now easy emigration to Western Europe for work.

THE TURKISH EQUATION

Traditionally Turkey, or should we say the Ottoman Empire, had posed a clear and present military danger to the Balkans, Hungary, and to the very gates of Vienna. No wonder that in 1497 Jacob Locher, a German Court poet to Maximilian I the Holy Roman Emperor, wrote a political play, "Of the Turks and Their Sultan," which underscored the pernicious threat from the Muslim Ottomans to Western Europe.

In the post-WWII era, Turkey has been viewed in geopolitical terms; from this angle, a strategic, strong and secular Turkish Republic has always had its lobby and supporters in both Brussels and Washington. Turkey's large land forces have traditionally formed a bulwark of NATO but during the nervous countdown to the Iraq conflict, the new *Islamic-lite* government in Ankara sent conflicting signals to Washington. Ultimately Turkey did not commit ground forces to the war nor allow U.S. forces to stage land operations from its territory. Yet with a formidable 500,000 men military force integrated in NATO, combined with its strategic location bridging Europe and the Middle East, Turkey is increasingly viewed as a unique geo-strategic piece on the European chessboard. In this new equation, the proposed EU membership offers Turkey economic growth, while Turkey provides enhanced security for the EU.

I recall being in Istanbul in December 1997 during the icy aftermath of the EU slap to Turkish membership. Prime Minister Mehmut Yilmaz was livid and was openly playing the American card against what Turkish government officials were deriding as the Old Europe. At issue was not formal Turkish EU membership, but *talks about* membership which would presumably lead to Brussels. Both the Clinton and Bush Administrations had lent strong support for Turkish membership. From an American viewpoint Turkey is viewed as both a strategic asset and moreover a secular example of a moderate Muslim state in the troubled Middle East. The Turks will always remind you they have wanted "in" to the European Union for the past forty years; an agreement signed with Ankara in 1963 was the first step. Practically speaking, the deal allowed for easier Turkish access to European markets, but kept formal membership, at arms length. Over the years Turkey's domestic political and economic instability provided the perfect excuse to keep this land of 70 million people at the gates of Brussels. Ankara achieved a breakthrough only in 1999, when the EU made Turkey a candidate for membership. By 2004, Turkey was presumably on the road, albeit a long one, to full EU membership.

Despite Turkey's large population, its economic clout remains limited by EU standards. Prime Minister Recep Erdogan addressing the Brussels based think tank Friends of Europe, stressed that "Turkey joined the customs union in 1996 and first began building relations with the (predecessor to) the EU in 1966; we are still trying to become a member of the European Union.." Erdogan stated that his country is already the 6th largest economy in Europe and the 17th largest in the world. Given Turkey's population, of 70 million "young and dynamic people" the EU would mutually profit from its membership. But beyond economic implications Ankara's democratic credentials have been a particular source of concern to the EU. "The key issue is still Turkey's domestic policy making; we have to decide on Turkey's capacity to deepen and widen its internal democracy," advised Olli Rehn, the EU Commissioner for Enlargement.[42]

Beyond having Europe's largest population and biggest voting bloc, many Europeans, especially the French, openly fear the integration of this Muslim country into the EU. Though the Ankara government has scrupulously supported a secular state model, the socio/economic integration of the rural Anatolian hinterland into the EU poses Herculean challenges. Moreover Turkish EU membership would bring the frontiers of the European Union to Iraq, Islamic Iran and Syria. The prosperous European Union would border the Middle East by the arbitrary stroke of a pen! *Brilliant??*

There's truth to the assertion Turks have argued that the EU views itself as a "Christian Club" of nations. Still the integration of such a huge, historically different and religiously diverse region into the EU would *ipso facto* have deep socio/economic ramifications. Beyond the oft cited economic subsidies to such a new member, one must concede that Turkey beyond its cosmopolitan confines in parts of Istanbul, Ankara and Izmir, remains a fundamentally different society than any of the other members of the *New Europe.*

A Parisian academic one told me, that had General de Gaulle not allowed for Algerian independence, and France still hypothetically retained its former constituent province, this North African land would be sending a disproportionately large number of Muslim deputies to the National Assembly in Paris! Equally the very face of the European Parliament would change from its nominally Judeo/Christian and decidedly secular mode to one comprising a formidable Muslim minority. Nonetheless, there's a quiet counter-current in the EU which views Turkey as the magic lamp for Europe's lurking demographic crisis; its population shortfalls with the ensuing deficit in a younger workforce, and military numbers. But seen another way Turkey's accession to the EU would bring the frontier of *Euroland* with Iraq, the Islamic Republic of Iran, not to mention Syria. Its modern *janissaries* would moreover be guarding the EU's ramparts.

Addressing the issue of Turkey joining the European Union Cardinal Josef Ratzinger (before he became Pope) opined, "To identify the two continents together would be a mistake. It would be a loss of the cultural richness to the profit of the economy. Turkey which considers itself a secular state but on the founding of Islam, could attempt to put in place a cultural continent with neighboring Arab countries and also become the protagonist of a culture possessing its own identity but in communion with the great humanistic values we should all recognize." This idea is not against some forms of narrow association with Europe and would permit the emergence of a united force opposition of all forms of fundamentalism."[43]

The accession of the Turkish Republic with its seventy million plus citizens would bring a younger non-immigrant population pool for the European labor force as well as a large NATO-integrated military force which exceeds the size any other European army. Its membership would presumably allow a *controlled* flow of workers into the labor-short European economy. This presumes a logical outcome where the EU could then formally close to doors to unbridled illegal immigration from the Third World. Such flows of people from South Asia and sub-Saharan Africa have little concern with EU membership minutiae but rather the lure of the *EU's Beaucoup Benefits.*

Europe faces a rise in welfare migration. One does not have to wander far in Amsterdam, Berlin, London, Paris, or Rome to see that migration into "rich" Europe is driven by two constants; good income and lifestyle possibilities as well as the opposite pole of the undeniable magnetism of the benefits of the social state. Many migrants, seeking the benefits will move legally or illegally to the Western EU countries. Such migration has already financially crippled many European states and forced a seemingly bottomless pit in social spending.

Dr. Henry Kissinger advised, "The emergence of a unified Europe is one of the most revolutionary events of our time. The impetus for it has sprung from a variety of motives. Initially Europe saw integration as a way to overcome the suicidal rivalry that led it into two catastrophic world wars and to overcome the economic ravages of those wars by cooperative action...a new impetus for European integration developed when Germany was unified in 1990." He stresses, "Throughout this process of unifying Europe, the United States has played a major supporting role, at first as a passionate advocate, more recently as a foil."[44]

Yet the European Union faces serious political malaise too. The resounding French and Dutch rejections of the proposed Euro constitution jolted political elites and shadowed plans for future continental integration. *Le Figaro* headlined "*NON*—The Shattered dreams of Jacques Chirac. The dream was equally shattered for much of *Euroland's* political class.

Both the Olympic Games and the 2006 World Football Cup in Germany (soccer) presented an extraordinary political barometer of EU sentiments. These global games very quickly boil down to high-octane nationalism. National Teams are often a perfect synthesis of national pride and aspiration— England, France, Germany, Italy, Portugal. The talk of one world and globalization comes down to a few very national teams facing each other on the green field of sport like rival armies. They are cheered on or jeered at by throngs of near frenzied fans waving national flags with near tribal abandon. Anyone who doesn't think this is national pride should hear the din of the English fans or see even the reserved Swiss in absolute abandon! In many ways Soccer is like diplomacy, illustrating the constant ebb and flow of fortunes, the consistent movement but little scoring, and the tedious and tiring pace which approaches the goal, nearly scores, only to be sent reeling back across the field. Unalloyed nationalism and patriotism reign. While powerhouse teams from the European Union were in the semi-finals, France, Germany, Italy, and Portugal, there was hardly a hint of EU mania but there certainly was a surge of old fashioned patriotism complete with flags, banners, and chants. The finals in Berlin saw a very nationalistic Italy triumph over France. The Euro cup finals in 2008 were no different as the sporting titans faced off to the intoxication of nationalistic euphoria, which reached its crescendo when Spain defeated Germany.

Sadly during the recent political evolution of *Euroland*, anti-Americanism has proven a useful socio/political scapegoat for the political class in explaining away many problems as well as solidifying the political base. Nonetheless there's a deep socio/ political malaise affecting the public especially in places like France where the once formidable institutions of the State are now subject to derisive ridicule and an eroding lack of trust. Despite its demographic constraints, its less than stellar economic growth rates and entrenched political angst, the EU states nonetheless have emerged as a formidable social, economic and political force. The extraordinary symbolism of the EU whole and free clearly stands as a model for the world.

NOTES

1. Olli Rehn, EU Enlargement Five Years On—A Balance Sheet and What Next?," European Policy Centre Breakfast/Brussels, 31 March 2009, pp. 2–3.

2. More Unity European Union 2003, pp. 5, 10–11.

3. "No Massive Diversion of Foreign Direct Investment Seen on Eve of European Union Enlargement," UN Press Release 30 April 2004, pp. 1–3.

4. "Assessing the early Benefits of EU Membership," *IMF Survey* Vol. 35 No 21, 20 November 2006, p. 331.

5. Cech, Zdenek and John MacDonald, "The Celtic Tiger Learns to Purr," ECFIN Country Focus/European Commission (Vol. 1, Issue 18), 19 November 2004, pp. 1–2.

6. Alan Barrett, "Quarterly Economic Commentary/Spring 2009," Economic and Social Research Institute/Dublin, April 2009.

7. NATO Review/Statistics, Vol. 47, no. 1 Spring 1999, p. 5.

8. Dennis Bark, Reflections on Europe, p. IX.

9. "Trade and Europe's Economy; All in the Same Boat," *Atlantic Times* April 2009, pp. 12–13.

10. Paul Johnson, "What Europe Really Needs," Reprinted from The *Wall Street Journal* © 17 June 2005, p. A14 Dow Jones & Company. All rights reserved.

11. Foreign Policy Association Lecture, Ana Palacio Foreign Minister of Spain 25 September 2003, pp. 1–2.

12. Italian Mission to the UN/Address by Prime Minister Prodi 25 September 2007, p. 3.

13. Treaty on European Union (Maastricht Treaty), (Luxembourg; Office for Official Publications of the European Communities, 1992), p. 123.

14. James Joyner, "Henry Kissinger in Quotes," New Atlanticist, Atlantic Council of the United States, Washington D.C, 16 January 2009.

15. Javier Solana, "Shaping an Effective European Union Foreign Policy," Speech/ *Konrad Adenauer Foundation*/Brussels 24 January 2005, p. 2.

16. Paul Johnson, "What Europe Really Needs," *Wall Street Journal* 17 June 2005, p. A14.

17. Walter Laqueur, "The Last Days of Europe; Epitaph for an Old Continent," (New York: Thomas Dunne Books, 2009), p. 115.

18. Tony Barber and John Murray, "Irish 'No Curbs EU Hopes," and "Irish Poll Delivers Big Blow to EU Morale," *Financial Times* 14/15 June 2008, pp. 1–2.

19. "Jerzy Buzek Elected President of European Parliament," Europa.eu 14 July 2009.

20. Kagan, Paradise and Power, p. 117, 119–120.

21. Rifkind, European Dream, 2004 pp. 296, 297.

22. Transatlantic Trends 2005, (Washington D.C.; German Marshall Fund of the U.S., 2005), p. 10.

23. German Mission to the UN/Address by Joshka Fischer 23 September 2004, p. 6.

24. The Enlarging European Union at the United Nations (Luxembourg: Office for Official Publications of the European Communities, 2004), pp. 5–7, 15–17.

25. Ibid., p. pp. 28–29, 38 and United Nations Secretariat, "Status of Contributions as of 30 June 2008," United Nations: New York, pp. 6–10.

26. Rifkind, European Dream, p. 301.

27. Ibid., p. 300.

28. "The Future of U.S.-German Relations" Council on Foreign Relations Debate, 2 July 2003.

29. Theo Sommer, "Tinker, Tailor, Soldier, Spy; Berlin Denies the Truth of Reports about US-German Intelligence Cooperation," *Atlantic Times*, March 2006, p. 1.

30. Dufourcq and Faber, "Transatlantic Dialogue," November 2006, p. 37.

31. Revel, *American Enterprise Magazine*, June 2004, pp. 36–37.

32. Vaclav Klaus, Speech of the President of the Czech Republic in the European Parliament/Brussels.19 February 2009, pp. 2–3 and "World Economic Outlook 2009," International Monetary Fund April 2009, imf.org.

33. "Fewer Children," *Atlantic Times*, April 2006, p. 23.

34. Patrick Buchanan, *Death of the West*, (New York: St. Martin's Press, 2002), pp. 13–17.

35. James Harkin, "The Great Leveler," *Financial Times*, 18–19 June 2005, p. W3.

36. "EU's Ageing Population Transforming the Bloc," *EUBusiness.com*, 27 April 2008.and EUROSTAT "Population Predictions 2008–2060" 26 August 2008.

37. "Belgium's Challenge; Making the Good Times Last," *IMF Survey* Vol. 36 No. 9, 28 May 2007, p. 136.

38. "Human Development Report 2004; United Nations Development Programme" (New York: Oxford University Press, 2004), pp. 152–154.

39. UNFPA "State of the World Population 2008," (New York: United Nations Fund for Population Activities, 2008), pp. 90–93.

40. Population and Vital Statistics Report, New York: Department of Economic and Social Affairs, United Nations, 2009, pp. 18–19.

41. Anne Chemin, "L'Exceptionnelle natalite Francaise est portee par la politique Familiale," *Le Monde* 28–29 October 2007, p. 8. see also Anne Chemin, "Natalite: la France consolide ses atouts dans une Europe vieillissante," *Le Monde* 23 August 2008, p. 9.

42. Friends of Europe/Brussels, "Turkey's European Future," January 2009, see also Alexandre del Valle, "Les Raisons de Refuser la candidature d'Ankara," *Le Figaro* 26 July 2004, p. 9.

43. Sophie de Ravinel, Cardinal Josef Ratzinger Interview, *Le Figaro Magazine* 13 August 2004, p. 34.

44. Kissinger, Does America Need a Foreign Policy?, p. 47.

Chapter Eight

Why Can't We Be Friends?

In the memorable closing scene of Casablanca, the hero the taciturn and once cynical American Rick Blaine and his new French friend Major Renaud, walk into the evening mist; "This is the beginning of a beautiful friendship." The implication was clear; not only had the Franco/American relationship been vigorously revived in 1942, but the film's onetime antagonists Humphrey Bogart and Claude Raines had become friends. In a way Casablanca could stand as a metaphor for Franco/American relations—the image of a once indifferent America grudgingly, and then convincingly, coming to the rescue of its old friend France.

The moral, as was the film, was *black and white*—Free France *versus* the Nazis. It presented a cinematic morality play of *good versus evil*. America was helping the oppressed, to the strains of the *Marseillaise* heroically playing in the foreground drowning out a German military march. Fast forward to Fahrenheit 911 and one discovers the murky moral relativism of the Gulf War II, not WWII. Here the Americans are clearly not the *good guys*, the Iraqis are clearly not the *bad guys,* and the French are indifferent to the American case against an Arab despot. Here "Mr. Rick" would remain indifferent, or at worst a clear antagonist. Yet, Hollywood has its lessons.

Naturally the time, place and generations are different but many of the root causes remain the same. The inability to identify, and then to confront, evil early on has often been a political fault among many countries. A root cause to the current transatlantic tempest rests not so much in the personalities or the issues, recall that General de Gaulle and an acerbic Texan President LBJ were really larger than life characters, but the fact that instant communication—24 hour *wall to wall* media, in need of news stories and the vastness of cyberspace through the internet, offers a platform which becomes a *trompe l'oeil* for complex foreign policy issues. The media, in its vastness and insatiable appetite for a story, magnifies the issue out of all political proportion. This is not to naively under-estimate the depth of genuine trans-Atlantic political problems with France, Germany and many other Europeans, but to place the issues in proper context. Given America's lack of historic context, viewing this crisis as something unique, new and unprecedented, and one has the grist for the major misunderstandings which are then magnified out of all proportion by the major media whose foreign policy learning curve is not far ahead of the general public.

"Europe is widely viewed in the United States as impotent, obstructionist, and simultaneously, utopian and cynical," according to Prof. Andrew Moravcsik.[1]

Though the Iraq war became a vexing symptom of what divided America from Europe, the wider malaise rests in differing interpretations of how to reconcile the use of force against dangerous tyrants. The European view for the most part embraced the maze of international legal constraints while Washington's view, especially in the jolting wake of September 11th took a pro-active approach—Preemptive attack and regime change. American policy, paraphrasing former Secretary of State Dean Acheson, sought support from the United Nations as little more than an aid to blessing overall American diplomacy and policy objectives. For the EU, seemingly any policy first needs the diplomatic benediction of the Security Council before any armed action even against the most hideous of despots. Put bluntly, Washington was willing to go the UN route towards military action in Iraq *providing* the Security Council would endorse a timely and robust resolution against Saddam. If the Council failed to do so, the U.S. and a *self-styled* alliance of the willing would then unilaterally go ahead and do the job. For the Europeans endless palaver seemed almost a goal in itself in trying to cajole, coerce, and compromise with Saddam. Lacking any substantial cooperation from the Iraqis, the EU would then essentially reschedule yet another round of breathless crisis negotiations only then to settle for half a loaf. This policy had maintained a unique inertia for a decade and could have easily been drawn out a few more years.

The case of Munich and the 1938 Anglo/French diplomatic betrayal of Czechoslovakia haunted contemporary Anglo/American policy makers. *It should.* And it should especially shadow the Europeans. A policy of appeasement whetted the appetite and strengthened the resolve of Nazi Germany to press a seemingly feckless Europe for yet more concessions *in the name of peace.* That peace was short lived. To this day, no political figure in Britain or America wishes to carry Mr. Neville Chamberlain's umbrella, and France's Edward Daladier remains a sorry footnote. While there was an awkward historical absurdity in comparing Saddam's Iraq's with the Third Reich, the sober fact remains that after September 11th 2001, Washington was not in the mood, nor the mindset, in offering the benefit of the doubt.

But the blame game over Baghdad must cease. What had become a diplomatic Tower of Babel where so many voices speaking in a self-righteous cacophony drowned out the real arguments, and have especially blurred the continuing case for strong trans-Atlantic ties in spite of Iraq. We must draw the line in the sand and move on. It's ludicrous to presume that the philosophical and cultural links between Europe and America don't exist or have been irreparably broken over Iraq.

Writing these lines from the near metaphysical detachment of a TGV train speeding across France at 300Mph, I'm reminded that high technology is not unique to the USA. Nor is national pride. America is justly proud of NASA and Europeans of the European Space Agency (ESA). We have Boeing and IBM, they have Airbus and Siemens. Still both French and Americans took pride in jointly celebrating Lance Armstrong's unprecedented six time win of the iconic *Tour de France* bicycle race. The point is that far too many Americans view Europe as a quaint "Old World" where political appeasement and incessant yammering have reached a fine art. To many Americans that's one of Europe's few world class achievements. And this belongs to the same nonsense as Europeans speaking about American "cowboy diplomacy" and vicious "Wild West capitalism." Both sides of the Atlantic are closer than they may think.

BUSINESS AND INVESTMENT

Look at the growing levels of cross investment. Years ago "business" was not something that *chic* upper class Europeans would feel comfortable with studying or doing. Today they study the "American way" in business schools, earn MBA's, and usually do so in the English language. These Entrepreneurial Europeans eagerly flock to America is search of more flexibility and economic freedom, fewer regulations and lower taxes. French and Germans often thrive in the *American business culture*. There are manifold reasons.

Germany, Europe's largest economy, presents an interesting case in business *education*. Few German business schools have a strong international standing compared with their U.S. or European competitors. In the *Financial Times* ranking of post-graduate MBA programs globally, the USA unabashedly led the list with the exceptions in France (INSEAD), Spain (IESE) and a notable few others. Of one hundred institutions listed, not a single exclusively German school rated. Of the top European MBA programs, only one had German connections.[2]

Sadly there's a creeping social state mentality in the USA which had put a regulatory and fiscal maze upon the very genius of American commerce. Thus as Europe grudgingly concedes that American business practices may hold some elusive answers for commerce, the U.S. side is often trying to construct the very same bureaucratic constraints and regulatory maze which has historically been the bane to European enterprise! Even the Euro *way of business*—and types of stores has dramatically changed across the continent. Hyper markets—food supermarket/department stores which look more like Wal Mart than Old World, are commonplace. In France names like Auchon, Carrefour, and Leclerc are ubiquitous. In Germany Home Depot-type stores are commonplace. The style of mega marketing—modeled on but exceeding the American inspiration—has been around for twenty years. And equally the hideous billboards which scar the outskirts of French cities and towns, evoke not the Old World but New Jersey.

This is a fact, a business reality, as much as is Mc Donald's and the ubiquitous KFC Chicken restaurants, which seem to have blossomed like mushrooms throughout Prague. One would be hard pressed to say the Euros want to distance themselves from everything American. America's traditional trade ties with Europe have been shadowed in the past twenty years by growing trade links with East Asia—especially with Japan, Korea and China. Our "Top Ten" trading partners *now include only four European countries*. Still U.S. commerce with the European Union remains formidable.

Nonetheless two-way trade between the USA and France, despite the stained political ties only marginally dipped from $50 billion in 2001 to $47 billion in 2002 and rebounded to $53 billion in 2004 and $61 billion in 2006. Commerce with Germany grew despite political tensions from $89 billion in 2001 to $88 billion in 2002, $97 billion in 2003 and to $109 billion in 2004. Interestingly during 2003, period of the most significant row with Washington, *both French and German exports to the USA* actually grew from the previous year.[3]

But while anti-Americanism ran at high levels, with consistent hostility towards President Bush and the Iraq war, few foreign consumers appeared to hold American firms accountable for the misgivings they had about Washington's policies. Earnings by U.S. affiliates in Europe more than doubled since 2001 rising to $147 billion in 2006. American affiliate income from Poland, the Czech Republic and Hungary in 2006 totaled $2 billion or larger than what American companies earned in India that year.[4]

U.S. policies may have dented sales in Europe. One in five Europeans say that they will avoid buying products most clearly associated with the U.S. according to a Global Market Insite Poll. That survey discovers most hostility is towards both iconic symbols and products: American Express, AOL, Ameri-

Figure 8.1. Imports from the USA/Exports to the USA in Billions of Dollars

	2001	2002	2003	2004	2005	2006	2007	2008
Japan	$57/126	$51/121	$52/118	$54/130	$55/138	$60/148	$63/146	$64/139
China	$19/102	$22/125	$28/152	$35/197	$42/243	$55/288	$65/322	$70/338
France	$20/30	$19/28	$17/29	$21/32	$22/34	$24/37	$27/42	$29/44
Germany	$30/59	$26/62	$29/68	$31/77	$34/85	$41/89	$50/94	$55/98
Italy	$10/24	$10/24	$11/25	$11/28	$12/31	$13/33	$14/35	$15/36
The UK	$41/42	$33/41	$34/43	$36/46	$39/51	$45/53	$50/57	$54/59

can Airlines, and McDonald's. Kevin Roberts chief executive of Saatchi and Saatchi fears that "public concerns over U.S. policy could hurt U.S. brands in foreign markets."[5]

Nonetheless American firms reign supreme in the pantheon of global brands with Eight of the Top Ten coming from the USA (Google, GE, Microsoft, Coca Cola, IBM, McDonalds's, Apple and Marlboro leading the list. French firms in the Top Hundred list include eight deluxe companies such as Louis Vuitton, L' Oreal, Chanel, Hermes, and Moet and Chandon, while German companies such as BMW and Mercedes are on the list. Among the top fifteen global brands, ten are American, (one is Finnish (Nokia), one British (Vodafone), two Chinese (China Mobile and ICBC) and one Japanese (Toyota).[6]

France, Germany and the Netherlands remain key American destinations for Foreign Direct Investment (FDI). In the first half of 2004 France attracted $4 billion in investment. Even during 2003, the year of the Iraq war and the hyper-strain in Paris/ Washington diplomatic relations, U.S. investment grew except for the one quarter just before the conflict. France ranks third in the world with foreign direct investment standing at $81 billion. The USA remains the largest investor, supporting 550,000 jobs. Almost one billion dollars in commercial transactions occur between France and the U.S. each day. "France has emerged as a primary recipient and provider of direct foreign investment since 1990," adds a study, "Currently France ranks as the third top destination for FDI in the world trailing only the U.S. and UK." FDI flows into France between 2000 and 2006 at $382 billion, were only slightly less than into China.[7]

Everyday shopping transactions illustrate this point. One of France's most popular coffees *Carte Noir* is owned by Kraft and the venerable mustard maker Maille is a subsidiary of Unilever.

Bill Drozdiak, President of the American Council on Germany adds, "Americans invested five times as much money in Germany last year (2006) as they did in China, and U.S. firms in total have four times as much money into tiny Belgium as they have into India. Europe provides three-quarters of all foreign investment in the United States, creating millions of American jobs."[8]

American firms have invested in the French high-tech sector; Xerox has 4,000 employees with a key "innovation center" at Grenoble; GE now in France for fifty years has 9,500 employees in R&D centers. GE's European CEO Nani Beccalli extols "The French have a passion for engineering and technology, for research and solutions that push back the boundaries." Motorola who established their first-semi-conductor site outside the USA in France in 1967 currently has 3,000 people in the R&D sector. But American investments go beyond France. As a point of comparison, the U.S. invests more in the Netherlands or UK than in Canada or Mexico. More surprising, between 2000–2008, U.S. investment on Mainland China was less than in Belgium or half of that into tiny Ireland![9]

The United States remains the primary destination for EU foreign investment. In 2005 the EU companies invested 29 billion Euros versus an investment of Euro 6 billion in China and Euro 2 billion in India. European affiliate firms earned 70 percent more in the U.S. than in all of Asia combined. Earnings from China and India combined represented less than 8 percent of earnings in the USA.[10]

Interestingly, the U.S. retained its position as the largest single host country for Foreign Direct Investment (FDI) at $233 billion in 2007. The United Kingdom, France and the Netherlands received record investments too. FDI flows into the 27 EU countries rose by 43 percent in 2007 to a total of $804 billion. Investment into France doubled reaching $158 billion.[11]

Indeed the U.S. has maintained a healthy lead over Europe in technology. According to the International Research and Development Scorecard, American companies increased R&D spending in 2006 by 13.4% or forty percent of the global total as compared to 8% for Europe. The scorecard compiled by the UK Department of Trade and Industry adds that Germany, France and the UK account for two-thirds of the Europe's total R&D spending of $180 billion. Global R&D spending grew 10%.[12]

The European Union's economic development has only now reached the level attained by the U.S. two decades ago, a study advises. The U.S. reached the EU's current level of GDP per capita in 1985, according to Eurochambers, a business lobby. The EU's Research and Development levels were reached by the U.S. in 1978. To match 2005 levels of American R&D spending, the EU's expenditure would have to grow by 14 percent annually until 2010. "The EU is still far from matching America's economic clout," the study adds.[13]

Importantly the U.S. has regained first place in global information technology rankings. A World Economic Forum Report advises that the leading countries excel in excellent physical infrastructure, market environment and high commercial and government usage of information technology. Singapore comes in second followed then by Denmark, Iceland, Finland, Canada, Taiwan, Sweden , Switzerland and the United Kingdom. The UK as number ten was the highest ranked of the major EU economies with Germany as number 17, France 22, and Italy 42.[14]

The USA also beats the EU states in innovation. A ranking by a prominent European business school INSEAD found the U.S. by far the world's most innovative country. According to the report by the Paris-based school, the U.S. is the top country generating ideas, adapting them quickly, and profiting from them. Germany was second, followed in the top five by Sweden, the UK and Singapore.[15]

Advances in biotech underscore another technology gulch across the Atlantic. The United States and Japan greatly outperform Europe. Biotech patents field by the University of California and University of Texas far outstrip the best European comparators. Only Denmark's companies and Universities can begin to compete with the overwhelming biotech advancement from the USA. Even Oxford University which has the best patent performance, holds less than half of number garnered by American institutions such as Columbia, Texas or Stanford.[16]

Europe has equally slipped in competitiveness too according to a survey by the Geneva-based World Economic Forum, a closely monitored indicator. The United States ranked first globally for its well-managed and competitive economy; Switzerland placed second. Denmark, Sweden and Germany followed and the Netherlands ranked 8th, Japan rated 9th, the United Kingdom rated 12th. Out of 131 comparators France ranked 16th, Ireland 22nd, Italy 49th and Poland 53rd.[17]

The status of E government among states provides another barometer. The ability of states to effectively deliver and offer government services and data through information technology has truly proven transformative. Leading the top countries in E-Government readiness are Sweden, Denmark, Norway, the United States and the Netherlands. Indeed the "end-goal of all e-governance and connected governance efforts must remain better public service delivery."[18]

Yet the challenges of global downturn have affected the EU and its trade partners. Vaclav Klaus, Czech President speaking before the European Parliament in Brussels warned, "The present economic system of the EU is a system of a suppressed market, a system of permanently strengthening centrally controlled economy." In a controversial address to the Parliament in his capacity as EU President he added, "Although history has more than clearly proven that this is a dead end, we find ourselves walking the same path again ...this results in both a constant rise in both the extent of government masterminding and constraining the spontaneity of the market process." Klaus opined "This trend has been further reinforced by incorrect interpretation of the causes of the present economic and financial crisis, as if it were caused by the free market, while in reality it is just the contrary—caused by political manipulation of the market." He advised that "the only solution is liberalization and deregulation of the European economy."[19]

SECURITY TIES—NATO AND BEYOND.

As Dr. Kissinger advised, "The leaders who created the Atlantic relationship had learned in the crucible of the Second World War that divisions among the democracies in a period of appeasement in the 1930's and during the long road to victory had nearly caused a worldwide catastrophe. They launched the Marshall Plan and NATO, overcame a series of direct and indirect Soviet challenges, and laid the basis for the eventual defeat of communism." He adds, "the generation in office or dominating elections in the 1990's in the countries bordering the Atlantic emerged from quite a different set of experiences... Their fathers were reared on confidence in American power and the importance of allied unity. The sons and daughters grew up during the protest movements of the 1960's and 1970's that had a profound distrust of American power...they identified foreign policy with non-strategic causes and were uncomfortable with the notion of national interest...the generation in office at the turn of the millennium in almost all of the countries of Western Europe represented center-left parties that had their formative experiences in some type of anti-American protest."

"During the Cold War there was indeed a common purpose," advises Kissinger adding, "but America's allies were convinced at every step that America would carry out its global responsibilities even when its allies fell short." Kissinger questions, "The ultimate issue is not technical but philosophical: Will Europe's emerging identity leave room for an Atlantic partnership?"[20]

Naturally NATO's success and the formal end of the Cold War made the case for wider European burden sharing. After all the Americans were phasing out some of their European based forces and thus the EU would have the historic and timely chance to pick up the strategic slack and fill the gap. Thus despite perpetual European polemics about a larger Euro role in defense, one would logically imagine that their national defense budgets would reflect this desire. They currently don't and they likely won't. European defense budgets are simply not commensurate with the economic power of the core EU players. Put less charitably, the Europeans are not pulling their weight. The expenditures of core NATO countries are, despite the near boundless enthusiasm about common European defense, a *Eurocorps*, and the sorts of prattle that emanate from Paris, simply don't add up. In 1994 for example, French defense spending stood at 3.3 percent of GDP—by 1999 it had fallen to 2.7 percent. The size of the French military moreover dropped from 410,000 to 317,000. Germany's GDP defense budget fell from 2 percent in 1994 to 1.7 percent in 1999 with corresponding cuts in troop strength from 367,000 to 333,000. In the UK the fall went from 3.4 percent to 2.6 percent with a troop cut from 254,000 to 216,000. As a point of comparison, Turkey's defense spending jumped from 3.2 percent in 1994 to 5.5 percent in 1999 with troop levels going from 504,000 to 639,000.[21]

So despite the crumbling of the Soviet Empire, the "peace dividend" and the corresponding downshift in defense spending—the USA's was cut from

4.3 percent in 1994 to 3.1 in 1999 with corresponding armed forces cuts during the Clinton Administration from 1.65 million to 1.37 million. By 2003 in the midst of the war on terror troop levels of NATO core country troop levels stood at 356,000 in France, 285,000 in Germany 214,000 for the UK, and 1.5 million for the USA. Turkey interestingly boosted its average armed forces strength to 823,000.[22]

Even after the horrors of September 11th and precisely due to wider troop commitments to fight the global war on terror, the Bush Administration decided to redeploy some of its forces posted in Germany. During Summer 2004, President George W. Bush's announced that 70,000 U.S. military forces will be gradually withdrawn from overseas bases, among them 30,000 based in Germany. The fact that large numbers of American troops remain in Germany nearly sixty years after WWII and fifteen years after the Cold War ended, on the face of it appears incongruous. But the timing of the redeployments were equally disconcerting to many Europeans in NATO. American forces in Germany had already been massively cut from the mid-1990's. At the end of the Cold War, the United States had 250,000 troops in Germany. In the years since, the total has dipped to about 50,000.[23]

In the wake of the Iraq war and strained political relations between Washington and Berlin, the cuts could appear as much as a political payback to the Schroeder government as an overdue restructuring. Yet Berlin's conservative *Die Welt* newspaper opined that it "rejects the rumors" that the pullout is intended to punish Germany for opposition to the Iraq war. The German government contributes $1 billion annually towards support for American bases. Even if the Pentagon's pullout schedule goes ahead as planned, don't expect the major EU states to offer to make up the difference in numbers. Through there will be yet increased talk about Eurocorps expansion and opportunities, it remains highly unlikely that the core EU members—France, Germany, Italy and the UK—will in effect make up the difference. The official reason is budgetary, but the fact remains that the populations are too small to sustain such expansions.

According to a respected Transatlantic Trends poll by the German Marshall Fund, support for NATO is dwindling Euro-wide from 69% in 2002 to 55% in 2006. Major declines came in Germany where support fell from 74% in 2002 to 56% in 2006; in Italy from 68% in 2002 to 52% in 2006, and in Poland from 64% in 2002 to 48% in 2006. In the U.S. however support for NATO grew from 56% in 2002 to 61% in 2006.[24]

Ironically when those same European states had far smaller populations a century ago, they were able to field huge land armies. One begins to see the logic some Europeans have of looking to the Turks to become the *Janissaries of the EU*. Turkey, with its expanding population and military tradition, can provide the troops to defend the tired and graying old world.

The *War on Terror* jolted both sides of the Atlantic. We must recognize that we are not dealing with traditional state players such as the former Soviet Union. This is stating the obvious but needs restating. After Japan's attack on Pearl Harbor, it was clear who the aggressor was. The attacking planes were clearly marked, the Imperial Japanese Navy flew the flag of the rising sun, and the Tokyo government had a clearly defined geographic place. In other words after the outrage of 7 December 1941, we knew the players and from where they operated. Targets were clearly defined. The enemy had a formal order of battle. There was no such luxury after September 11th. The shadowy Al Qaida terrorist organization had few identifiable leaders save for the mastermind Osama Bin Laden, there was no capital city, infrastructure, or even a formal flag. We were seeking shadows who emerged from places like Kabul, Karachi, and Baghdad, but likely had as many links in London, Hamburg and New York.

Precisely because of the nebulous nature of the enemy, often state supported but not a state in itself, it's difficult for policymakers and populations to focus on the threat. It is much easier to concentrate on a defined target than a mirage. While Washington generally has a better concept of the threat, European Union policymakers are hesitant to accept this reality. Why? Because as America has discovered, many of the culprits were apprehended in Buffalo and Brooklyn as in far off Baghdad. European police know that while places like Pakistan and Yemen remain an Al Qaida safe haven, there are mare than enough sleeper cells in the rough immigrant suburbs of Paris, Lyon and Le Mans than they would wish to admit. Islamic radicalism and the terrorism it often breeds remains a force as fundamentally opposed to Western Europe as it does to the USA. Though the European political class may wish to believe that if one magically removes the external issues such as the American role supporting Israel or Iraq, is only then to see the chimera of Islamic Iran, Chechnya, or Kashmir for that matter.

In the wake of the Iraq war there was nonetheless increasing Franco/American political cooperation on issues such as pressuring Syria out of Lebanon and anti-terrorist cooperation. Former French Foreign Minister Michel Barnier addressing the UN General Assembly illustrated the contradiction between both sides of the Atlantic; "The tragedy of 11th September, which I refer to with emotion in New York, was an attack on us all. Since then terrorism has continued to strike…We wage a merciless fight against terrorism… Global threats require a strong, and always collective response." But lest anyone think that the pernicious rift with Paris over Iraq policy can be patched by an election in the USA, Barnier then added "In Iraq violence is exploding. France, as everyone knows, did not approve of the conditions in which the conflict was unleashed. *Neither today, nor tomorrow, will it commit itself militarily in Iraq."*[25]

There's a deeper reason France hesitates to forcefully confront militant Islam, the fear of domestic political disorders and violence in the large and spontaneously unruly Moslem quarters of major French cities and towns. Two domestic intelligence agencies: the *Renseignements Generaux* intelligence gathering service and the *Direction de la Surveillance du Territoire*, the counter-intelligence agency were tasked with security. To reinforce and refine the fight against terrorism, the Sarkozy government has fused both agencies into a new force "Direction Centrale du Renseignement Interieur (DCRI). The new unit will field 4,000 highly specialized police and shall be "a veritable French CIA," adding a "new face to surveillance."[26]

The French State imposes an almost militant secularism for its citizens. Through a careful diplomatic cultivation of Arab states, keeping of a political arms length from the Anglo/ American coalition operations in Iraq, and offering rhetorical support to its own internal Muslim population through the sonorous secular mantra of *Liberte, Fraternite* and *Egalite*, the Chirac government presumed France was shielded by a *cordon sanitaire*. Such optimism proved horribly misinformed when the *Realite* of domestic youth discontent boiled over in the Parisian banlieues in October/November 2005. So in a prosperous and pivotal EU member state we see news headlines like "Facing the Suburban Crisis, Villepin Declares a State of Emergency (*Le Monde*) or "Villepin Goes Off to War" (*Liberation*), CNN evokes the risks of "Civil War," and ABC News headlines "French Violence," and even *The Economist* decried "France's Failure."

While many of the youth frustrations are indeed rooted in social issues (lack of jobs, alienation from society, and that all encompassing word *Respect*) the riots cannot be simply explained away as a social workers challenge. The primary spark for nearly three weeks of troubles—the accidental deaths of two youths fleeing the police—was not at all Islamic-based, but would soon mobilize many of the marginalized Muslims living near Paris and scores of French cities. The aggressive culture promoted by French Rap music, appeals to youth who happen to be second generations Muslims—in other words people born in France—but feeling marginalized, frustrated, and filled with rage for the society in which they grew up. Combine this with a highly stratified and restrictive labor market, whose perks and portals are jealously protected by socialist trade unions, and there is little chance for jobs for newcomers.

"The Rap expresses the violence of the banlieues, it permits the young of the cities to hurl, with their words, their rage against the society in which they feel marginalized," editorialized *Le Monde* adding, "The cries of hate are unacceptable." The French criminal justice system holds juridical powers which predate and likely surpass the provisions of the U.S. Patriot Act.

Nonetheless the political class seemed powerless to seriously confront the nightly violence; the rioting, the street battles and car burnings, which defined this misplaced *cult of respect*. And despite its proactive secularist (laicite) devotion, the French government wishes to set up schools to train the Muslim imams serving the nation's growing Islamic community. The concept is to offer imams courses in "secularism" as well as French institutions, and the French language.

If we take France's classically *Dirigiste* or Stateist approach and contrast it with the *laissez faire* multicultural course of the Netherlands, one finds a difference "In contrast, the Dutch governments minority policies, provided a large degree of cultural autonomy for "ethnic minorities" in the 1980's. Although this Dutch multiculturalism was partially reversed in the 1990's, the institutional effects are there for all to see," writes Paul Statham. He adds "The Netherlands has a state funded Islamic broadcasting network, an Islamic school board, an Islamic pedagogic center, and more than forty Islamic schools, all of which are government funded with a regular Dutch curriculum. Closer inspection reveals however, that the outcomes of Dutch policies are far from a multicultural utopia."[27]

One may opine whether such tolerance and social leeway encourages immigrants to become good Dutch citizens or simply allows for balkanized communities living in the Netherlands. Islamic headscarves, and "dressing ghetto," have been fused onto Holland's already libertine scene. Moreover the Netherlands military, which already has Catholic, Protestant, Jewish, Hindu and humanist chaplains has now added Muslim imams to its ranks. The name Mohammed (and varied spellings) has become the most popular name for baby boys born in the four largest cities (Amsterdam, Rotterdam, the Hague, and Utrecht) in the Netherlands. Traditional Dutch tolerance towards foreigners is often strained. While many observers will quickly rationalize that the roots of the Muslim discord in the "Old Europe" actually reflects the social spiral of Middle Eastern violence, this remains a symptom but not likely the problem.

The issue should be so narrow. While the West Bank and Iraq remain the obvious festering symptoms, the deeper problem goes to the roots of a fundamentally different worldview in which dogmatism, hatred, and violence form a virile political cult. While many will say the roots go back to the creation of the state of Israel in 1948, historically for many fundamentalists the deeper issue deals with 1492 and the *Reconquista* in Spain, or Charles Martel and the Battle of Poitiers, or Czarist Russia's conquest of the Caucuses. Fundamentalists hate Spain, France, and Russia as much as they do the United States; one has only to look at the grisly list of Islamic terrorist acts in France in the 1980's, Spain in 2004, Britain in 2005, to see a series of horrific actions beyond America's frontiers. Islamic Chechen attacks on Russian aircraft, subways and schools in August/September 2004, sadly illustrates what many Europeans are hesitant to concede; the threat of international terrorism is just that—an *international threat.*

Following the London Subway and bus bombing in July 2005, author Ian Buruma wrote; "The war in Iraq may not have been a sensible move. It probably did galvanize religious extremism. For the record, I was against it. But to claim that we should not have gone to war with Saddam Hussein because it puts us in the firing line of holy warriors seems a bad, and certainly cowardly argument." He adds, "Britain would have been in their firing line anyway. *Jihadis* do have an ax to grind with the Western world. Long before Iraq was a gleam in Blair's eyes, the West was in the holy warriors sphere of hate."[28]

Going beyond the stereotypes, most of the French and Spanish Muslims are of North African origin as well as half of those in Belgium and Italy. British Muslims tend to come from Pakistan and Bangladesh. "Thus the communities in Europe are anything by monolithic," advises Walter Lacquer adding, "except in France they have no common language; few of them have a command of Arabic. But even though their number is small their political influence is growing…religion is very important in the life of Muslim communities; the number of Mosques in France has grown from about 260 in the mid-1980's to more than 2,000 at the present time…Germany had some 700 little mosques or prayer rooms in the 1980's, there are more than 2,500 at the present time. There were 574 "certified mosques in Britain in 1999, but the real number is at least 2,000 at present." In his book *The Last Days of Europe,* Lacquer adds , beyond religion there is the actual demographic. About half the Muslims in Western and Central Europe were born there. While Muslims constitute only about fifteen percent of the population of Brussels, they are 25 percent or more of the cohort under 25…the respective percentages in Dutch cities are higher…the number of Muslims in Germany will double in the next decade while the native German population will decrease."[29]

CULTURE AND CIVILIZATION

Cultural cross-pollination insures English is often the *lingua franca for arts and popular culture.* Consider the cinema. The mega-cinemas in the Parisian Montparnasse quarter almost exclusively show American films. In Berlin besides the American *agit-prop* film Fahrenheit 911, there were openings for I Robot with lead actor Will Smith working the crowds in person and Vin Diesel, doing the same shortly thereafter.

Thus in France, the EU's leading, and may we say state subsidized—filmmaker we discover that during a time of sizzling "anti-Americanism," Hollywood took in the box office hands down. Of the top six grossing films of mid-Summer 2004, five were American—I Robot, Spider Man 2, Fahrenheit 911, Home on the Range, and Shrek 2. Over the past year the stats are even more impressive—the top ten box office attractions in the City of Light lead with the Nemo's World, Shrek 2, Pirates of the Caribbean, Spider man 2, and Terminator 3. *Hurray for Hollywood?* This was not short lived either; by 2009 Clint Eastwood was being lauded for his less than politically correct but blockbuster film *Gran Torino*. Eastwood's films have been wildly successful in France ranging from *Million Dollar Baby, Pale Rider* and the *Good, the Bad and the Ugly* back in 1968. TV viewers remain enthralled by the American series "24" and House.[30]

Pop music is no exception either...unless of course we concede that *French Rap* Music is uniquely French, that Country/Western music sung in Czech is uniquely Bohemian, or that just about every permutation of American pop music is played or copied in Germany or Spain for that matter . Though the French have legislated the "cultural exception" whereby fiction and films are state subsidized by the state and moreover the state imposes a minimum quota of French language radio programs (something Canada's *Quebecois* have long excelled at), such a linguistic Maginot Line seems near fruitless in today's media/movie marketplace. This is not unique to France. The share of American films in France averages about half; in Italy it is 60 percent, and 77 percent in Germany. Equally, the share of domestically produced movies in France hold holds at 42 percent but in the other countries just under 20 percent.[31]

The enormous cultural power of America is often not appreciated argues Dr. Josef Joffe of *Die Zeit*, "There's McDonald's but also Microsoft, there's Hollywood and Harvard."[32]

Beyond the appeal of American films and popular culture, there is another reason which goes far deeper than entertainment; the growing use of the English language for business and commerce throughout the EU and most especially in the *New Europe* countries. Though Russian had been the dominant *lingua franca* from the Baltics through Bulgaria, these former East Bloc states now have eagerly adopted English as their second language, especially for commerce.. The issues are manifold whether in the Baltic states or Brussels, for communication between an Estonian, Czech and Hungarian, the native tongue's use is extremely limited, but the former common tongue would have been and still is to a point Russian. Now it's clearly emerging as English. Despite valiant efforts by Paris to bring the French language to the new EU states, studying English is the overwhelming choice among high school students in new EU members such as Estonia, the Czech Republic, Poland and Slovenia. It's that way in Hungary too, but there German plays a strong second. Interestingly this has equally translated into the wider use of English among EU members in their governmental capacity in Brussels as well.

It's precisely in this context that linguistics form yet another natural bridge in spanning the trans-Atlantic divide. The English language as a tool of commerce, a medium of entertainment, and even a *lingua franca* of government is an established fact. And what about overseas travel-where do Europeans go? To the USA with Florida, New York and California being prime destinations. During 2007, despite the lingering trans-Atlantic *angst* due to the Iraq war, 8.7 million Western Europeans visited New York City for example, with British, (1.2 million), German (547,000), and French (423,000) comprising the top three European visitor groups.[33]

Conversely Western European music, drama and opera still form the backbone of classical arts in America. The continued cultural creativity of the EU countries, despite their eclipse in the realm of popular mass culture, should not be underestimated any more than many Europeans tend to underestimate the rich classical roots in America which transcend the New York and Boston Philharmonic and which extend to scores of serious symphony orchestras in cities from Sarasota, to Santa Fe and San Francisco. While European educational mores no longer exclusively form the core curriculum of American education, its roots remain Greco/ Roman. Still one must not underestimate the impact of the current Social Studies curriculums on the secondary and University level. Since the 1970's the traditional focus on European History and Cultures has significantly shifted towards courses dealing with non-Western studies. While this educational *globalization* has allowed for a welcome and important awareness of non-Western cultures, it has undeniably lessened the unique importance of European civilization in America and by design downplayed its context in the continuity of close Trans-Atlantic ties.

Significantly the number of Western European students in American universities has grown from 32,500 in academic year 1985–86, to 53,000 in 2000–2001. By 2008 the number of French students stood at 7,050 or one percent of foreign students. German students studying in the USA numbered 7,000 in 1990 and 8,900 in 2008 or just over one percent. By 2008, the number of Europeans studying in the USA had fallen to three places among the top twenty, the largest enrollment numbers coming from India and China. Indeed the trans-Atlantic divide and visa problems, have negatively affected higher education. At the same time record numbers of Americans are studying abroad with 242,000 students dispersed in nine European countries among the top twenty study destinations. By 2008 international students were at an all time high with 624,000 registered in the USA during the 2007/2008 academic year.[34]

Another notable change in the trans-Atlantic equation deals with declining numbers of Americans studying French and German in Universities. While the late 1960's to mid-1970's showed a surge in BA, MA and PhD's granted in the French language (7,624 BA, 1,409 MA and 181 PhD's in 1969–70), by 2000–2001 the numbers had dropped to 2,371 BA, 376 MA and 115 PhD's in French. In the German language the numbers reflect a similar decline going from the 1969–1970 period of 2,652 BA, 669 MA, and 118 PhD's granted in German. By 2000–2001 the degrees granted had fallen to 1,143 BA, 242 MA, and 73 PhD's.[35]

In fact foreign language study in American institutions of higher learning has an enrollment rate of 8.6 per 100 students; *that is about half of the 1965 rate*. While there has been marginal growth in French and German over the past decade, in 2006 some 206,000 students were enrolled in French and 94,000 in German.[36]

Interestingly on the other side of the scale, an OECD report shows that percentages of working age populations without secondary education while only 12 percent in the U.S. and 15 percent in Japan, reach over 30 percent in the U.K., France and Ireland, and exceed 50 percent in Italy and Spain. Only Germany and Sweden have numbers near the U.S. average.[37]

A landmark *Transatlantic Trends Poll 2006* taken by the US German Marshall Fund illustrates the complexity of the issues:

European support for the strong Americans leadership in the world has declined significantly over the past two years, as had the approval of President George Bush's international policies.

- Although U.S. and European policymakers report that official relations have improved in the past year, most observers agree that the image of the United States and President Bush among the European publics has not improved since their strong opposition to the Iraq war in 2003.
- Most Americans want to maintain a close partnership with Europe and support a stronger European partner to help manage global challenges.

However an earlier survey *Transatlantic Trends Poll 2005* stated, "After a first term marked by a crisis in transatlantic relations around the war in Iraq, the re-election of George W. Bush in 2004 seemed likely to some observers to prolong the estrangement between the United States and Europe. Strikingly, President Bush launched his second term with an ambitious diplomatic effort to improve relations with Europe, setting a new tone of cooperation and identifying democracy promotion as the centerpiece of his foreign policy…Bush traveled to Europe three times in the first six months of his second term. He became the first American President to officially visit the European Union in Brussels declaring, "The alliance of Europe and North America is the main pillar of our security."[38]

Yet some key *Transatlantic Trends Poll* 2008 findings include…

- Americans desire closer partnership with the EU while Europeans support a more independent approach.
- Europeans feeling towards the U.S. have remained cool. When asked how desirable it is for the U.S. to assert strong leadership in world affairs, Euro wide feeling reversed since 2002 from 64% positive to 37% in 2006, and 36% in 2008. Calls for Partnership between the U.S. and EU increased from 27 % in 2006 to 31% ; only three countries view such partnership with significant percentages, Romania, Poland and Italy. Support for this rests at just over a quarter in the Netherlands, Germany, Slovakia and the United Kingdom.
- Not surprisingly positive views of President Bush fell from 38% in 2002 to 17% in 2007 and 19% in 2008. Seen another way Bush faced a 75% disapproval in 2008.[39]
- Turkey is cooling to the U.S. and EU and warming towards Islamic Iran. Only eight percent of Turkish respondents viewed the U.S. "leadership" in world affairs as desirable. Warmth towards the USA dropped from 20 degrees in 2006 to 14 in 2008; feelings towards the EU fell from 45 degrees to 33 on a hundred point thermometer.[40]
- When asked how they felt transatlantic relations would be affected by the 2008 U.S. Presidential election regardless of who is elected, 47% of Europeans felt that relations will improve if Obama is elected, compared with 29% who felt relations will remain the same, and 5% who felt relations will get worse.[41]

Significantly disapproval of Bush's international policies hit 85% in France, 83% in Germany, 62% in the UK and 81% in Spain. Only in Poland was there a *relatively low* disapproval of 36%.[42]

Despite such clear links of kith, kin and common values, as noted earlier "While Americans and Europeans agree broadly on the threats they face, there is no transatlantic consensus on using force without multilateral approval," the poll stressed adding, "Unlike Americans, many Europeans are unwilling to act without an international mandate to defend vital interests, suggesting that the debate over the legitimacy of using military force was not peculiar to the Iraq war but is an enduring feature of transatlantic relations."[43] This point remains vital.

Yet, there's another level here touching on what Polish trade unionist Bronislaw Geremek alluded to "We have Europe, Now we need Europeans." In an important address "The Politics of European Values," presented in The Hague, Dutch Prime Minister Jan Peter Balkenende described a deep malaise among the European populations due to "indifference and skepticism." "Europe is a project with great historical significance for all of us," he stated, "but in the hearts and minds of many people the project has no resonance. And we have failed to recognize this for too long." He added, "The generation which lived through the Second World War is disappearing. Post-war generations see Europe's great achievements –liberty, peace and prosperity—as a given." Prime Minister Balkenende implored, "The horrors of the Second World War, the chilling winds of the Cold War and the crushing weight of the Iron Curtain are little more than fading memories, Ideals that once commanded great loyalty are now taken for granted...For many people, the idea of Europe as a heritage and a mission does not mean much anymore. But without the ideals, Europe's very foundations will begin to erode. Without ideals, the basis of continued European cooperation will crumble."[44]

Tragically the murder of filmmaker Theo Van Gogh by Islamic militants, caused the tolerant Dutch to reappraise their once lenient immigration policies. The Netherlands has been a swamped by Muslim immigration and has become a haven for many radicals. Van Gogh's killing galvanized a wide spectrum of political opinion which had allowed an almost laughable tolerance to fundamentalists.

Questioned whether "With regard to religious fundamentalism, was the growth in France of secularism, not a protective reaction to this phenomenon?" Vatican Cardinal Josef Ratzinger opined in a celebrated *Le Figaro* interview, "According to me for one part the rise of fundamentalism is provoked by a surge of secularism. It concerns the rejection of a world which refuses God and the sacred, which feels itself totally autonomous, and reconstructs man according to its own themes and thoughts. This loss of the sense of the sacred and respect for the other, provokes a reaction of self-defense in the bosom of the Arab and Islamic world. A deep distain expresses itself facing the loss of the sense of the supernatural which is perceived as the decadence of man." He added poignantly, "This absolutist secularism is not the response to the horrible challenge of fundamentalism. Only a reasoned religious sense in strict union with reason can moderate these radical- isms and permit the finding a balance in the dialogue of the cultures."[45]

Cardinal Ratzinger (before his elevation to Pope) told the Italian daily *La Repubblica*, "We have moved from a Christian culture to aggressive and sometimes intolerant secularism...A society from which God is completely absent self-destructs. We saw that in the major totalitarian regimes of the last century."

Historian Paul Johnson opines that there is another in the EU's malaise, "Europe has turned its back not only on the U.S. and the future of capitalism, but also on its own historic past. Europe was essentially a creation of the marriage between Greco-Roman culture and Christianity. Brussels has in effect, repudiated both." He adds "There was no mention of Europe's Christian origins in the ill-fated Constitution."[46]

Cardinal Miloslav Vlk, the head of the Czech Roman Catholic Church, stresses that behind the failure to adopt the euro-treaty is the absence of what Europe feels natural about—Christian values. Demographically Europe is dying out, Cardinal Vlk feels Europe will become markedly more Muslim in the 21st century because of the low fertility of Europeans the majority of whom are non-believers. "Muslims in Europe have much more children than Christian families. That is why demographers have been trying to come up with a time when Europe will become Muslim," the Cardinal claimed. While European Muslims are living their religion, the Europeans are "pagans, as they do not respect their religion". Europe needs spiritual rehabilitation. "If we do not restore Europe in terms of Christian values, we will surely die out," Cardinal Vlk said.[47]

Islam's growth in Europe is often underestimated; Chris Patten former EU Commissioner for External Relations advises that in the United Kingdom "More Muslims go to Mosque on Friday than Church of England members go to Church on Sunday."[48]

According to some observers, church attendance in Britain has declined so fast that the number of regular church goers will be fewer than those attending mosques within a generation, states Religious Trends, a statistical analysis of religion in the UK. "In contrast, the number of actively religious Muslims will have increased from about one million today to 1.96 million in 2035." Though traditional Christian denominations in Britain are in decline, Islam and Hinduism are thriving.

Islam is the largest religion in Amsterdam; twelve percent of people identify with the faith more than with Catholicism or the Protestant denominations combined! In a recent survey by the city council, only 34 percent of citizens felt connected to any religion of which Islam at 12 percent, and Catholicism at 10 percent formed the largest block. The traditional Dutch Reformed and Protestant churches registered fewer than ten percent. At issue is not that the Muslim population is so large by but the traditional Christian churches have became often spirituality stagnant in hyper-secular humanistic societies such as Britain and Holland. Dutch Prime Minister Peter Balkenende remarked before the UN, "The Netherlands wants to join forces with all those who want to promote tolerance and dialogue between civilizations. But we must not allow this dialogue to put the universal validity of our common values in question."[49]

The USA and Western Europe are primarily Judeo/Christian cultures. Both sides equally share a strong minority of agnostics. Still when asking the citizens of five European Union states (France, Germany, Italy, Hungary Finland), "In your opinion what best way describes the cultural patrimony for the EU?" 67 % of French, 76% of Germans, 81%of Italians, 78% of Finns and only 8 % of Hungarians cited Churches and Religious buildings. Equally high numbers related to the patrimony being embodied in the Museums and Palaces and Chateaux. With the exception of Hungary which is still scarred by the lingering residue of communist rule, the Europeans surveyed related to the classic religious and historic symbols of the "Old Europe."[50]

Though many observers glibly say that the Catholic Church is rapidly losing adherents in Europe, the visit by Pope Benedict XVI to France proved a most curious counterpoint. During a visit to Paris, Benedict XVI celebrated mass for 250,000 and in the words of *Le Figaro*, "A Friend of France, Seduces Paris." Another mass at Notre Dame cathedral saw 50,000 youth celebrate the Pontiff's visit. Yet even in secular France, President Sarkozy discussed the role of religion in society. "Positive secularism is an invitation to dialogue, to tolerance and to respect. It is legitimate to speak with religions, it would be a folly to deprive ourselves of that by a fault in our thought. That is why I call for positive secularism...I have often had the occasion to speak of the Christian roots of France, that does not stop us from doing everything so that our Muslim compatriots can live their religion with all the others."[51]

"The role of religion in public life is markedly different on both sides of the Atlantic," remarked Karsten Voigt, Coordinator for German American Co-operation, adding, "In most European countries, ties with Christian churches and creeds they profess, as well as church attendance have grown weak. Less than 15 percent of Germans, go to church every week. The United States, in contrast, is a country of believers and churchgoers. Four out of ten Americans say that they go to a church service every week."[52]

During an extraordinary Papal visit to the USA, Pope Benedict XVI stated at a White House ceremony, "From the dawn of the Republic, America's quest for freedom has been guided by the conviction that the principles governing political and social life are intimately linked to a moral order based on the dominion of God the Creator. The framers of this nation's founding documents drew upon this conviction when they proclaimed the 'self-evident truth' that all men are created equal and endowed with inalienable rights grounded in the laws of nature and of nature's God."[53]

Chapter Eight

THE ROAD AHEAD—THE PAST AS PROLOGUE?

Is Europe's close political relationship with the USA really over? Hardly, but the epic political events in Europe itself—from 1989 to the creation of the enlarged EU supra state in 2004, have fundamentally changed and redefined the context and structures of those ties. This presents a logical political evolution, not a threat, and certainly an opportunity.

The EU's Javier Solana states the case well. Speaking before the Konrad Adenauer Foundation, he advised; "When it comes to forging partnerships with key states, no task is more urgent than the need to revive the spirit of the Transatlantic cooperation. We must talk less of inevitable clashes in worldviews and put more emphasis on practical cooperation. We should re-learn the earlier habit of mutual compromise." He added, "We want the US/European relationship to become a more equal partnership."[54]

The classic U.S./European cooperation during the Cold War, something not quite as close as many memories may recall—has passed; there is a new historic phase—a united, democratic and prosperous Europe. This Europe *whole and free* is not a strategic antagonist as much as a commercial rival and often a moral Pharisee. And both Europe and America have more to gain by cooperation than by confrontation. Though the 2004 Presidential election campaign did not make relations with Europe a central issue, there's little doubt that American perceptions of the "Old Europe" and the "New Europe" were just below the political radar. After all the constant drumbeat of Iraq policy, and coalition support, had been a consistent theme of both President Bush and his Democratic challenger Senator John Kerry. Though the British played a pivotal role in Iraq, equally Poland, Italy, Denmark and the Netherlands all formed part of the military coalition.

The Media has often magnified transatlantic troubles and underplayed the quiet successes in trade, tourism and culture. With its undulating 24 hour news cycle and a tendency to hype stories, it has highlighted disputes and diplomatic rifts but often has missed the bigger story. On both sides of the Atlantic, the electronic media especially, has encouraged a not so subtle jingoism, which has needlessly widened the gap among Western Europeans and Washington by playing up the *political bogeyman* of the Bush Administration. Indeed U.S. foreign policy classically exhibits continuity amid change and shall naturally adapt to the emerging realities in *Euroland* much as it adapted to rebuilding post-war Europe, defending a divided West/East Europe, defining a united Europe, and now rediscovering this *New Europe* of the 27. For Washington this presents a challenge to be certain. But for the Europeans from Lisbon to London and Paris to Prague, keeping close links with the USA remains an absolute necessity.

Clearly while the Iraq war accelerated a deep political rift between prosperous and self-satisfied *Euroland* and the Bush Administration, the social, commercial and indeed wider political values that bind America and Europe remain stronger. The Bush visit to Europe in 2005, early in his second term, was a politically well timed but equally necessary gesture couched in the parameters of the traditional Atlantic Alliance. Diplomacy can be defined as many things, but basically it's a process which comes down to accentuating the positive, attaining the possible, while often deferring the probable. In other words states will stress what unites them rather than what divides them. Based on that assessment George W. Bush's visit to Europe was a political success, precisely because the U.S. team tirelessly sought common ground not confrontation with our European allies. Going beyond the counterproductive Trans-Atlantic blame game raging since 2002, the visit aimed at re-affirming the President's second term as well as the successful free elections in Iraq and Afghanistan. As Bush told a Brussels audience, "The Alliance of Europe and North America is the main pillar of our security. Our robust trade is one of the engines of the world's economy." He added significantly "Our strong friendship is essential to peace and prosperity across the globe. No temporary debate, no passing disagreement of governments, no power on earth will ever divide us." If one foolishly views the entire U.S./European relationship thorough the prism of Iraq, the U.S. had serious challenges which given the current governments in Paris, Berlin, Brussels would *not* change appreciably. But mortgaging the entire post-WWII political partnership on a single policy in Iraq is simply shortsighted. When George Bush met with French President Jacques Chirac, clearly the most articulate and obstinate opponent to the Iraq operation, the discussion centered on the ongoing Franco/American political cooperation on getting Syrian occupation troops out of Lebanon. This is a shared French and American political objective and thus naturally brought common ground to discussions. In other words discuss Beirut, not Baghdad.

Just prior to the U.S. Presidential election, *Le Figaro* reported ecstatically "The Planet Votes for Kerry." The story reflected a *global poll* in which citizens in Germany backed Kerry 74% to 10% for Bush, the French voted 64% for Kerry versus 5% for Bush and Italians 58% for Kerry versus 14% for the President.[55]

Such hostility towards the American President defined the EU's political landscape in 2004. In the lead-up to the 2008 elections Europeans equally favored Democratic contender Barack Obama. *Der Spiegel* magazine in an article "Obamamania Infects Germany," swooned, "Berlin political circles—both liberal and conservative—are fawning over US presidential candidate Barack Obama. Many in Germany see him as a cross between John F. Kennedy and Martin Luther King, Jr., but expectations may be exaggerated."[56]

Viewing the U.S. 2008 election, another article stressed, "Germans have long had an ambivalent relationship with their powerful friends across the Atlantic and now seem eager to discard their anti-Americanism. But there is good reason to suggest that there is a clear divide between German hopes and reality...Obama, on the other hand, is as fascinating to German politicians as a mirage. He seems promising from afar, and yet no one knows what he actually stands for. In fact, hardly anyone knows him at all."[57]

Almost giddy paeans to the Democratic candidate appeared in France too with *Le Monde* devoting an effusive supplement "Barack Obama; An American Destiny." No wonder that in an *Le Figaro* poll for, 85% of the French saw Obama's election as positive for the U.S. image in the world and 77% viewed his election as positive for Franco/ American relations. Europeans voted overwhelmingly for Obama in such surveys.[58]

As the EU's articulate President Jose Manuel Barroso once stated, "One thing the Europeans have to understand is that it is not Europe that elects the President of the United States, it's the Americans. Sometimes the Americans have to understand that it is not the Americans that elect Europe's leaders, that is the Europeans."[59]

The Europeans did not have to like Bush but they had no realistic choice but to work with him. And for the U.S. the political obverse, with Chirac and Schroeder, was equally true. George Bush's meeting with Chancellor Gerhard Schroeder in the historic Rhineland city of Mainz allowed for a needed rapprochement. Not that Schroeder (whose Socialists were reeling from a series of self-inflicted electoral setbacks) was going to change course on Iraq, but that Germany and the USA supported common goals in Afghanistan, Iran and Tsunami Relief. Bush stated; "Europe is America's closest ally....And in order for Europe to be a strong, viable partner, Germany must be strong and viable. And in order for us to have good relations with Europe, we must have good relations with Germany." Viewing the Bush visit to Europe, Germany's conservative *Die Welt* newspaper stated rather stoically "The encounters between Europe and America over the past few days are reminiscent of a pair of lovers who are now separated. They know that the affair is over, but shouldn't they try it one more time for the sake of the children?" The tabloid *Bild* editorialized in blunt but needed perspective, "Without the Yanks, Berlin would be Khrushchev-grad. Without the Yanks, we would still have the Berlin Wall and barbed wire. Without the Yanks, the Nazis would still be around.. You Americans are sometimes crazy guys, but you're also damned good friends."

Even the left-leaning German magazine *Der Spiegel* curiously compared the unpopularity of the USA during the Bush Presidency with the era a more generation ago; when President Ronald Reagan's visit to Berlin in 1987. "The

Germany Reagan was traveling in, much like today's Germany, was very skeptical of the American president and his foreign policy. When Reagan stood before the Brandenburg Gate—and the Berlin Wall—and demanded that Gorbachev 'tear down this Wall,' he was lampooned the next day on the editorial pages. He is a dreamer, wrote commentators. *Realpolitik* looks different." Still *Der Spiegel* adds, "But history has shown that it wasn't Reagan who was the dreamer as he voiced his demand. Rather, it was German politicians who were lacking in imagination—a group who in 1987 couldn't imagine that there might be an alternative to a divided Germany." The article concedes "Germany loves to criticize U.S. President George W. Bush, just like Germany loved to criticize former President Ronald Reagan. But Reagan, when he demanded that Gorbachev remove the Berlin Wall, turned out to be right. Could history repeat itself?"[60] *Der Spiegel* seems haunted by this possibility.

Naturally this dovetails with the entrenched anti-Americanism of many Germans. Mathias Dopfner, Chairman of Germany's influential Springer publishing stated that "there has always been a left wing, anti-capitalist and a right wing nationalist, culturally conservative" anti-Americanism. Now however a, "A new anti Americanism has been added to the younger generation; the idea being to *live* American, but *talk* anti-American. Surveys show that some 50% of the population is in the grip of this phenomenon. Nine out ten dislike Mr. Bush. Vladimir Putin is more trusted in this country than the American President." he added, " and 70% are convinced that they no longer owe the Americans a debt for their help in reunification." In a wider context Dopfner laments, "The German-American relationship has sustained lasting damage, and Europe's role is pitiful when it comes to combating international terrorism, pacifying the Middle East, and defending the free West against Islamic fundamentalism."[61]

Equally gloomy was former German Foreign Minister Joshka Fischer who said that ending Serbian aggression in Kosovo remains for him a model of transatlantic political and military cooperation, an ideal to strive fore in "redefining the transatlantic relationship." In an address sponsored by the German Historical Institute, Fisher thought the Iraq war was a "very bad idea" from the start. While making it clear that the transatlantic closeness of the Cold War period cannot be recaptured, and that a new transnational period had dawned, he felt that the two sides of the Atlantic were bound together by trade and finance and by many shared values.[62]

Moreover German Foreign Minister Frank-Walter Steinmeier, speaking at Harvard University affirmed, "For the past 60 years, the transatlantic relationship has been the world's transformative partnership. America's relationship with Europe—more than with any other part of the world—enables both of us to achieve goals that neither of us could achieve alone. This is what makes the transatlantic relationship unique: When we agree we are at the core of any effective global coalition; when we disagree no global coalition is likely to be effective." As if diplomacy was not exciting enough, Steinmeier lather threw out the first pitch at a baseball game between the rival Boston Red Sox and the New York Yankees at Fenway Park. In separate remarks in Washington D.C. with his American counterpart Condoleezza Rice he stressed, "The USA is our most important ally."[63]

This rhetorical question, or should one say challenge, confronts many Europeans who are not willing to think outside the traditional confines of rigid *status quo* politics, and whose self-satisfied political classes are philosophically loathe to accept the enduring optimism of the Americans. While George W. Bush has intoned the virtues of freedom like the Greek chorus, many of the comfortable EU city-states choose instead to celebrate the status quo. Though few Europeans will doubt the philosophical and often military dangers from dictatorships, be they in the Middle East or East Asia, Americans will assume a far more pro-active role in practically *doing something* about them. To the Europeans, Burma's left-wing military regime is viewed as politically repulsive, though Castro's communist dictatorship is seen as somewhat noble through its instinctive tweaking of Uncle Sam's nose, never mind a place for cheap holidays and exquisite cigars. Still at the end of the day neither Burma nor Cuba are vital to EU interests.

Naturally the trans-Atlantic relationship will continue to be tested and not necessarily within the traditional realm of NATO but of what are described as *out of area* challenges. Beyond the War on Terror states must confront the nuclear proliferation plans of Islamic Iran. Though both the EU and the USA agree that Iran should not possess atomic weapons, achieving that result offers many options. Though the Europeans will pursue a path of dialogue at practically any price, the USA will take a far more pro-active approach should diplomacy reach an impasse. Responding diplomatically to Teheran's Atomic Ayatollahs can likely divide, or possibly reunite, Europe and America. While Washington has largely been in close diplomatic accord with Britain/ France/Germany conserning policy towards Iran's nuclear proliferation, the fact remains that the Islamic Republic of Iran remains a primary trading partner with Germany, France and Italy.

Though Europe and America have basked in moments of political enthusiasm concerning working together to pressure Syria over its military occupation of Lebanon, (UN resolution #1559) or a mutual aversion to the Islamic fundamentalist Taliban regime in Afghanistan, this may prove the exception. In July 2006 Lebanon unexpectedly exploded in violence. The renewed crisis however provided another case of Franco/ American accord.

Sustained Hizbollah terrorist rocket attacks on Israel provoked a massive Israeli counter-attack, the ensuing crisis in Lebanon caused nearly a million internally displaced civilians. The U.S. and France worked for a Security Council resolution to stop the fighting. After weeks of tense negotiations and a number of false dawns in presenting a cease-fire resolution to the UN Security Council, Washington and Paris passed a resolution. Following a month of conflict, Resolution #1701 brought about a fragile cease-fire between Israel and Hizbollah, provided for Israeli troop pullouts, and importantly agreed to reinforce the size of the long-standing UN peacekeeping presence in southern Lebanon to prevent renewed violence.[64]

Closer Franco/American amity was highlighted by Nicolas Sarkozy's visit to Baghdad, the first such trip by a French President since the overthrow of Saddam. "We say to French companies that the time has come to return to Iraq," Sarkozy said at a joint press conference with the Iraqi Premier. "I came to show France's willingness to take part in the economic development of Iraq, in the rehabilitation of its infrastructure. Our collaboration has no limits." A week later German Foreign Minister Frank-Walter Steinmeier arrived with a similar message in a trip which also saw the opening of a new Consulate and Commercial office was the first visit by a German official to Iraq since 1987. One recalls substantial French and German commercial ties to pre-war Iraq.[65]

The French initiative proved a political watershed after the sharp disputes between George W. Bush and Jacques Chirac; the German gesture was no less important given the uneasy relationship between the American Administration and Gerhard Schroeder.

For example, the geopolitical role played by the emergence of a stronger China is viewed quite differently on each side of the Atlantic. Many EU countries, most arguably the French, have courted a strong People's Republic of China as a political and strategic counter-weight to the USA's superpower status. Calling for a multi-polar world, Jacques Chirac has long stressed the need to counter the America *hyperpower* through building a multipolar world order. During a state visit to Peking in 2004, while basking in the afterglow of his strident opposition to the Iraq war, Chirac declared that France and China shared visions of *multipolar world.*[66]

Thus while the PRC's growing economic and military power can been viewed as a theoretical counter-balance, practically speaking a potentially aggressive PRC can uniquely threaten the *status quo* in East Asia most especially towards democratic Taiwan, South East Asia and the South China Sea. And without question this directly impinges on American and Japanese interests. As Josef Joffe advised, "The Franco-German axis will continue to oppose the American behemoth, and it will seek to recruit other players such as China and Russia into the neo-containment game. These are the ways of international politics when power is so grievously unbalanced in favor of a single giant."[67]

Such sentiments clearly reflect part of the problem on both sides of the Atlantic but should not be allowed to become self-fulfilling political prophesy. Rather than building up or strengthening autocracies to achieve a presumed *balance of power*, the European Union's democracies should reinforce their friendship with the U.S. and states of similar values such as Australia, Canada and Japan.

Historian Paul Johnson stressed, "The rise of anti-Americanism, a form of irrationalism deliberately whipped up by Messer's Schroeder and Chirac, who believe it wins votes, is particularly tragic. For the early stages of the EU had their roots in admiration of the American way of doing things and gratitude for the manner in which the U.S. had saved Europe first from Nazism, then from the Soviet Empire, by the Marshall Plan in 1947 and the creation of NATO in 1949." Johnson adds, "Europe's founding fathers; Monnet himself, Robert Schuman in France, Alcide de Gasperi in Italy and Konrad Adenauer in Germany, were all fervently pro-American and anxious to make it possible for European populations to enjoy U.S.-style living standards. Adenauer in particular assisted by his brilliant economic minister Ludwig Erhardt, rebuilt Germany's industry and services, using the freest possible model. This was the origin of Germany's "economic miracle," in which U.S. ideas played a determining part."[68]

Addressing the prestigious American Council on Germany, Ambassador Nicholas Burns, stated unambiguously, "though our geopolitical focus may have shifted, our partnership with Europe remains at the center of U.S. diplomacy. Our diplomatic challenges and priorities are not coincidently also, Europe's. So are our core values. The overlap in both is nearly perfect....The Cold War may have ended, but our alliance, with Germany continues to be a cornerstone of our engagement with the world."[69]

Significantly the election of pro-American figures in Germany, France and Italy, has changed Europe's political geography. The balance has tilted to Washington's advantage. In his first foreign policy address, British Prime Minister Gordon Brown described the Anglo/ American relationship as Britain's "most important bilateral relationship." And in response to the coolness in relations between Gordon Brown and George Bush, the Prime Minister stated, "I have no truck with anti-Americanism in Britain or elsewhere in Europe and I believe that our ties with America, founded in the values we share, constitute our most important relationship." Brown added, "it was good for Britain, for Europe and for the wider world" that Nicolas Sarkozy, French president, Angela Merkel, German Chancellor, were building stronger relationships with the U.S.[70]

During his visit to Europe to attend the NATO Summit, President Obama told a Strasbourg audience that sixty years ago, "We ensured our shared security when 12 of our nations signed a treaty in Washington that spelled out a single agreement; an attack on one was an attack on all. Without firing a single shot this alliance would prevent the Iron Curtain from descending on the free nations of Western Europe. It would lead eventually to the crumbling of a wall in Berlin and to the end of the communist threat. Two decades later, and with 28 member nations that stretched from the Baltic to the Mediterranean, NATO remains the strongest alliance the world has ever known."

Obama conceded, "In recent years we have allowed our alliance to drift. I know that there have been honest disagreement over policy, but we know there is something more that has crept into our relationship. In America, there a failure to appreciate Europe's leading role in the world. Instead of celebrating your dynamic union and seeking to partner with you to meet common challenges, there have been times when America has shown arrogance and has been dismissive, even derisive. But in Europe, there is an anti-Americanism that is at once casual but can also be insidious. Instead of recognizing the good that America so often does in the world, there have been times where Europeans choose to blame America for much of what's bad. On both sides of the Atlantic, these attitudes have become all too common. ….they threaten to widen the divide across the Atlantic and leave us both more isolated."[71]

Chris Patten put the matter succinctly, "We should be partners not rivals of the U.S."

NOTES

1. Andrew Moravcsik, *Foreign Policy*, May/June 2005, p. 72.
2. "Global MBA 2009 Rankings" *Financial Times*, 26 January 2009, p. 13.
3. U.S. Census.org 2007, 2008 Foreign Country Trade Statistics.
4. Daniel Hamilton and Joseph P. Quinlan, "The Transatlantic Economy 2008/ Executive Summary," Washington D.C.: Center for Transatlantic Relations, School of Advanced International Studies (SAIS) Johns Hopkins University, 2008.
5. Dan Roberts and Gary Silverman, "U.S. Policy Dents Brands' Reputation in Europe as Consumers Snub Products," *Financial Times* 23 November 2004, p.1.
6. "Global Brands," *Financial Times*, 29 April 2009, Special Report, pp. 1–3.
7. *Invest-in-France.org* November 2007. Daniel Hamilton and Joseph P. Quinlan, "France and Globalization," Washington D.C.: Center for Transatlantic Relations, School of Advanced International Studies (SAIS) Johns Hopkins University, 2008.
8. William Drozdiak, "4 Myths About America Bashing in Europe," *Washington Post* 13 May 2007, p. B3.

9. NewFrance.com 2005, Hamilton and Quinlan, "The Transatlantic Economy 2009," p. vi.
10. Hamilton and Quinlan, "The Transatlantic Economy 2008," Executive Summary.
11. World Investment Report 2008, pp. 72–73.
12. John Willman, "U.S. Leads Way as Global R&D Spending Rises 10%," *Financial Times* 12 November 2007, p. 2.
13. Tobias Buck, "EU Economy is 20 Years Behind, U.S., Says Study," *Financial Times* 6 March 2007, p. 4.
14. World Economic Forum/Geneva Weforum.org 28 March 2006.
15. "Global Innovation Index 2009," Insead.edu 21 January 2009.
16. Clive Cookson, "Universities Drive Biotech Advancement," *Financial Times* 7 May 2007, p. 3.
17. "The Global Competitiveness Report 2008–2009," World Economic Forum/Geneva 2008.
18. United Nations E-Governance Survey 2008; From E governance to Connected Governance. United Nations: New York, 2008, pp. 10, 20.
19. Vaclav Klaus, "Speech of the Czech Republic President to the European Parliament," Brussels, 19 February 2009, pp. 3–4.
20. Kissinger, Does America Need a Foreign Policy?, p. 41, 48.
21. NATO Review Autumn 2001, p. 34.
22. NATO Review Autumn 2001 and Summer 2004.
23. Troop cuts were announced in August 2004; by 2009 only 50,000 remain in Germany.
24. Transatlantic Trends Poll 2006, (Washington DC: German Marshall Fund of the United States, 2006), p. 6.
25. French Mission to the UN/23 September 2004, pp. 9–10.
26. Christophe Cornevin and Jean-Marc Leclerc, "DCRI: le Nouveau Visage du Renseignement," *Le Figaro* 30 June 2008, pp. 1–2.
27. Paul Statham, "Resilient Islam—Muslim Controversary in Europe." *Harvard International Review* Vol. 26 (3) Fall 2004, p. 58.
28. Ian Buruma, "Homeland Insecurity," *Financial Times* 16/17 July 2005, p. W1.
29. Laqueur, The Last Days of Europe, pp. 38–41.
30. Paris Scope, 11 August 2004, pp. 92–93. Olivier Delcroix, "Eastwood, la Longue Marche d'un heros, *Le Figaro* 18–19 April 2009, p. 29.
31. Human Development Report/United Nations Development Programme 2004, p. 87.
32. Josef Joffe, Lecture Council on Foreign Relations 16 June 2006.
33. Nycgo.com/statistics, 2009.
34. National Center for Education Statistics, "International Comparisons of Education, 2002," p. 483 and "Open Doors 2008" Institute of International Education/online, New York, 2008.
35. United States Department of Education, "National Center for Education Statistics/Degree-Granting Post Secondary Degrees, 2002, p. 339.

36. "New MLA Survey Shows Significant Increases in Foreign Language Study at U.S. Colleges and Universities," Modern Language Association Survey November 2007, pp. 1–3.
37. "Number in the News; Education," *Financial Times* 18 January 2006, p. 16.
38. Transatlantic Trends 2005, (Washington DC: German Marshall Fund of the United States, 2005), pp. 3–5.
39. Transatlantic Trends 2008, (Washington DC: German Marshall Fund of the United States, 2007), pp. 6–7.
40. Ibid., pp. 19–20.
41. Ibid., p. 8.
42. Transatlantic Trends 2005, p. 6.
43. Transatlantic Trends 2004, (Washington DC: German Marshall Fund of the United States, 2004), p. 29.
44. Jan Peter Balkenende, Address to the Conference The Politics of European Values, The Hague/Netherlands, 7 September 2004, pp. 3–4.
45. Sophie de Ravinel, Cardinal Josef Ratzinger Interview, *Le Figaro Magazine*, 13 August 2004. p. 34.
46. Paul Johnson, *Wall Street Journal* 17 June 2005, p. A14.
47. Simona Holecova, "EU is Headed for Muslim Future, Says Czech Cardinal," *Aktualne.cz* , 6 January 2009.
48. Chris Patton Remarks at Council on Foreign Relations, 5 February 2006.
49. Simon Kuper, "Amsterdam's Soft Approach to Jihadists," *Financial Times* 11 September 2007, p. 8 and Netherlands Mission to the UN/Statement by Dr. Jan Peter Balkenende, Prime Minister 27 September 2007, p. 2.
50. Emmanuel de Roux, "L'Europe sonde son Patrimoine," *Le Monde* 20 March 2007, p. 29.
51. Jean-Marie Guenois, "Benoit XVI, L'Ami de la France," *Le Figaro* 13–14 Septembre 2008, pp. 9–10.
52. Karsten Voigt, Atlantic Community, 31 August 2007.
53. His Holiness Pope Benedict XVI Visit to the U.S. Washington/Welcome Ceremony, *L'Osservatore Romano*/weekly 23 April 2008, p. 2.
54. Javier Solana, "Shaping an Effective EU Foreign Policy," Address before Konrad Adenauer Foundation 24 January 2005, p. 4.
55. "The Planet Votes for Kerry," *Le Figaro* online 10 September 2004.
56. Ralf Beste, "Obamamania Infects Germany," *Der Spiegel.* Online 26 May 2008.
57. Ralf Beste and Konstanin von Hammerstein, "Will Berlin's Love fest with Obama be Shortlived?" *Der Spiegel.* Online 9 June 2008.
58. "Barack Obama; Un Destin Americain," Le Monde/Supplement 29/30 June 2008 and Le Politoscope/American Presidential Election 5 November 2008 and Bruno Jeudy, "Obamania Plus Forte en France qu'aux Etats-Unis," *Le Figaro* online 5 November 2008.
59. Stephen Castle, "Barroso Sings the Praises of Bush to Skeptical Europeans," *Independent.* Online 18 February 2005.
60. Claus Christian Malzahn, "Could George W. Bush Be Right?," *Der Spiegel* 23 February 2005.

61. Mathias Dopfner, "Help Us, America," Reprinted from *The Wall Street Journal* © 3 March 2005, p. A12, Dow Jones & Company. All rights reserved.

62. Robert Gerald Livingston, "Blind and Weak Joshska Fischer is Gloomy over Transatlantic Relations," *Atlantic Times* June 2007, p. 6.

63. Foreign Minister Steinmeier Visits MIT, Harvard, Fenway Park in Boston, Germany .info 14 April 2008, p. 1–2.

64. "Le Cessez-le-Feu a l'Epreuve," *Le Figaro*, 14 August 2006, pp. 1–3.

65. James Joyner, "France and Germany Suddenly Interested in Iraq," *New Atlanticist*/Atlantic Council of the United States/Washington DC, 17 February 2009, pp. 1–2.

66. "France-China Cooperation to Serve World; Chirac," *People's Daily* Online/China 12 October 2004, and see Richard Bernstein, :Europa: Chirac Bends to China, Keeping Gaullist Legacy," *International Herald Tribune*, 15 October 2004.

67. Josef Joffe, "Shifting Atlantic Alliance; Europe and the U.S. Have Learned that they Need Each Other," *Washington Post*, 14 February 2005, p.A17.

68. Paul Johnson, *Wall Street Journal*, 17 June 2005, p. A14.

69. Nicolas Burns, "The United States, Germany, and Europe: Building a Global Agenda," Address to the American Council on Germany, 27 November 2006, pp. 1–2.

70. Gordon Brown/Lord Mayor's Banquet Speech/Number 10.gov.uk, 12 November 2007.

71. Remarks by President Obama at Strasbourg Town Hall, The White House/Office of the Press Secretary, 3 April 2009, p. 2.

Chapter Nine

What Is to Be Done? The Road Ahead

Eugeniusz Smolar, president of Warsaw's Centre for International Relations stated unambiguously, "For Poland, security comes from America, and development comes from Europe." Indeed Russian efforts to re-assert its influence through energy policy has served to reinforce ties between Middle Europe and the United States.[1] One could hypothesize that Russia's greater political assertiveness, combined with its tightening grip on Europe's energy supplies, could in direct counterbalance, revitalize trans-Atlantic ties. Stated plainly the primary trans-Atlantic rift stems from geopolitics, not trade, and thus needs a political solution. Since the end of the Cold War, American policies have been driven by both a moral impulse, (Haiti, Balkans, Kosovo, Darfur, Burma,) and a moral/military combination. (Kosovo, Iraq). The political drumbeat of rogue regime status, while aptly describing many states, nonetheless implies that force remains an option in dealing with them. This polemic towards such regimes, while warranted, encourages a dynamic which will tend towards "solving" the crisis militarily.

Though the Europeans often support Washington over political isolation of rogue states, there was a clear parting of the ways over the U.S. propensity to use force as an option. "The Clinton Administration's translation of rogue state rhetoric into strategy exposed three major liabilities," advised Robert Litwak of the Woodrow Wilson Center. First the term "rogue state" was an American political rubric without standing in international law. ...Second, the rogue-state approach incurred significant political costs. During the second Clinton Administration, the policy emerged as a major source of contention with America's closest allies—Europe, Japan, and Canada. Third, the translation of the rogue state concept into policy sharply limited strategic flexibility. . . Once a country was branded as a "rogue" or "outlaw" state and placed in that category, critics viewed and deviation from hard-line containment as tantamount to appeasement."[2]

The above assessment sets the polemical template for much of post-Cold War American policy in places from the Bosnia, to Kosovo, but most especially Iraq. Saddam's rule had been demonized by both the first Bush Administration and increasingly so by Bill Clinton who often spoke of "regime change" in Baghdad. The sheer inertia of such rhetoric, as well as the implied "the clear and present danger" which Saddam posed, was the grist for the 2003 Iraq war. September 11th provided the slow fuse. Recriminations aside, the rhetoric against the Iraqi regime, combined with Saddam's open and boastful violation of fourteen United Nations Security Council resolutions, provided the momentum towards military confrontation. The countdown to the invasion and subsequent occupation of Iraq, thus sadly emerged as the prime focus of trans-Atlantic tensions.

In June 2000, the State Department announced its decision to change the term "rogue state" from the foreign policy lexicon in favor of the more diplomatic sounding "states of concern." As Robert Litwak advised, "The rogue state approach tapped into one American foreign policy tradition (moralism) but was at odds with another (pragmatism)." He added, "The underlying issue remains the character of these regimes, and their regulation to the rogue category has communicated to the target states that the U.S. objective remains regime change regardless of any change in their behavior.[3]

Based on this analysis, both Saddam Hussein and Slobodan Milosevic knew they were irredeemably targeted whereas; Libyan leader Muammar Qaddafi actually turned the tables, came figuratively clean of WMD, and allowed regime survival. Undeniably, the overthrow of the Iraqi regime, caused massive collateral damage for the United States both politically and militarily.

Zbigniew Brzezinski opines on the outcome, "By 2006, it was clear that the costs of the war had exceeded its one positive accomplishment: the removal of Saddam Hussein." Writing in his book *Second Chance—Three Presidents and the Crisis of American Superpower,* Jimmy Carter's National Security Advisor describes the George W. Bush presidency as "Catastrophic Leadership" and then lists a litany of failures from the Iraq conflict. "First, the war has caused calamitous damage to America's global standing... America's global credibility has been shattered...Distrust has also undermined America's international legitimacy...America's moral standing in the world , an important aspect of legitimacy, was also compromised by the prisons at Abu Ghraib and Guantanamo...Most of all, the war has discredited America's global leadership." He adds, "The War in Iraq has been a geopolitical disaster. It has diverted resources and attention from the terrorist threat...the physical toll of the war has been steadily rising."[4]

Such hypotheses while common across much of the academic and media spectrum, are counterpoised by Tony Blair. Before leaving office, Blair wrote an extraordinary essay in the *Economist* of London, which bears serious attention, "Be very clear about global terrorism. I fear the world, and especially a large part of Western opinion, has become dangerously misguided about this threat. If there was any mistake made in the aftermath of September 11th , it was not to realize that the roots of this terrorism were deep and pervasive." On transatlantic relations he opines, "I have real concern that on both sides of the Atlantic there is, in certain quarters, an indifference, even a hostility, to an alliance that is every bit as fundamental to our future as it has been to our past... He warned "In Britain now there are parts of the media and politics that are both Euro-skeptic and wanting 'an independent foreign policy' from America. Quite where Britain is supposed to get its alliances from bewilders me. There is talk of Britain having a new strategic relationship with China and India bypassing our traditional European and American links. "Get real." Blair stressed, "For all our differences, we should be very clear. Europe and America share the same values. We should stick together. That requires a strong transatlantic alliance."[5]

Nonetheless most European governments have readily opted for a "soft power" approach on virtually any issue, whereas the USA has kept credible military options on the policy table. This does not denigrate military participation in both Afghanistan and Iraq since 2002–2003 by countries such as Britain, Estonia, and Poland.

In separate comments in *Der Spiegel* concerning Germany's and Europe's "deep distrust of American power" Kissinger looking ahead, stated that after a new American Administration assumes power in 2009, "We will then discover to what extent the Bush administration was the cause or the alibi for European-American disagreements. Right now, many Europeans hide behind the unpopularity of President Bush. And this administration made several mistakes in the beginning... But I do believe that George W. Bush has correctly understood the global challenge we are facing, the threat of radical Islam, and that he has fought that battle with great fortitude. He will be appreciated for that later."[6]

So what is at issue? The French journal *Defense Nationale* outlined the traditional structure of transatlantic relations:

1. There can be no viable Western security without the United States just as there can be no U.S. security without the contributions of Europe and the Western world.
2. At least in the short term, neither North America nor Europe can do without NATO, regardless of what European 'activists' and American 'unilateralists' might say to the contrary.

3. A strong European Security and Defense Policy does not automatically mean a weaker NATO. In terms of security, fears of a zero-sum game between NATO and the European Union are unfounded.[7]

Building upon that partnership becomes the obligation of governments on both sides of the Atlantic. Strengthening cooperation comes in many forms but can best be achieved through government and non-governmental structures. Avoiding political rivalry takes statesmanship. So what should be done following the watershed of the 2008 Presidential elections?

FIRST; LISTEN THEN SPEAK AT SPECIAL FOCUSED U.S./EU SUMMITS

The United States must be willing to listen to European security and economic concerns and equally Europe must more fully appreciate U.S. viewpoints. Beyond the confines of the G8 Economic gatherings, more focused venues would address the specific political and economic concerns of the American and European sides as well as promote a regular open channel for discussions. The Transatlantic Economic Council, established by the United States and Germany, is one such important step which smoothes out any barriers in the $500 billion bilateral business ties.

Meetings could proceed on a rotating six month process—the *Economic Basket* in Winter following the Davos Economic Forum, while the *Political Basket* would follow in the Fall during the United Nations General Assembly. Thus one set of meeting would take place in Europe the other in North America. Both settings would stress not only high profile leadership but would encourage practical *working level* contacts in the financial and policy sectors.

SECOND; REVIVE SPACE, SECURITY, AND SCIENTIFIC COOPERATION

NASA and the European Space Agency (ESA) should renew cooperation. Though the Boeing/Airbus rivalry has clouded much of the trans-Atlantic debate on commercial aircraft, Space Cooperation between the U.S. and Europe should be enhanced. The NASA/ ESA "Columbus Lab" Space Mission in 2008 highlighted such cooperation.

After having proven itself as a guarantor of West European defense, now in the post-Cold War era, NATO must redefine its operational rationale and goals. The Alliance must rethink its mission and very selectively accept out of area deployments such as those it has successfully participated in Kosovo (KFOR) and Afghanistan. Promoting munitions and equipment standardization among Atlantic Alliance members and honing operational skills through joint training maneuvers remains vital. So too are focused and dedicated efforts to coordinate military stabilization and humanitarian efforts through NATO in select and carefully defined missions in Africa and the Mid-East.

Facing the common public health threat of epidemic disease often transported from parts of the developing world, both the U.S. and Europe should establish a common vaccine research, production, and distribution centers as to better respond to future flu or avian flu type epidemics. Such plans could enlist both private pharmaceutical industries as well as national governments to jointly tackle what could be an catastrophic epidemic outbreaks on the threat level of terrorism, or in fact a byproduct of terrorist violence. The potential public health crisis on both sides of the Atlantic resulting from an Asian Avian Flu pandemic can quickly replicate the influenza outbreaks of 1918 and can pose contemporary politicians with a crisis dwarfing current levels of terrorism. Europe and America must redouble research and development of anti-flu vaccines.

U.S./EU scientific cooperation on climate change issues and environmental issues must be enhanced in the spirit of cooperation but not seen as simply reacting to or following EU initiatives. Climate cooperation should reflect global participation, the EU and U.S., *but also including* such major industrial states as Brazil, China, India, and Russia.

THIRD; STRENGTHEN EU/USA DOMESTIC SECURITY

Despite the overwhelming sympathy for the U.S. in the post September 11th period, so much of that emotional political capital has since disappeared. Nonetheless Washington and its NATO allies, who also happen to be European Union members, need to enhance and strengthen domestic security. We are not speaking about NATO armies in the field, but EU/USA police and intelligence cooperation to strengthen internal security especially in facing the very real threat from domestically based Islamic fundamentalist forces.

Poor coordination between Homeland security watch lists on trans-Atlantic flights often leads to embarrassing *faux pas* by the U.S. side causing flight delays and disruptions needs to be ironed out with European carriers. Moreover if there is one thing which nearly universally upsets and raises the ire of visitors from the European Union, it is the mandatory finger-printing and photographing when entering the USA at airport point of entry. Such steps are of dubious value, but almost certainly cause resentment from many of Europeans otherwise prone to be well disposed to America.

As importantly maritime and port security cooperation, though especially good with the Netherlands, warrants considerable enhancement. Container vessels offer terrorists the opportunity to infiltrate a nuclear device, dirty bomb, or chemical agents into key ports. Equally computer and financial security needs wider cooperation especially among European Banks and Stock Exchanges, and Public Health Data banks to guard against cyber warfare attacks. Such cooperation could decrease the threat level from both hackers as well as dedicated and focused terrorist attacks on the cyber infrastructure. There is ample evidence which links Islamic militants to proficiency with computer viruses to cause financial or air traffic havoc.

FOURTH; STRESS POINTS OF CONSENSUS

Going beyond the polarizing Iraq debate, to dealing with the evolving situation with the Islamic Republic of Iran, one finds increasing consensus between Europe and the United States. American policy often parallels European Union initiatives in key Human Rights issues too. The cooperation concerning humanitarian aid in Sudan's Darfur region, the support for political democratization in Burma, and the EU's enduring commitment to Kosovo's sovereignty, are among the points of consensus. In Darfur, the United States and the European Union are basically on the same political page in confronting the Sudanese regime over widespread human rights abuses. Political initiatives in the Security Council have been hampered and sidetracked by Russia and People's Republic of China but U.S./EU cooperation has been smooth since the start of the crisis in 2004. The U.S. and France have cooperated closely on Lebanon as well as Zimbabwe. Strong European and American support for joint efforts to curb sea piracy, UN Resolution 1816 (2008), offers another example as did close American/EU coordination during the Georgia crisis.

Importantly in Burma, the Bush Administration long stressed the need for democratization and pressed for wider sanctions on the Myanmar's military rulers. EU Foreign Ministers echoed the American policy and in many cases exceeded it. During the 2007 UN General Assembly, the Foreign Minister of Austria was particularly eloquent in her call for Burmese democracy. Following the Cyclone Nargis natural disaster in 2008, the United States and Europeans pressed both for humanitarian aid and political reforms in Burma. The USA and EU may have returned to a more normal cycle of relations where trade disputes will return to the fore rather than flashpoint political disputes. While Washington has often been tempted to employ the *Euroland soft power* approach to international relations, hard reality has a nasty habit of getting in the way especially in places like Iran.

FIFTH; PROMOTE PUBLIC DIPLOMACY

Enhancing educational and cultural contact between American states and European states/provinces. The State Department has unwisely trimmed public diplomacy posts from 2,500 in 1991 to 1,200 in 2003, the real issue in a European context no longer relies on American libraries. Through media, the movies, the internet, and travel, Europeans are hardly starved of American media content. But what is presented beyond entertainment? *People to People contact is surprisingly sparse outside the tourist world.*

Presuming that with the end of the Cold War, the need for explaining America abroad had basically ceased, the Clinton Administration abolished the United States Information Agency (USIA), merged its public affairs functions with the State Department, and then proceeded to trim the overseas information budgets.

In 1983, during heightened "anti-Americanism" the bi-partisan German-American Parliamentary Friendship was founded. The group which links American and German legislators form all parties, has proven effective in strengthening bi-lateral relations. Such concepts linking Congressmen or state legislators with their European counterparts should be expanded. Though Europe(especially the UK, Italy, Spain and France), hosts 57 percent of the 242,000 American students studying abroad, a mere 5 percent stay for an academic year according to the respected Open Doors Education Report for 2008. Wider and more comprehensive study should be encouraged, especially in languages.

Rather than proceeding on an purely official government level—a top down approach—it may be wiser to present the richness of American States and European Regions through a more user friendly character. Though not working through formal and top-heavy governmental channels this plan would stress regional links. Both American states and European regions/provinces have sponsored trade/tourism/genealogical and cultural expos in key cities. Scotland, Spain, Germany and Scandinavia have sponsored such expos in the USA. Indeed many U.S. states maintain major export relationships with European countries and such obvious ties are usually overlooked.

Commemorations in 2008 marking the 60th anniversary of the Berlin Airlift, which saved two million blockaded civilians, have recalled strong

German/American bonds in the post-war era. Given the Ethnic, cultural and religious links of the majority of the American population, with historic or current familial links to Germany, Ireland, England, Italy, Poland, and Scandinavia, such family ties across the Atlantic remain a foundation upon which to build.

Though few Americans really think much about, the Balkans region holds an amazing reservoir of goodwill for the USA. Moreover large communities of Croatians, Bosnians and Albanians living in the United States are testament to these ties. In February 2008, Kosovo, the overwhelmingly ethnic Albanian province of Serbia declared its independence. Amid sea of the double-eagle Albanian flags celebrating secession from Serbia were a surprising number of American flags too. Kosovar Albanians have long looked to the USA as a special guarantor for their future sovereignty. When President Bush visited neighboring Albania in June 2007, he was feted like the proverbial rock star by the crowds in the predominantly Muslim country. His support for Kosovo's independence was viewed as a powerful pledge from a friend from afar. Seeing the U.S. stars and stripes alongside the Albanian double eagle should have come as no surprise, but rather a reaffirmation of how America is still positively viewed in many places not necessarily in the headlines.

COMMERCIAL SEA CHANGE

Still the very nature of Europe's global business prominence is fast changing. While Germany remains the world's number one exporter, France's share of global commerce over the past five years has dropped dangerously from 4.5 percent to 4 percent. Germany's export trade at the same time grew to 8.9 percent. Tracking world commerce from a 1996 starting line one finds that France stood at 6 percent, Germany at 10 percent, Japan at 8 percent and the United States at 12 percent of total global trade. China was just coming on the charts with 3 percent. A decade later France and Japan have been in decline, Germany has slipped, and the USA has slumped from 12 percent in 2001 down to 8 percent today. Today China with 8 percent of the world trade is slightly behind the U.S.[8]

The very nature of Euro dominance is changing *vis-a-vis* China not because Europe is slipping but because *China is climbing fast*. French business initiatives to stay competitive include plans to assemble Airbus 320 orders in Tanjin China, and assembly of French automobiles in North Africa.

The European Union's trade with China is "deeply unequal" according to EU Trade commissioner Peter Mandelson. In a frank letter to the European Commission in Brussels, he suggested that China took business in Europe for granted. Given that China is now the EU's largest source of manufactured goods, the commissioner added that tariff barriers were limiting EU exports to China. In fact the EU sold more to Switzerland than to China and that the deficit with the PRC was growing at a rate of $20 million per hour. His warning was summed up as "The Chinese juggernaut is, to some extent, out of control."[9]

Mandelson's candid remarks concerning China caused a firestorm of criticism—and before long *clarification and revision* from EU officials. Yet on the eve of a Sino/European trade summit he stated "During the six days I spent in China, the trade deficit will grow over by over 2 billion Euros or 15 million Euros an hour…this that is what I call unsustainable. There are real issues of market access, legal protection, as well as the other issues we are dealing with like counterfeiting and export of fake goods."

Astoundingly China has replaced the United States as the biggest source of exports to the European Union. The EU is China's biggest trading partner and their two-way trade topped $470 billion last year. Still as Charles Grant argues, "Meanwhile the EU is bumping up against China all over the world, when dealing with issues such as Darfur, Burma, the Iranian nuclear program, or curbing carbon emissions. These kinds of problems cannot be solved without Chinese help." Peter Mandelson argued that Beijing's economic nationalism is hindering European investment. European companies often complain of encountering in China "an unspoken economic nationalism that implies that foreign investment is no longer wanted or needed," he advised. In fact EU investment in China dropped from $8.7 billion in 2006 to $2.6 billion in 2007. China accounted for only two percent of Europe's foreign direct investment.[10]

European attempts to redress the difference have rested with technology transfer and high-tech investment. A landmark trip to China by President Nicolas Sarkozy, garnered over $30 billion in business for French firms. Airbus, nuclear reactors and telecommunications equipment contracts led the list. Some 160 Airbus aircraft were ordered. A $12 billion deal between EDF and China Guangdong Nuclear Power will see France deliver two 1,600 megawatt reactors to the Mainland with construction starting in 2009.[11]

Yet not all French trade is high-tech. France's wine and spirit industry reached record exports in 2007, with major surges in China and an exuberant performance from the star of French wines, Champagne. France sent nearly 9.3 billion euros, or about $14 billion, worth of wines and spirits abroad in 2007, an increase of nearly 7 percent, according to the French Federation of Wine and Spirits Exporters. Growth in China more than doubled to nearly 247 million euros ($365 million). Champagne had a cork-popping year, too, with more than 147 million bottles exported in 2007, a 5 percent increase from 2006. Still the strength of the Euro compared to the U.S. dollar makes French wines more expensive in the United States, France's largest market by value despite an estimated 3 percent decline in exports across the Atlantic in 2007. Seen another way, wine exports equaled the sale of 180 Airbus aircraft or 400 TGV high speed trains.[12]

Trans-Atlantic trade remains vital for both North America and Europe. Commerce between even many of the smallest American states and European countries is generally unknown. Educational efforts which would highlight ties between U.S. states and Europe would be surprising for most Americans. Naturally such efforts can extend into the educational arena, especially on the secondary school level where existing student exchanges can be expanded and enhanced. Religiously the exchange of pastors between Europe and America, practiced in the past, can be revived. The Rotary and Chambers of Commerce can achieve such goals.

The American Chamber of Commerce in Germany was founded in Berlin in 1903 and is the second oldest AmCham in the world. With over 3,000 members, it's also the largest American Chamber of Commerce in Europe. Membership includes 85% of all U.S. investment in Germany, accounting for approximately 800,000 direct jobs and over 130 billion Euro in investment. Addressing the wider picture there's the reality that the EU and USA "represent the largest and most interconnected bilateral trading and investment relationship in the world, accounting for approximately 40 percent of world trade and 60 percent of global GDP. Transatlantic trade measures around 1.7 ($2billion) a day registering more than 440 billion in 2007." Jobs created on both sides of the Atlantic are estimated between 12 and 14 million, of which half are in the USA.[13]

Naturally there's the political equation. Traditional American links, with Euroland, based on shared values, must supersede the transitional political differences as large as the Iraq war or climate issues.

RUSSIA TO THE RESCUE?

"Vladimir Putin has transformed Russia from a relatively weak, partially democratic country, into an authoritarian mercantilist system," opines a report by the Atlantic Council. "Strengthened by Russia's resource wealth, the Kremlin has wielded political, economic and energy power and has employed military force to intimidate its neighbors, and assert a self-proclaimed right to "privileged interests" throughout Eastern Europe and the post-Soviet space, attempt strategic control over key energy transportation corridors, and establish itself as an independent Eurasian power." The report adds, "Strong domestic support for the

Putin-Medvedev system rests on two pillars. The first is economic performance and resource wealth. The second is the specter of foreign enemies."[14]

Ironically but not surprisingly, the Russian resurgence during the late Putin era may lay the foundation for closer Euroland/American political relations. President Vladimir Putin's implicit threats over energy supply to Europe, threatened neighboring Ukraine with missiles should it join NATO, scorned the independence of Kosovo from Serbia, and has engaged in crude intimidation towards Poland and the Czech Republic, over missile defense radar sites. U.S. Secretary of State Condoleezza Rice called Putin's threats "reprehensible."

While much of this can be characterized as high octane Russian rhetoric echoing the former Soviet era, the deeper reasons rest in Vladimir Putin's confident calculation that Russia is a reinvigorated and revived State. His bluster, threat and probing actions are not just part of Moscow's boorishness but a calculated move on the geopolitical chess board. Putin's game plan, invigorated by an influx of petrodollars to Kremlin coffers, served by a web of energy pipelines supplying heat and fuel acting as an undeniable noose to European Union supplies, and propelled by a self-righteous political desire to revive the control over of former Soviet satraps now becomes clearer. Ukraine, now independent and sovereign but Moscow's sorely missed "heartland," got the frontal blast while Georgia, the former southern satrap got Moscow's backhand. The desire of Ukraine and Georgia to join NATO is seen as geo-strategic provocation to the Kremlin. Yet the frosty ties between Moscow, Kiev, and Tbilisi, could become colder if Russian energy giant Gazprom decides to interfere with Ukraine's energy supplies as it has already done. The *Financial Times* dubbed Gazprom editorially as not a commercial enterprise but "It is the single most important instrument of the resurgent Russian state."

In a bold move Moscow offered Kiev favorable prices (about half the market rate) for natural gas which is shipped to Europe. Taking advantage of deep internal divisions in the Ukrainian government, and using the energy incentive as a wedge to gain greater geopolitical control over Ukraine which had sided with Georgia in the Summer 2008 conflict, Vladimir Putin personally orchestrated this tact through Gazprom to undeniably bind Ukraine with Russia. Moscow's natural gas pipelines form a web of energy dependence in Western Europe and thus implicit control. Countries like Finland, the Baltics, Slovakia, Greece and Bulgaria depend almost exclusively on Russian gas. Austria (67%), Hungary (65%), Poland (46%), Germany (39%), Italy (27) and France (16%) dependent on Russian supplies to warm and run both homes and industries.[15]

As interestingly and largely unreported, Russia has written off Iraq's $12 billion dollar debt, a sum incurred when Saddam Hussein's regime was an eager buyer of Soviet arms. Baghdad's debt to Moscow, long seen as a key reason why Russia supported Saddam to the last moment, was written off in exchange for Russian firms including Lukoil being allowed to invest, prospect and develop the Qurna oil fields, one of Iraq's largest. The deal quietly returns Russia to Iraq as a key player in the petroleum game. Gazprom and the Italian energy giant ENI have signed a deal to gain access to Libya's oil and natural gas deposits. ENI already Europe's biggest buyer of Russian gas, is already cooperating with Gazprom in gas export projects such as a pipeline across the Black Sea from Russia to Bulgaria. The Libyan deal, which was finalized by a personal visit of President Putin to meet with his counterpart Muammar Gadaffi in Tripoli, would further tighten Gazprom's "stranglehold on European markets," according to the *Financial Times*. In a separate sign of renewed Russian/Libyan ties, Moscow will write off $4.5 billion in debt incurred from Soviet era arms purchases. The Putin visit "highlighted Russia's determination to strengthen its influence in North Africa and aggressively pursue deals around the globe."[16]

Energy supply tensions between Russia and EU heightened during the fall of 2006. A confidential NATO study warned that Russia plans for a "natural gas OPEC" which would include Algeria, Libya and Iran. The study by NATO's economic policy group warned that "Russia was seeking to use energy policy to pursue political ends, particularly in dealings with Ukraine and Georgia. Russia already supplies 24 percent of Europe's natural gas."[17] During a dangerous pricing dispute between Russia and Ukraine in 2009, this energy dependency emerged as a reality. During a harsh winter, Moscow shut down gas supplies to Ukraine, the effect of which had a downstream effort on supplies transiting to Western Europe. Serious shortages ensued in the dead of winter.

Alexander Medvedev, Vice President of Gazprom exports stated, "Gazprom is a global player. It controls 17 percent of the global gas reserves. The history of links between Russia and Europe go back forty years, with deliveries to Austria 1968. Cooperation between Gazprom and GDF started in 1975. The portion of Russian Natural gas to France goes to 25 percent of consumption of gas representing 20–30 percent of commerce between our two countries....in 2006 Gazprom furnished 160 million cubic meters from 147 million in 2005. This corresponds to 26 percent of the gas needs of the Union." He added, "Since 2006 Gazprom can furnish to the French market up to 1.5 million cubic meters a year."[18]

"One of the most powerful forces shaping Europe in the 21st century is the juxtaposition of the world's second biggest gas market, the European Union, with the owner of the world's biggest gas reserves, Russia," states a *Financial Times* Energy Survey. "The EU depends on Russia foe about a quarter of its gas supplies. By 2030 as demand rises and the EU's own production declines, that proportion is expected to rise to a half." The article states sagely, "Everything that Europe thinks about energy security is shaped by its relationship of simultaneous dependence and antagonism with Russia. In this chess game between East and West, the pipelines are the most powerful pieces." Europe has become increasingly reliant on Russian gas; such dependence will only grow as older nuclear and coal plants are being phased out. In 2007, 50 percent of EU imports came from Russia, while 29 percent originated in Norway and another 11 percent from Algeria. Germany alone relies on Russia for 40 percent of its natural gas imports. Nuclear power presents an alternative illustrating electric energy independence. France using 58 reactors, generates 77 percent of its electric from nuclear power, Belgium 54 percent, Sweden 46 percent, and Germany 26 percent.[19]

"One of the most striking developments in European security is the new Russian assertiveness," opines Nicole Gnesotto, former Director of the European Union Institute for Security Studies. "Russia has rejected the post-Cold War 'Western Order,' This goes particularly for the enlargement policies of Western institutions, the evolution of the Balkans (Kosovo), the Caucuses (Georgia) and maybe other parts of the former Soviet Union." She adds, "Strategic revisionism and a more authoritarian nationalism have become the new pillars of Russian foreign policy, both in its commercial and strategic dimensions." [20]

The Balkans too may is illustrate the law of unintended consequences. Namely American and European political recognition of Kosovo may have reenergized a Russian political backlash in Europe which will have the effect of driving EU states into the American embrace. Russia has rhetorically backed up its "little brother" ally Serbia in Belgrade's last ditch-bid to hold on to the majority Albanian province of Kosovo. Russia's representatives in the UN Security Council have provided Serbia with rhetorical cover fire for keeping Kosovo, and have echoed Putin's most recent warning that recognition of an independent Kosovo would be "immoral and illegal." Russia has equally warned the U.S. that Kosovo's declaration of independence from Serbia endangers international stability. Comments by Russian Foreign Minister Sergei Lavrov, came in the aftermath of Kosovo's declaration of independence from Serbia.. The USA and key European states soon offered diplomatic recognition to Kosovo.

Kosovo has reenergized Russian geopolitical policy rhetoric. Regarding Kosovo's Albanian assembly's unilateral declaration of independence, speaking before the UN Security Council, Russian Ambassador Vitaly Churkin stated, "The 17th February declaration of the Serbian province Kosovo's local Assembly is a blatant breach of the norms and principles of international law...the illegal acts of the Kosovo Albanian leadership's and of those who support them set a dangerous precedent. They are fraught with an escalation of tension and inter-ethnic violence in the province, destructive consequences for international relations that took decades to build." President Putin was even more blunt calling the Kosovo's unilateral declaration of independence as setting a "horrible precedent."[21]

Nearly a month following the unilateral declaration, the Kosovo issue still simmered in the UN Security Council. Firmly denouncing Kosovo's breakaway and vowing never to recognize the province's self-declared independence, Serbian Foreign Minister Vuk Jeremić warned the Security Council that the events in Kosovo had left the international system "wobbling precariously", and may be a precedent that could be replicated in other parts of the world. "Kosovo shall remain a part of Serbia forever," Minister Jeremić said in a briefing to the Security Council, adding that Kosovo's "illegal and illegitimate" 17 February declaration of independence was undermining the international system. "The Republic of Serbia will not accept the imposition of an outcome that fundamentally violates our legitimate national interests," he declared.[22]

More than a year later Jeremic told the Security Council that as a result of Kosovo's unilateral declaration of independence, "this has become a test case of global significance. Should it be allowed to stand, a door would open challenging the territorial integrity of any UN member state." Indeed many multinational states from China to India and Indonesia and even Spain fear the Kosovo precedent.[23]

The most recent installment of the Kosovo Crisis has been going on since 1999, when the Clinton Administration used military force to stop Serbia from attacking its ethnic Albanian population. An editorial in the *Ottawa Citizen* opined, "Indeed, driving the Serbian government and Serbian people into the protective embrace of ex-Soviet Russia, and ultimately her ex-KGB strongman, was among several counter-productive dimensions in the war that Madeleine Albright organized, along with other ruinous Clinton interventions in areas of peripheral interest to the U.S. (Haiti, Somalia, Bosnia). President Bush, who was prompted to recognize the self-declared Kosovar state together with most European powers), feels obliged to accept the *fait accompli* he inherited from the preceding administration."[24]

Putin's formal step down from the Russian Presidency to become the watchful Prime Minister has likely insured continuity. Elections in 2008 installed his dutiful successor Dmitri Medvedev. Putin, an ex-KGB man after all, is expected to rule from the shadows. Interestingly, President Medvedev's inauguration was followed the very next day by reviewing the official Victory Day celebrations commemorating the end of WWII; the first massive military parade in Red Square since the end of the Soviet Union.

Medvedev in the meantime once directed GAZPROM. British author Edward Lucas brings a poignant focus to the new Russia's plans; "Communism is gone but in its place has come 'sovereign democracy' a potent cocktail of self-righteousness, nationalism and xenophobia that fuels the Kremlin's power grab abroad. In the swing states of Eastern Europe--Bulgaria, Latvia and Moldova, we are already losing the new Cold War." Russia's increasingly assertive foreign policies and political probing are part of Vladimir Putin's ongoing legacy. With a renewed and more vigorous Russia on the horizon, American and European policymakers must adapt and adjust to this geo-political change. It was no coincidence that Vladimir Putin's first trip as Russian Premier was to Paris for a meeting with President Nicolas Sarkozy and meetings with former President Jacques Chirac. Though France remains Russia's eighth largest trading partner, the visit was to foster political ties, and possibly rejuvenate the close Franco/Russian cooperation of recent years.[25]

The Georgia Crisis was naturally a key concern of delegates to the UN General Assembly debates. French President Nicolas Sarkozy, speaking in his capacity of European Union President made an impassioned European case for civility and reason; "Europe does not want war. It does not want a war of civilizations; It does not want a war of religion; It does not want a new Cold War. Europe wants peace, and peace is always possible when one truly wants it." He stressed, "What Europe is telling Russia is that we want links with Russia, that we want to build a shared future with Russia. Why not build a continent-wide common economic space which would unite Europe and Russia?" He cautioned however, "But Europe is also telling Russia with the same sincerity that it cannot compromise on the principle of states' sovereignty and independence, their territorial integrity, or respect for international law." He stated forcefully, "Europe's message to all states is that it cannot accept the use of force to settle a dispute."[26]

The EU's High Representative Javier Solana speaking at the 2009 Munich Security Conference stated, "It is quite clear that among the three pillars of the pan-European security order, the U.S., Europe, Russia, one of them feels uncomfortable in it. For whatever reasons…Certainly no new 'Cold War' is in the making but all this is taking place against a wider backdrop of mistrust." American Vice President Joe Biden, addressing the same venue added importantly, that in the ties between Washington and Moscow , 'it is time to press the re-set button' in the important relationship with Russia. Biden equally addressing the wider bonds with Europe added poignantly, "America will do more—that's the good news. The bad news is that America will ask for more from our partners, as well." He added, "We'll listen. We'll consult. America needs the world, just as I believe the world needs America."[27]

The 2008 NATO Summit held in Romania went a long way to narrow some key differences in defense policy between Washington and its European partners. NATO leaders agreed to endorse the U.S. missile defense plans, and for Europe to provide more troops for Afghanistan. Nonetheless the Europeans, most especially France, Germany and Spain, rejected the Bush Administration's plan to get both Georgia and Ukraine on the fast track to NATO membership. Indeed such moves equally enraged Moscow and may have indirectly prompted the ensuing confrontations in both Georgia and Ukraine.

Vladimir Putin, visiting the Bucharest Summit bluntly stated that the NATO alliance had engaged in "the total demonization" of Russia. Later, Russian Foreign Minister Sergey Lavrov decried a "new dividing line was being created with the expansion of the North Atlantic Treaty Organization, and the moving of its military assets into the territories of new members." [28]

Founded in 1949, the Atlantic Alliance has expanded well beyond its original core geographic mission to the shores of the Baltic and Adriatic. But military spending remains a major distinguishing factor today as it often did, among members. While the USA spends 4 percent of GDP on defense, the United Kingdom 2.3 percent, such large countries as France and Poland allocate 1.9 percent, but Canada, Denmark and Germany spend only 1.3 percent and Belgium and Hungary allocate a mere 1.1 percent. Javier Solana advised, "The transatlantic relationship has been changing. The days that it was primarily about security in Europe are, thankfully, long gone. It is now a partnership for action around the world. This in turn requires two things: First, a shared strategy, which means a U.S. willing to listen; and second, resources, which means a Europe able to act."[29]

Though most EU members belong to NATO, their security strategy focuses overwhelmingly on soft power. Clearly the EU states, and Canada for that matter, prefer the amorphous soft power option, which equally allows the moral rationalization that Euroland is "somehow above" a recourse to military solutions as are the Americans.

Indeed America's political parties view Europe as vital. In the 2008 party platform "Renewing America's Promise," the Democratic National Committee under the heading, "Strengthen Transatlantic Relations" asserts "Europe remains America's indispensable partner. We support the historic project to build a strong European Union that can be an even stronger partner for the United States. NATO has made tremendous strides over the past 15 years, transforming itself from a Cold War security structure into a partnership for peace." Yet they lament "NATO's challenge in Afghanistan has exposed a gap between its missions and capabilities. To close this gap, we will invest more in NATO's mission in Afghanistan." There is mention of supporting a closer U.S. relationship with states "that seek to strengthen their ties to

NATO and the West, such as Georgia and Ukraine." There is no specific call for Georgian or Ukrainian membership in the Atlantic Alliance per se. The 2008 Republican Platform under the heading "Strengthening Our Relations with Europe" offers a deeper explanation. "Our country's ties to the peoples of Europe are based on shared culture and values, common interests and goals. We particularly appreciate our close friendship with the United Kingdom, a relationship that has led the forces of freedom for generations. The enduring truth, that America's security is inseparable from Europe's, was reaffirmed by our European allies after September 11th, 2001. NATO, the most successful military alliance in history, has been greatly strengthened by the addition of new members in Central and Eastern Europe." Importantly it states, "We believe the door to NATO membership should remain open to all democratic nations who share our values and meet the requirements for NATO membership."[30]

"Engaging with Europe is not an option, it is a nearly automatic foreign policy action, especially for an American president committed to working with allies and partners," advised a policy briefing by Germany's Bertlesmann Foundation. The report added, "Washington frequently tends to consider Europe as unnecessary of attention because it is "solved." Yet the continent is a worthy recipient of Washington's time precisely because partners there are stable and reliable." It adds, "European governments add value to U.S. policy because they often dedicate resources to the same global challenges and national-security threats that America faces."[31]

The historic election of Barack Obama as President of the United States created a groundswell of euphoria throughout Euroland during the campaign and after the election. The European media gushed with positive pro-American headlines ranging from *Le Monde's* "Hope of a New International Era," to *Le Figaro's* messianic front page photo of Obama with the headline "Historic." French philosopher Bernard-Henri Levy viewing Obama's role in the world context opines, "Anti-Americanism will not suddenly magically disappear. But it will have a hard time surviving and it will be forced to revisit its sales pitch." He adds, "One thing is certain, the new president will feel a meta-historical weight on his shoulders: never before has an American election aroused in the rest of the world so much wild and yet reasonable hope."[32]

Presenting his national security team, Barack Obama stated, "The national security challenges we face are just as grave and just as urgent as our economic crisis... To succeed, we must pursue a new strategy that skillfully uses, balances and integrates all elements of American power: our military and our diplomacy; our intelligence and law enforcement; our economy and the power of our moral example."[33]

Secretary of State Hillary Clinton focused on the point stating, "There are three legs to the stool of American foreign policy: defense, diplomacy, and development. And we are responsible for two of the three legs. And we will make clear, as we go forward, that diplomacy and development are essential tools in achieving the long-term objectives of the United States."[34]

Germany's former Chancellor Helmut Schmidt writing a "Dear America" Letter in the influential political weekly *Die Zeit*, opined, "The global policies that the new president will inherit in January 2009 appear more complex, more wide ranging and oppressive than the legacy in Vietnam that Richard Nixon took over from his predecessors John F. Kennedy and Lyndon B. Johnson. As it turned out, neither Nixon nor his successors, Gerald Ford and Jimmy Carter managed to restore America's self-confidence. That would have to wait until Ronald Reagan." Schmidt stated that ever since the United States was founded, isolationist, imperialist, and internationalist tendencies have to varying degrees, played a major role in U.S. foreign policy. Many Europeans believe that the current Administration's largely unilateralist approach, is an expression of imperialist tendencies. Still we have kept our faith in the American peoples democratic instincts." Schmidt, a Social Democrat who was Chancellor between 1974–1982, added, "Europe's faith in the United States may be shaken, yet we wish to maintain the transatlantic partnership . We want to be able to love America again."[35]

Following the jarring Global Financial Crisis in Autumn 2008, there's also a new global economic template as Philip Stephens warns editorially, " Yet, the big lesson is that the West can no longer assume the global order will be remade in its own image. For more than two centuries, the U.S. and Europe have exerted an effortless economic, political and cultural hegemony. That era is ending."[36]

During his visit to the United States Pope Benedict XVI , implored, "Freedom is ever new. It is a challenge held out to each generation, and it must constantly be won over for the cause of good. Few have understood this as clearly as the late Pope John Paul II. In reflecting on the spiritual victory of freedom over totalitarianism in his native Poland and in Eastern Europe, he reminded us that history shows time and again that "in a world without truth, freedom loses its foundation," and a democracy without values can lose its very soul. Those prophetic words in some sense echo the conviction of President Washington, expressed in his Farewell Address, that religion and morality represent "indispensable supports" of political prosperity."[37]

There's a renewed Transatlantic era between the United States and such key European allies as France, Germany, Italy, and the United Kingdom. Indeed neither the USA nor Europe should allow self-fulfilling prophesy about the permanent rift in relations to actually become the case. Both the EU and

What Is to Be Done? The Road Ahead   215

Figure 9.1. Convergence of Agreement between the USA and the EU Six*

Topic / Issue	2000–2004			2004–2008		
	Strong	Moderate	Low	Strong	Moderate	Low
Afghanistan	•					
African Relief	•					
Bosnia and the Balkans		•		•		
China		•		•		
Cuba					•	
Darfur	•			•		
Global Warming			•		•	
Iran		•			•	
Iraq			•		•	
Kosovo	•			•		
Lebanon	•			•		
Myanmar/Burma		•		•		
Nuclear North Korea	•				•	
Palestine		•		•		
Piracy at Sea	•			•		
Russia		•		•		
Terrorism/al Qaida		•		•		
United Nations Tribunals	•			•		
West Africa	•			•		
Zimbabwe				•		

*For focus I define the EU Six as original core members Belgium, France, Germany, Italy, Netherlands and the United Kingdom from 1973.

U.S. are compelled by their clear national interests to put recent divergences, and especially misperceptions, behind as to strive for harmony. Smoothing of the Atlantic waters may take tough love but remains paramount for the long run relations with Europe both on the geopolitical and commercial levels. *We can treat the symptoms or the problems, but we must start with the misperceptions.* Neither side of the Atlantic should allow emotions and self-fulfilling prophesies to override the reality that the U.S. and EU are natural friends and trading partners. To admit the obvious, we both need each other.

NOTES

1. Robert Anderson, "Central Europe Casts Doubts Aside to Welcome U.S. Embrace," *Financial Times* 21 June 2006, p. 4.

2. Robert Litwak, "Regime Change: U.S. Strategy Through the Prism of 9/11," (Washington : Johns Hopkins, 2007), pp. 32–33.

3. Ibid., p. 36.

4. Zbigniew Brzezinski, "Second Chance—Three Presidents and the Crisis of American Superpower," (New York: Basic Books, 2007), pp. 146–148.

5. Tony Blair, the *Economist* newspaper Ltd. London, 2 June 2007, pp. 26–27.

6. Henry Kissinger Interview, "Europeans Hide Behind the Unpopularity of President Bush," *Der Spiegel*. Online , 18 February 2008.

7. Dufourcq and Faber, "Transatlantic Dialogue," November 2006, pp. 33–34.

8. Cyrille Lachevre, "La France Malade de son Commerce Exterieur," *Le Figaro*, 9 August 2007, p. 14.

9. "Trade Commissioner Mandelson toughens stance on mainland China ahead of trade defense reform proposal" Business Alert/EU, Hong Kong Trade and Development Council, 2 November 2007. see Charles Grant with Katinka Barysch, "Can Europe and China Shape a New World Order,?" Centre for European Reform/London, May 2008.

10. Charles Grant, "Europe Must Build a Strategic Alliance with China," *Financial Times*, 9 June 2008, p. 9 and Ralph Atkins, "China Replaces U.S. as Biggest Source of Exports to EU," *Financial Times*. Online 23 March 2007 and Geoff Dyer, "EU Hits out at Beijing's Economic Nationalism," *Financial Times* 26 September 2008, p. 10.

11. "Plus de 20 Milliards d'Euros de Contracts Commerciaux," *Le Monde*. online 27 November 2007; Charles Gautier, "EDF Finalise un Accord Nucleaire avec la Chine," *Le Figaro* 11 August 2008, p. 15.

12. Marie-Jose Cougard, "Le Marché Americain inquiete les Exportateurs de Vins et Spiritueux," *Les Echos* 21 February 2008, p. 21.

13. American Chamber of Commerce (AMCHAM), Frankfurt, Germany/2008 and EU Focus, "The Indispensable Partnership," March 2009, p. 4.

14. Daniel Hamilton, "Alliance Reborn; An Atlantic Compact for the 21st Century," Atlantic Council of the United States/Washington D.C., February 2009, p. 17.

15. Roman Olearchyk and Catherine Belton, "Ukraine Reaches Accord on Russian Gas," *Financial Times*, 3 October 2008, p. 4, and International Energy Agency/Paris 2008.

16. Neil Buckley, "Gazprom Signs Supply Deal with Libya," *Financial Times*, 18 April 2008, p. 3.

17. Daniel Dombey and Neil Buckley, "NATO Fears Russian Plans for 'Gas OPEC'," *Financial Times,* 14 November 2006, p. 1.

18. Alexandre Medvedev, "Paris et Gazprom partenaires pour la Securite Energetique de l' Europe," *Le Figaro* 14 February 2008, p. 14.

19. Ed Crooks, "Search for Alternative Routes," *Financial Times*, Gas Industry Special Report, 10 March 2008, p. 2. and Chris Bryant, "Germany Considers Building Strategic Reserve," *Financial Times* 5 September 2008, p. 3. and International Energy Agency IAEA.org.

20. Nicole Gnesotto, "Europe's Strategic Equation," *The Atlantic Times/Security* (Berlin) February 2009, p. 2.

21. Russian Mission to the UN/Remarks by Ambassador Vitaly Churkin 18 February 2008, pp. 1–3. and Le Monde 24–25 February 2008, p. 7.

22. UN Security Council SC/9273 Kosovo Meeting 11 March 2008.

23. Statement by Vuk Jeremic, Minister of Foreign Affairs of the Republic of Serbia, UN Security Council Meeting 17 June 2009, p. 2.

24. David Warren, "Rewarding Separatists Will Haunt the West," *Ottawa Citizen*, 23 February 2008. See also, Bernard Kouchner, "Independence, le Joli Mot," *Le Figaro*, 19 February 2008, p. 14.

25. Fabrice Node-Langlois, "Le Premier Ministre Poutine en 'visite presidentielle' a Paris," Putin in Paris, " *Le Figaro.* online 28 May 2008.

26. French Mission to the United Nations/Speech of President Nicolas Sarkozy delivered to the 63rd Session of the General Assembly, 23 September 2008, pp. 5–6.

27. Javier Solana, EU High Representative/Munich Security Conference 7 February 2009, pp. 1–2. and Remarks by Vice President Biden at 45th Munich Conference on Security Policy, whitehouse.gov 7 February 2009, pp. 2, 5.

28. UN Press Conference/Minister of Foreign Affairs of Russian Federation, 29 September 2008.

29. Laurent Zecchini,"Nouvelles Frontiers pour l'OTAN," *Le Monde* 2 April 2008, p. 20.

And Javier Solana, "Europe in the World," Speech at Kennedy School, Harvard University, 17 September 2009, p. 3.

30. "Renewing America's Promise" Democratic National Committee Platform Washington D.C. 2008, p. 33; Republican Platform, Washington D.C. 2008, p. 11.

31. *Trans-Atlantic Briefing Book*; "Managing Expectations, Expanding Partnerships, Shaping the Agenda for 2009." Washington, D.C.: Bertelsmann Foundation, 2008, p. 5.

32. Bernard-Henri Levy, "Obama Arouses a Wild yet Reasonable Hope," *Financial Times,* 6 November 2008, p. 13.

33. "Key Members of Obama-Biden National Security Team Announced," 1 December, 2008, change.gov. The Office of the President-Elect.

34. Hillary Clinton, Welcome Remarks to Employees, state.gov./secretary 22 January 2009.

35. Helmut Schmidt, "Dear Americans…What Can the World Expect from You?" *Atlantic Times*, February 2008, p. 1.

36. Philip Stephens, "The Financial Crisis Marks out a New Geopolitical Order," *Financial Times*, 10 October 2008, p. 9.

37. His Holiness Pope Benedict XVI, U.S. Visit Washington; Welcome Ceremony *L'Osservatore Romano*/weekly 23 April 2008, p. 2.

Bibliography

NEWSPAPERS

Atlantic Times (Berlin)
Die Welt (Berlin)
Financial Times (London)
International Herald Tribune (Paris)
Le Figaro (Paris)
Le Monde (Paris)
Les Echos (Paris)
New York Times (New York)
Wall Street Journal (New York)

PERIODICALS

American Enterprise (Washington DC)
Aussenpolitik (Bonn)
Economist (London)
Defense Nationale (Paris)
Der Spiegel (Hamburg)
Foreign Affairs (New York)
Foreign Policy (New York)
Harvard International Review (Cambridge, Mass)
United Nations Documents/Security Council and UN Diplomatic Missions
Washington Quarterly (Washington DC)
World Policy Journal (New York)

BOOKS

Amme, Charles, Jr. *NATO Without France; A Strategic Appraisal.* Stanford; CA: Hoover Institution Press, 1967.

Bark, Dennis, ed. *Reflections on Europe.* Stanford, CA: Hoover Institution Press, 1997.

Barysch, Katinka, ed. *Pipelines, Politics and Power; The Future of EU-Russia Energy Relations.* London: Centre for European Reform, 2008.

Blix, Hans. *Disarming Iraq.* New York: Pantheon Books, 2004.

Boot, Max. *War Made New*: Technology, War and the Course of History 1500 to today. New York: Gotham Books, 2006.

Buchanan, Patrick. *The Death of the West*; How Dying Populations and Immigrant Invasions Imperil Our Country and Civilization," New York: St. Martin's Press, 2002.

Brezinski, Zibgniew. *Second Chance; Three Presidents and the Crisis of American Superpower.* New York: Basic Books, 2007.

Carpenter, Ted, ed. *NATO's Empty Victory; A Post-Mortem on the Balkan War*, Washington, D.C.: CATO Institute, 2000.

Crozier, Brian. *DeGaulle.* New York: Charles Scribner, 1973.

Eksteins, Modris. *Rites of Spring; The Great War and the Birth of the Modern Age.* Boston: Houghton Mifflin, 2000.

Ghali, Boutros-Boutros. *Unvanquished; A U.S.—U.N. Saga.* New York: Random House, 1999.

Hamilton, Daniel, and Joseph P. Quinlan, *The Transatlantic Economy 2008/* Executive Summary, Washington D.C.: Center for Transatlantic Relations, School of Advanced International Studies (SAIS) Johns Hopkins University, 2008.

France and Globalization, Washington D.C.: Center for Transatlantic Relations, School of Advanced International Studies (SAIS) Johns Hopkins University, 2008.

Joffe, Josef. *Uberpower—The Imperial Temptation of America.* New York: WW Norton, 2006.

Kagan, Robert. *Of Paradise and Power/America and Europe in the New World Order,* New York: Vintage Books, 2003.

Kissinger, Henry. *Does America Need a Foreign Policy?* New York: Simon & Schuster, 2001.

Kuisel, Richard. *Seducing the French; The Dilemma of Americanization.* Berkeley: University of California Press, 1997.

Laqueur, Walter. *The Last Days of Europe—Epitaph for an Old Continent.* New York: Thomas Dunne Books, 2009.

Litwak, Robert. *Regime-Change U.S. Strategy Through the Prism of 9/11.* Baltimore: Johns Hopkins, 2007.

Nadeau, Jean-Benoit, and Julie Barlow. *Sixty Million Frenchmen Can't Be Wrong.* London: Robson Books, 2004.

Revel, Jean-Francois. *L'Obsesion Anti-Americaine.* Paris: Plon, 2002.

Rieff, David. *Slaughterhouse; Bosnia and the Failure of the West*. New York: Simon & Schuster, 1995.

Rifkin, Jeremy. *The European Dream/How Europe's Vision of the Future is Quietly Eclipsing the American Dream*. New York: Tarcher Penguin, 2004.

Zelikow, Philip, and Condoleezza Rice. *Germany Unified and Europe Transformed; A Study in Statecraft*. Cambridge, MA: Harvard University Press, 1995.

DOCUMENTS

Population and Vital Statistics Report. New York: Department of Economic and Social Affairs, United Nations, 2009.

State of the World's Cities 2008/2009. Nairobi: United Nations Habitat, 2008.

State of the World Population 2008, New York: United Nations Population Fund, 2008.

The Enlarging European Union at the United Nations; Making Multilateralism Matter. Luxembourg: European Communities, 2004.

The Partnership between the UN and the EU. Brussels: UN Office in Brussels, 2006.

Trends in Europe and North America 1995. Geneva: Economic Commission for Europe, 1995.

Urban Population, Development and the Environment 2007. New York: Department of Economic and Social Affairs/United Nations, 2008.

World Economic Situation and Prospects 2009. New York: United Nations 2009.

World Investment Report/2008; Transnational Corporations and the Infrastructural Challenge. New York: United Nations Conference on Trade and Development, 2008.

World Population Policies 2007. Department of Economic and Social Affairs. New York: United Nations, 2008.

Index

Acheson, Dean, 28, 166
Adenauer, Konrad, 27, 75, 81, 120, 137
Afghanistan: Blair and, 88; Al-Qaida and, 103; Taliban in, 87–88; UK and, 88; USSR and, 87
Ahern, Bertie, 151
Ahtisaari, Martti, 17
Albright, Madeleine K.: Balkan wars and, ix, 16, 18, 210; indispensability term and, 4–5, 20, 99; Iraq and, 114; as UN ambassador, 14
Algeria, 26–27, 54–55, 160, 208–9
Allen, Woody, 62
Alliot-Marie, Michele, 33
American Chamber of Commerce in Germany, 82, 206
American Council on Germany, 170, 192
Anglo/American alliance, 3, 51, 124, 134, 176
Anim, Moises, 54
Annan, Kofi, 14–16, 18, 93–94, 112, 118
Anti-Americanism, xi; Chirac and, 141; in Europe, 100, 120, 122, 151–52, 162, 168, 173, 192–93, 213; in France, 25, 30, 35–36, 47–48, 51, 64, 179; in Germany, 71–74, 76–77, 80–82, 95, 97, 128, 141, 188–89; unilateralism and, 82
Anti-American Obsession (Revel), 52
Anti Ballistic Missile Treaty, 34
anti-globalization, 35, 47, 60, 152
anti-Semitism, 56
Ashton, Catherine, 146
Asian avian flu, 201
Austrian Foreign Policy Yearbook, 11
authoritarianism, 147
"axis of appeasement," 120
"axis of evil," 59, 92–93
"axis of weasel," 62
Aziz, Tariq, 121
Aznar, Jose Maria, 124, 148
Azores Summit, 124

Baader-Meinhof Gang, 77
Baker, Gerard, 51, 100
Baker, James, 125
"balance of terror," 1
Balkan wars, x, 10; Albright and, ix, 16, 18, 210; Clinton, B., and, 10–16; Islam and, 12–13; Kosovo and, 15–21, 201; Russia and, 19–20; Sarajevo, war in, 10–15
Balkenende, Jan Peter, 183–84
Baltic Accord, 153–54

Bandow, Doug, 18
Bark, Dennis, 141
Barnier, Michel, 175
Barroso, Jose Manuel. *See* Durao Barroso, Jose Manuel
Bastiat, Frederic, 58
Beer, Patrice de, 51, 61
Benedict XVI (pope), 160, 183, 185, 214
Bereuter, Doug, 95
Berlin Airlift (1948–1949), 11, 79, 203
Berlin Wall, 78–79, 138, 143; Merkel and, 38, 83; Reagan and, 75, 188–89
Biden, Joe, 211
Bin-Laden, Osama, x–xi, 87–88, 175
biotech industry, 172
birthrates, 54, 58, 155, 158
Blair, Tony: Afghanistan and, 88; Bush, G. W., and, 7; foreign policy of, 35, 42, 60–61, 124; Iraq and, 178; as Prime Minister of UK, 110, 122, 126–27; war on terror and, 199
Blix, Hans: *Disarming Iraq*, 131; Kyoto Treaty and, 50; WMD's and, 114, 117–19, 121–23, 126–27, 131
Bogart, Humphrey, 165
Bohlen, Charles E., 29–30
Bosnia, ix, 8, 14
Bousquet, Pierre de, 56
Boutros Ghali, Boutros, *Unvanquished: A U.S.-UN Saga*, 14
boycotts, of goods from France, 62–65, 97
Brahimi, Lakhdar, 132
Brandt, Willy, 68
Bremer, Paul, 131
Brezhnev, Leonid, 71
Brown, Gordon, 192
Brzezinski, Zbigniew, 28–29, 99, 198; *Second Chance—Three Presidents and the Crisis of American Superpower*, 198
Buchanan, Pat, 155; *A Republic Not an Empire*, 5
Bukoshi, Bujar, 15

Burns, Nicholas, 192
Buruma, Ian, 178
Bush, George H. W., 2–5, 9, 39, 83, 133
Bush, George W., ix, 4–5; administration of, 6–7, 15, 33, 110, 126; Blair and, 7; Brown and, 192; EU and, 59, 190; Europe and, 48–49, 187; foreign policy of, 31, 101, 151, 181; Germany and, 78; Iraq and, 115–16, 120–24, 127–30, 133, 186; Kosovo and, 204; 9/11 terrorist attacks and, 59, 65, 85–88; Reagan and, 49–50, 78; Sarkozy and, 39–42; Schroeder and, 67, 94–95, 129; unilateralism and, 31, 93, 100, 128; United Nations Security Council and, 110, 113, 122; unpopularity of, 7, 95; war on terror and, 88–95, 98, 100–103, 174
business environment, in Europe, 167–72, *169*
Butler, Richard, 114
Buzek, Jerzy, 146

CARE packages, 76
Carter, Jimmy, 68–70, 198, 214
Casablanca (film), 165
Castro, Fidel, 52, 61
Catholic Church. *See* Roman Catholic Church
Cato Institute, 18
Chamberlain, Neville, 166
Chechnya, 56, 175, 178
Checkpoint Charlie, 78–79
Cheney, Richard, 92
Chernomyrdin, Viktor, 17
China: Cold War and, 34; embassy bombing and, 16–17; EU and, 204–6; nuclear power program of, 205; Sarkozy in, 205; United Nations Security Council and, 18, 202
Chirac, Jacques, *108*; Anti-Americanism and, 141; anti-Semitism and, 56; de Gaulle and, 23, 30–33; foreign policy of, 60, 62, 89–90, 95–97, 187–88,

191–92, 211; as French president, 35–37, 40, 51–52, 63, 161, 176; Iraq and, 120, 123, 127–28; Putin and, 211
Christopher, Warren, 10
Churchill, Winston, 25–26, 117
city population growth, *156*
Clinton, Bill, 4–5; administration of, ix–x, 5–6, 33, 86, 93, 98, 197; Balkan wars and, 10–16; foreign policy of, 8, 20; Iraq and, 94, 126, 133, 198; Serbia and, 20; Somalia and, 8–9, 14, 210; unilateralism and, 20; United Nations Security Council, 17
Clinton, Hillary, 214
Coker, Christopher, 17
Cold War: aftermath of, 1, 3, 5–6, 8, 20, 52, 68–75, 197–98; China and, 34; de Gaulle and, 28, 165; Eastern bloc and, 132, 209, 211; Europe and, 183, 186, 189, 211; Germany and, 68–75, 78–81, 192; NATO and, 200, 212; US and, 132, 140, 150, 173–74; USSR and, 28–29, 34, 49, 68–72, 75, 132, 142
collapse, of USSR, 2, 11, 75, 78, 173
Colombani, Jean-Marie, 99
Common Market, 31–33, 141
communism, 2, 211
Comparison of City Population Growth/ Europe *versus* Developing World, *156*
consensus-building, 202–3
Convergence of Agreement between the USA and the EU Six, *215*
Cook, Robin, 18, 110
Crozier, Brian, 25–26, 31
Cruise missiles, 3
Cuban Missile Crisis, 28
culture, 178–85
Czech Republic, 120, 132, 136, 147, 153, 158, 207

Daladier, Edward, 166
D'Ancona, Stephen, 7
Danubian Concert, 153
Dauth, John, 125
Dayton diplomatic conference, 14
Deferre, Gaston, 31
De Gasperi, Alcide, 137, 141
de Gaulle, Charles, 23, 25–33, 35, 38; Algeria and, 160; Chirac and, 23, 30–33; Cold War and, 28, 165; *The War Memoirs*, 24
Democracy in America (Tocqueville), 44
demography, of Europe, 154–58, *156*
Deneuve, Catherine, 44
Disarming Iraq (Blix), 131
Does America Need A Foreign Policy? (Kissinger), 4
Donati, Pierpaolo, 155
Dopfner, Mathias, 80, 189
Dromoland Castle Summit, 150–51
Drozdiak, Bill, 170
Dueck, Colin, 9–10
Durao Barroso, Jose Manuel, 124, 151, 188

Eastern bloc: Cold War and, 132, 209, 211; John Paul II and, 2, 70, 75, 214; NATO and, 142–43, 192; Roman Catholic Church in, 70
Eastwood, Clint, 179
Economic Commission for Europe, *xii*
economic development, of EU, 167–72
educational globalization, 179–81, 206
Eisenhower, Dwight D., 26
Ekeus, Rolf, 114
Ellsberg, Daniel, 74
embassy bombing, Chinese, 16–17
Emnid Institute, 72
English language, 178–80
Erdogan, Recep, 159
Erhardt, Ludwig, 141, 192
ESA. *See* European Space Agency
EU. *See* European Union
Euro Disney (theme park), 47
Euroland. *See* Europe; European Union

Europe: Anti-Americanism in, 100, 120, 122, 151–52, 162, 168, 173, 192–93, 213; Bush, G. W., and, 48–49, 187; business environment in, 167–72, *169*; Cold War and, 183, 186, 189, 211; demography of, 154–58, *156*; map of, *xii*; Roman Catholic Church in, 70, 184–85; WWII and, 142

European Space Agency (ESA), 167

European Union (EU), xi, 6; Bush, G. W. and, 59, 190; China and, 204–6; economic development of, 167–72; growth of, 136–64; Ireland and, 137, 139–41, 145, 147; John Paul II and, 145; NATO and, 136–37, 140–43, 152, 154–55, 172–78, 199–200; religion in, 183–85; superpower status of, 141, 150; UK and, 147, 181, 184, 203; United Nations Security Council and, 148–49, 154, 166; US and, xi, 90–92, 94, 99, 101–3, 165–93, 205–6, 212–16, *215*

exports to the USA in billions of dollars, *169*

Fahrenheit 9/11 (film), 100, *109*, 165, 178–79

FDI. *See* Foreign Direct Investment

Ferguson, Niall, 137

Fischer, Joshka, 77–78; as German Foreign Minister, 6, 91, 96, 122, 149, 189; Iraq and, 120

Fontaine, Andre, 26

Foreign Direct Investment (FDI), 139, 170–71

foreign policy: of Blair, 35, 42, 60–61, 124; of Bush, G. W., 31, 101, 151, 181; of Chirac, 60, 62, 89–90, 95–97, 187–88, 191–92, 211; of Clinton, B., 8, 20; of France, 25–27; of Putin, 206–12; of Reagan, 75, 79, 83, 151, 188–89, 214; of Russia, 206–12; United Nations Security Council and, 146

France, 23–24; Anti-Americanism and, 25, 30, 35–36, 47–48, 51, 64, 179; boycotts of, 62–65, 97; foreign policy of, 25–27; Hussein and, 33, 49–50, 59–60; Iraq and, 33–36; Islam in, 35–36, 52–58, 176; Jews in, 49, 56; John Paul II in, 59; NATO and, 27; nuclear power program of, 38; nuclear weapons and, 26–28; Roman Catholic Church in, 24, 58–59; superpower status of, 23, 36; UK and, 30, 32, 37–38, 51, 60–61; United Nations Security Council and, 25, 31, 37, 40, 51, 61; US and, 44–49, 100–101; WWII and, 47

Franco, Francisco, 147

free trade agreements, 2

French Institute for International Relations, 128

Friedman, Tom, 155

fundamentalism: in Islam, xi, 53, 55, 87–88, 98, 183, 189–90, 201; religious, 160, 183

G-8 Summit, 60

Gazprom, 207–8, 211

Gedmin, Jeffrey, 150

genocide, x

Georgia, 207, 211–13

Geremek, Bronislaw, 183

German Marshall Fund, 174

Germany: Anti-Americanism in, 71–74, 76–77, 80–82, 95, 97, 128, 141, 188–89; Bush, G. W., and, 78; Cold War and, 68–75, 78–81, 192; Schroeder and, 76–81, 120–21, 141, 188, 191–92; unification of, 3; United Nations Security Council and, 61; US and, 67–84; USSR and, 11, 74; WWII and, 174

Gingrich, Newt, x, 4

Giscard d'Estiang, Valery, 144

Giuliani, Rudy, 88

globalization: anti-globalization, 35, 47, 60, 152; educational, 179–81, 206; language and, 58–61
Global Market Insite Poll, 168
Glucksmann, Andre, 102
Gnesotto, Nicole, 209
Gorbachev, Mikhail, 75, 79, 189
Grant, Charles, 205
Great Britain. *See* United Kingdom
Gulf war (first), 2, 8, 33
Gurfinkiel, Michel, 36, 54, 56–57
Gutknecht, Gil, 91

Halberstam, David, 20
Hamas, 98
Hamilton, Daniel, 97
Hanseatic League, 153
Han Seung-soo, 89
Hayek, Friedrich von, 141
Heisbourg, Francois, 60–61, 102
Hennequin, Denis, 47
Henriksen, Thomas, 3–4
Hezbollah, 98, 191
Hitler, Adolf, 72, 74, 79
Honecker, Erich, 71
Hoover Institution, 3–4
humanitarian intervention, 9, 13
human rights, 9, 41, 138, 149, 202
Hungary, 74, 91, 120, 132, 136, 147, 153
Huntington, Samuel, 20
Hurricane Katrina, 63–64
Hussein, Saddam: France and, 33, 49–50, 59–60; Gulf War (first) and, 2; Iraq war and, 124–28, 130–33, 178; UN Security Council and, 6–7, 9, 51, 111–13; war on terror and, 91–94, 96; WMDs and, 114–18, 122–24
"hyper-power" status, of US, 20, 35, 52, 191

IAEA. *See* International Atomic Energy Agency

ICC. *See* International Criminal Court
IFOR. *See* Implementation Force (Bosnia)
Ikenberry, G. John, 5
IMF. *See* International Monetary Fund
Implementation Force (Bosnia) (IFOR), 14
imports, from US, *169*
imports from the USA/Exports to the USA in billions of dollars, *169*
indispensability term and Albright, 4–5, 20, 99
Indochine (film), 44
information technology, 171–72
International Atomic Energy Agency (IAEA), 114, 134
International Criminal Court (ICC), 149
International Monetary Fund (IMF), 139, 154, 157
Iran, 13, 59; nuclear power program of, 147, 190, 205
Iraq: Albright and, 114; Blair and, 178; Bush, G. W., and, 115–16, 120–24, 127–30, 133, 186; Chirac and, 120, 123, 127–28; Clinton, B., and, 94, 126, 133, 198; Fischer and, 120; France and, 33–36; Hussein and, 124–28, 130–33, 178; nuclear weapons and, 111, 133; Putin and, 123, 129; regime change in, 59–60, 198; Russia and, 207–8; Sarkozy and, 191; Schroeder and, 127–29, 148, 151–52, 174, 188; UK and, 122, 124, 134, 178; UN and, 110–35; United Nations Security Council and, 6, 9, 31, 60, 93–96, 102, 110–27, 130–33, 142, 198; war in, xi, 7–8, 30; WMDs and, 111–14, 116–20, 125, 131–32
Ireland: birthrate in, 155, 158; EU and, 137, 139–41, 145, 147; Northern Ireland question, 18, 86; UN Security Council and, 111, 115
Islam: Balkan wars and, 12–13; in France, 35–36, 52–58, 176;

fundamentalism in, xi, 53, 55, 87–88, 98, 183, 189–90, 201
isolationism, x–xi, 8, 214
Israel, and United Nations Security Council, 191
Ivanov, Ivan, 123

Japan, *169*
Jeremić(c1), Vuk, 210
Jervis, Robert, 4–5
Jews, in France, 49, 56
Joffe, Josef, 5, 78, 179, 191
John Paul II (pope): Aziz and, 121; Eastern bloc and, 2, 70, 75, 214; EU and, 145; in France, 59; 9/11 terrorist attacks and, 85–86
Johnson, Lyndon B., 29–30, 165
Johnson, Paul, 141, 145, 184, 192
Jones Parry, Emyr, 132

Kagan, Robert, 17, 20; *Of Paradise and Power*, 93, 98
Kaiser, Karl, 71
Kant, Immanuel, *Perpetual Peace: A Philosophical Sketch*, 150
Kelly, Michael, 77
Kelly, Petra, 74
Kelly, Ray, 65
Kennedy, John F., 26, 39, 79, 83, 151
Keohane, Robert, 83
Kerry, John, 101, 186–87
Kim Jong-il, 52
Kissinger, Henry, 87, 144, 161, 172–73, 199; *Does America Need A Foreign Policy?*, 4
Klaus, Vaclav, 154
Koch, Ed, 50
Kohl, Helmut, 2, 70–71, 73–75, 120
Kohut, Andrew, 95
Korea, nuclear weapons of, 114
Kosovo: Balkan wars and, 15–21, 201; Bush, G. W., and, 204; Schroeder and, 17; Serbia and, 189, 204, 207; United Nations Security Council and, 19, 21, 209–10

Kouchner, Bernard, 40
Kuisel, Richard, 25, 30
Kyoto Treaty, xi, 34, 50, 67, 150

Lacquer, Walter, *The Last Days of Europe*, 178
Lafayette, marquis de, 35, 41–42
Landsbergis, Vytautas, 136
language, and globalization, 58–61
Laqueur, Walter, 145
The Last Days of Europe (Lacquer), 178
Lavrov, Sergei, 118, 209, 212
Layne, Christopher, 16
Levy, Bernard-Henri, 213
Libya, 33, 39, 198, 208
Lisbon Treaty, 145–46
Litwak, Robert, 197–98
Lugar, Richard, 91
Luthy, Herbert, 24

Macapagal Arroyo, Gloria, 88
MAD. *See* mutual assured destruction
Mandelson, Peter, 204–5
Marshall Plan, 41, 137, 141, 173, 192
Marxism, 18, 60, 77, 152
McDonald's restaurants, 46–48, 168
Mearsheimer, John J., 6
Meding, Michael, 90
Medvedev, Alexander, 208
Medvedev, Dmitri, 207, 210
Merkel, Angela, 38, 79–83, 155, 192
Milosevic, Slobodan, 15–17, 198
Mladic, Ratko, 12
Moisi, Dominique, 23, 25, 31, 59
Monnet, Jean, 137, 141, 192
Moore, Michael, 100, *109*
Moravcsik, Andrew, 166
Mortimer, Edward, 14
multilateralism, 82, 128
mutual assured destruction (MAD), 1

Napoleon, 32, 35
NATO. *See* North Atlantic Treaty Organization
Nauman, Michael, 126

Nazi regime, 25, 141, 147, 165, 188
Negroponte, John, 88–89, 116, 118
Netherlands, 147, 171, 183–84, 202
New World Order, 2–3, 5
9/11 terrorist attacks, xi, 4–7; Bush, G. W., and, 59, 65, 85–88; John Paul II and, 85–86; Al-Qaida and, 34, 48, 98, 175; Schroeder and, 90; United Nations Security Council and, 87–88; war on terror and, 85–89, 94, 167, 174
Nixon, Richard M., 67, 214
North Atlantic Treaty Organization (NATO), xi, 1, 6, 11–12, 18–20; Cold War and, 200, 212; Eastern bloc and, 142–43, 192; EU and, 136–37, 140–43, 152, 154–55, 172–78, 199–200; France and, 27; Serbia and, 6, 19; SHAPE and, 26; summit in 2008 of, 212; Turkey and, 151–52, 158–60, 173–74; unilateralism and, 199
Northern Ireland question, 18, 86
North Korea, 59
nuclear power programs, 209; of China, 205; of France, 38; of Iran, 147, 190, 205
nuclear weapons, 3; France and, 26–28; Iraq and, 111, 133; Korea and, 114; UN Security Council and, 118; of US, 26, 70–71, 74; of USSR, 1, 29, 74
Nuremberg Tribunal Against First Strike and Mass Destruction Weapons in East and West, 74, 77

Obama, Barack, xi, 182, 187–88, 193, 213
Obamamania, 102, 187
Of Paradise and Power (Kagan), 93, 98
Olszowski, Stefen, 71
Operation Desert Fox, 17
Operation Iraqi Freedom (2003), 6

Palacio, Ana, 124, 143
Pamir, Umit, 89

Parmentier, Guillaume, 128
Patten, Chris, 184, 193
Patton, George, 125
peace dividend, x, 2, 8, 173
people to people contact, 203–4
Perle, Richard, 61
Perpetual Peace: A Philosophical Sketch (Kant), 150
Pershing missiles, 3, 70–71, 74
Perthes, Volker, 82
Pew Center, 95
Peyrefitte, Alain, 27–28, 33
Piaf, Edith, 44
points of consensus, 202–3
Poland, 132, 136, 147, 153, 158, 199, 207
population growth, *156*
Powell, Colin, 61, *107*, 116, 119, 123–24, 126
Primakov, Yevgeny, 17
Prodi, Romano, 91, 141, 143, 151
public diplomacy, 203–4
public health cooperation, 200–201
Putin, Vladimir, 69; Chirac and, 211; foreign policy of, 206–12; Iraq and, 123, 129; as Russian President, 157, 189, 206, 211

Qaddafi, Muammar, 33, 39, 198, 208
Al-Qaida: Afghanistan and, 103; 9/11 terrorist attacks and, 34, 48, 98, 175; Taliban regime and, 87

Raines, Claude, 165
Rambouillet agreement, 16
Ranke, Leopold von, 137
rap music, 176, 179
Ratzinger, Josef, 160, 183, 185, 214
Reagan, Ronald, 2, 38; administration of, 68–71, 73, 140; Berlin Wall and, 75, 188–89; Bush, G. W., and, 49–50, 78; foreign policy of, 75, 79, 83, 151, 188–89, 214; Libya and, 33; war on terror and, 86
Rehn, Olli, 138, 159

religion, in EU, 183–85
religious fundamentalism, 160, 183
A Republic Not an Empire (Buchanan), 5
Revel, Jean-Francois, 58, 152; *Anti-American Obsession*, 52
Rice, Condoleezza, 92, 116, 190, 207
Rieff, David, *Slaughterhouse: Bosnia and the Failure of the West*, 12
Rifkin, Jeremy, 146, 150
rogue states, 92, 120, 126, 197–98
Roman Catholic Church: in Eastern bloc, 70; in Europe, 70, 184–85; in France, 24, 58–59
Rommel, Manfred, 74
Rompuy, Herman Van, 146
Roosevelt, Franklin D., 25–26, 92, 142
Rose, Charlie, 61
Rose, Michael, 13
Rousselin, Pierre, 40
Royal, Segolene, 36–37
Rumsfeld, Donald, x, 92, 100, 143
Rusk, Dean, 29–30
Russia: Balkan wars and, 19–20; foreign policy of, 206–12; Iraq and, 207–8; Serbia and, 17–18, 209–10; United Nations Security Council and, 202, 209; US and, 197
Ryan, Richard, 115

Sabri, Naji, 112
Sarajevo, war in, 10–15
Sarkozy, Nicolas: Bush, G. W. and, 39–42; China and, 205; as French Interior Minister, 57, 65; as French president, 36, 185, 211; Iraq and, 191
Schild, Georg, 13
Schily, Otto, 77
Schlesinger, Stephen, 15
Schmidt, Helmut, 70–73, 120, 214
Schroeder, Gerhard: Bush, G. W., and, 67, 94–95, 129; as Chancellor of Germany, 76–81, 120–21, 141, 188, 191–92; Iraq and, 127–29, 148, 151–52, 174, 188; Kosovo and, 17; 9/11 terrorist attacks and, 90
Schuman, Robert, 137, 141
scientific cooperation, 200–201
Second Chance—Three Presidents and the Crisis of American Superpower (Brzezinski), 198
Serbia: Clinton, B., and, 20; Kosovo and, 189, 204, 207; NATO and, 6, 19; Russia and, 17–18, 209–10; United Nations Security Council and, 10, 15–16
SHAPE. *See* Supreme Headquarters Allied Powers Europe
Shultz, George, 93–94, 96
Slaughterhouse: Bosnia and the Failure of the West (Rieff), 12
Smith, Adam, 58
Smolar, Eugeniusz, 197
Solana, Javier, 14, 144, 186, 211
Somalia: Clinton, B., and, 8–9, 14, 210; United Nations Security Council and, 103
Sommer, Theo, 83, 152
Soviet Union. *See* Union of Soviet Socialist Republics
space program cooperation, 200–201
Starbucks, 47
Steinmeier, Frank-Walter, 82, 189–91
Stephens, Philip, 214
Straw, Jack, 123
Suez crisis, 26–27, 82
superpower status: of EU, 141, 150; of France, 23, 36; of US, 3–6, 20, 52, 92, 146, 191
Supreme Headquarters Allied Powers Europe (SHAPE), 26
Szent-Ivanyi, Istvan, 92

Taheri, Amir, 54
Taliban regime, 87–88, 91, 103, 190
terrorism. *See* 9/11 terrorist attacks; war on terror
Thatcher, Margaret, 2–3, 38, 70, 75

The Third Man (film), 1
Third World, 1
Tocqueville, Alexis de, *Democracy in America*, 44
totalitarianism, 141, 147, 214
trade relationships, 204–6
Transatlantic Trends polls, 174, 181–82
Treaty of Rome, 137
Trittin, Jurgen, 77
Turkey: NATO and, 151–52, 158–60, 173–74; war on terror and, 89, 182

UK. *See* United Kingdom
UNHCR. *See* United Nations High Commissioner for Refugees
unification, of Germany, 3
unilateralism, 6; Anti-Americanism and, 82; Bush, G. W., and, 31, 93, 100, 128; Clinton, B., and, 20; NATO and, 199; war on terror and, 126, 132
Union of Soviet Socialist Republics (USSR): Afghanistan and, 87; Cold War and, 28–29, 34, 49, 68–72, 75, 132, 142; collapse of, 2, 11, 75, 78, 173; Germany and, 11, 74; military power of, 1, 3, 6–7, 173, 192; nuclear weapons of, 1, 29, 74; WWII and, 25, 74
United Kingdom (UK), 2–3; Afghanistan and, 88; EU and, 147, 181, 184, 203; France and, 30, 32, 37–38, 51, 60–61; Iraq and, 122, 124, 134, 178; Suez crisis and, 26; US and, 70, 75, 169–70, 214; war on terror and, 99–101, 199
United Nations (UN), and Iraq war, 110–35
United Nations High Commissioner for Refugees (UNHCR), 10, 19
United Nations Protection Force (UNPROFOR), 10–14
United Nations Security Council, x, *106*, *107*; Bush, G. W., and, 110, 113, 122; China and, 18, 202; Clinton, B., and, 17; EU and, 148–49, 154, 166; foreign policy and, 146; France and, 25, 31, 37, 40, 51, 61; Germany and, 61; Hussein and, 6–7, 9, 51, 111–13; Iraq and, 6, 9, 31, 60, 93–96, 102, 110–27, 130–33, 142, 198; Ireland and, 111, 115; Israel and, 191; Kosovo and, 19, 21, 209–10; 9/11 terrorist attacks and, 87–88; nuclear weapons and, 118; Russia and, 202, 209; Serbia and, 10, 15–16; Somalia and, 103
United States (US): Cold War and, 132, 140, 150, 173–74; EU and, xi, 90–92, 94, 99, 101–3, 165–93, 205–6, 212–16, *215*; France and, 44–49, 100–101; Germany and, 67–84; "hyper-power" status of, 20, 52, 191; imports from, *169*; nuclear weapons of, 26, 70–71, 74; Russia and, 197; superpower status of, 3–6, 20, 52, 92, 146, 191; UK and, 70, 75, 169–70, 214
United States Information Agency (USIA), 203
UNPROFOR. *See* United Nations Protection Force
Unvanquished: A U.S.-UN Saga (Boutros Ghali), 14
USIA. *See* United States Information Agency
USS Cole, attack on, 86
USSR. *See* Union of Soviet Socialist Republics

Van Gogh, Theo, 183
Vedrine, Hubert, 20, 35, 52, 93, 96
Velayati, Ali Akbar, 13
La Vie en Rose (film), 44
Viera de Mello, Sergio, 40
Villepin, Dominique de, 23, 51, 60, 93, 95–96, *107*, 116, 119, 121–23
Vlk, Miloslav, 184
Voigt, Karsten, 82, 185

The War Memoirs (de Gaulle), 24
war on terror, 85–109; Blair and, 199; Bush, G. W., and, 88–95, 98, 100–103, 174; Hussein and, 91–94, 96; 9/11 terrorist attacks and, 85–89, 94, 167, 174; Reagan and, 86; Turkey and, 89, 182; UK and, 99–101, 199; unilateralism and, 126, 132
Warsaw Pact, 28, 34, 68
Weapons of Mass Destruction (WMD), 29, 93–94, 198; Blix and, 114, 117–19, 121–23, 126–27, 131; Hussein and, 114–18, 122–24; Iraq and, 111–14, 116–20, 125, 131–32; Nuremberg Tribunal Against First Strike and Mass Destruction Weapons in East and West, 74, 77

welfare states, 37, 46, 59, 79, 161
Welles, Orson, 1
Wilson, Woodrow, 5, 9
WMD. *See* Weapons of Mass Destruction
Wojtyla, Karol, 2. *See also* John Paul II
Wolf, Martin, 100
World War I (WWI), 24, 32, 49, 152
World War II (WWII): Europe and, 142; France and, 47; Germany and, 174; USSR and, 25, 74

Yalta Conference, 25–26, 142
Yeltsin, Boris, 17
Yilmaz, Mehmut, 159

Zebari, Hoshyar, 131
Zhu Rongji, 18